THE
UNITED FRUIT COMPANY
IN LATIN AMERICA

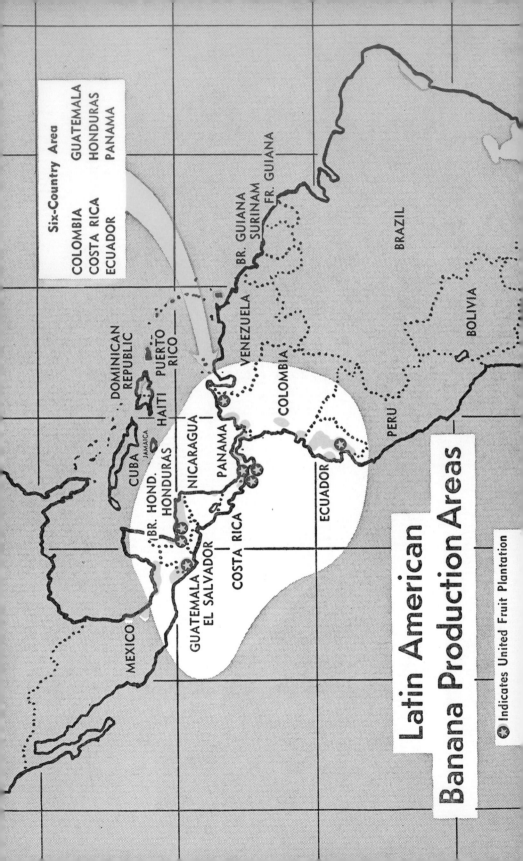

Latin American Banana Production Areas

Six-Country Area

COLOMBIA GUATEMALA
COSTA RICA HONDURAS
ECUADOR PANAMA

⊕ Indicates United Fruit Plantation

THE
UNITED FRUIT COMPANY
IN LATIN AMERICA

BY STACY MAY AND GALO PLAZA

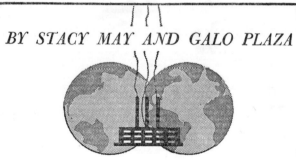

SEVENTH CASE STUDY IN AN NPA SERIES ON

United States Business Performance Abroad

338.174
M46Tu

United States Business Performance Abroad

First Case Study

SEARS, ROEBUCK DE MEXICO, S.A. May 1953. 88pp. $1.00

Second Case Study

CASA GRACE IN PERU. November 1954. 112pp. $1.00

Third Case Study

THE PHILIPPINE AMERICAN LIFE INSURANCE COMPANY. March 1955. 94pp. $1.00

Fourth Case Study

THE CREOLE PETROLEUM CORPORATION IN VENEZUELA. December 1955. 116pp. $1.00

Fifth Case Study

THE FIRESTONE OPERATIONS IN LIBERIA. December 1956. 140pp. $1.00

Sixth Case Study

STANVAC IN INDONESIA. June 1957. 144pp. $1.00

Seventh Case Study

THE UNITED FRUIT COMPANY IN LATIN AMERICA. June 1958. 316pp. Cloth bound $4.50; paper bound $2.00

Library of Congress
Catalog Card Number
58-12402

iv

★

ACKNOWLEDGMENT

This Case Study was made possible in part by funds granted by the Carnegie Corporation of New York and by the John Hay Whitney Foundation. These foundations are not, however, authors, owners, publishers, or proprietors of this publication, and are not to be understood as approving by virtue of their grants any of the statements made or views expressed therein.

★

CONTENTS

Flood Fallow; Contract Farms; Research
Center; Standard Fruit and Steamship
Company; Impact on the Local Economy;
Stable Contribution

Contribution to the Economy; Comparisons
With Other Activities; United Fruit's Contribution to Development

Contract Operations; Land-Use Problems;
International Railways of Central America; Contribution to the Economy

United Fruit Share; Problems of Ecuadorian Producers; Contribution to the Local
Economy

Brief History; Possible Future Pattern;
Contribution to the Local Economy

United Fruit Company Contributions to
Countries of Production; Appraisal of the

United Fruit Company as an Investment; The
United Fruit Company Record in Social
Welfare, Labor, and Public Relations;
Why the Image Is Blacker Than the Record

Future of the World Banana Market; Persist-
ence of Large-scale Integrated Organization;
Future Position of the United Fruit Company
in Bananas; Future Programs for Using
Abandoned Banana Lands; Gradual Emanci-
pation from Extraneous Services; The Problem of Company-Government Contracts

ORGANIZATION OF AMERICAN STATES

ARGENTINA · BOLIVIA · BRAZIL · CHILE
COLOMBIA · COSTA RICA · CUBA · DOMINICAN
REPUBLIC · ECUADOR · EL SALVADOR

GUATEMALA · HAITI · HONDURAS · MEXICO
NICARAGUA · PANAMA · PARAGUAY · PERU
UNITED STATES · URUGUAY · VENEZUELA

GENERAL SECRETARIAT
PAN AMERICAN UNION
Washington 6, D. C., U. S. A.
(Cable Address PAU WASHDC)

May 23, 1958

My dear Mr. Symington:

I appreciate your sending me a copy of the text of your latest case study in the series relating to United States business operations abroad. I also note with interest, that in the preparation of this volume, "The United Fruit Company in Latin America" you had the good fortune of securing the services of Mr. Galo Plaza, my friend of many years standing, as co-author.

Your series of studies to date has clearly shown that United States enterprise is being moved more and more by a growing sense of social responsibility in its activities abroad and that it has demonstrated how profitable operation, on the one hand, and general economic improvement and development, on the other, can be mutually accelerative.

Economic and social development throughout the Americas is one of the fundamental objectives of the Organization of American States and its various organs. Your case studies reflect the many areas in which United States business enterprise has contributed to these ends in particular countries in Latin America. I call attention especially to such constructive steps as are exemplified in the founding of the Escuela Agrícola Panamericana al Zamorano, Honduras, by the President of the United Fruit Company in 1942. This is but one of many instances in which the foresight of enlightened business leaders has resulted in practical measures and in the type of collaboration which is bound to strengthen the bonds of inter-American economic, social, and cultural relations.

Sincerely yours,

José A. Mora
Secretary General

Mr. Charles J. Symington
Chairman, Policy Committee for NPA Case Studies
National Planning Association
230 Park Avenue
New York 17, New York

AUTHORS' NOTE

T HE AUTHORS of this report share a deep conviction that there is need for an ever-increasing degree of understanding and collaboration between the citizens of the Latin American republics and of the United States. Trade exchanges excepted, the flow of capital from the United States to Latin America in the form of direct private investments has been the most important factor in the economic interrelationships of the two areas. In addition to their evident contribution to development, there is growing recognition that direct private investments have exerted a very large influence upon the volume and structure of United States-Latin American trade.

When we were invited by the National Planning Association to report upon the United Fruit Company's operations in Latin America as a case study of this type of investment, as a condition of our acceptance, we asked for assurance of full access to all relevant accounts and reports of the company. This assurance was given by the management of United Fruit, and was carried out not only in letter and spirit by the company's representatives in Boston and in the field, but with a generosity and freedom that has earned our respect as well as our sincere gratitude.

We owe an equal debt to numerous government officials, including heads of state, in the six countries in which our field studies were centered. They gave unstintingly of their time and in many cases provided special compilations of unpublished economic data that were a necessary background against which United Fruit's impact on local economies could be measured. An equal measure of generous and gracious response and cooperation was afforded by private citizens of the six countries—by businessmen, independent banana growers, members of the company's work force, labor union officials, and others too numerous to catalog. And the debt multiplies to include the help of U.S. officials in Washington and in the embassies abroad, to officials of the Organization of American States who made available to us the findings of their own forthcoming study of the banana industry, to officers of United Fruit's competitors, and to jobbers and retailers whose establishments we visited.

All of these gave us their help in a measure that far transcended the accepted amenities of social courtesy. We acknowledge their assistance with gratitude and with a deepened awareness of the meaning of inter-American cooperation.

We wish, also, to record our indebtedness to the following who assisted us directly upon various phases of this study: William Butler, who accompanied us on our field trips, contributed valuable advice in planning the study, and wrote one chapter; John Gillin, Miguel Albornoz, and Miss Lilo Linke who conducted field investigations under Galo Plaza's direction; and Shaw Livermore, Ferdinand Mehrlich, and Miss Erika Teutsch who carried out specific research assignments or assisted with statistical calculations and editing with Stacy May.

A large measure of any worth that the study may have is due to the help we have received as recorded above, but the authors assume full and joint responsibility for what has been presented.

In the hope that this report might contribute to the methodology of studying an important field, in addition to throwing light upon one company's operations abroad, we have tried to employ objective measurement to the greatest practicable degree and to spell out sources and procedures that might be useful to others embarking upon comparable undertakings. We realize that this imposes upon the reader a greater burden than many who are interested mainly in the study's findings may be willing to assume. Accordingly, tempering our zeal with mercy, we recommend that those who would prefer to go directly to conclusions without the pain of sifting evidence should turn to Chapter IX. That chapter summarizes the major findings of this study, with some indication of where, in earlier chapters, the reader may find a fuller exposition of issues about which his curiosity may have been aroused.

T HIS SEVENTH STUDY in the National Planning Association's series on United States Business Performance Abroad turned out to be a much more ambitious project than we intended when the United Fruit Company first agreed to cooperate in a study of its operations abroad. Subsequent inquiry indicated that it would not be meaningful to restrict the study of the company's banana operations —which are its principal operations—to a single country. However, it seemed unreasonable from the point of view of research and cost to include every country in which the company had banana operations. The solution seemed to point to studying the company's banana business in the six banana-producing countries in Central and South America (Colombia, Costa Rica, Ecuador, Guatemala, Honduras, and Panama) that produce 60 percent of the world's banana tonnage and 90 percent of U.S. imports of this exotic fruit.

Happily, this six-nation limitation lent itself at least to partial geographical and cultural similarity in coverage. In addition, it facilitated concentration in this study on the company's banana operations which account for over 60 percent of its gross sales and 85 percent of its gross profits before taxes. Without these obviously minor limitations, the study could not have been sufficiently simplified for presentation in this series. Neither the authors nor officials of United Fruit, however, feel that the frank appraisal of the company's banana activities in the six nations—as reflected in this study— would be modified if *all* of its operations outside the United States had been included for study.

The National Planning Association is grateful for the wholehearted cooperation of the United Fruit Company in releasing for publication much factual information supplied from its own records. Employees throughout the company here and abroad were uniformly courteous and helpful to the authors in their search for facts. Much credit also should be given to the many individuals in governmental and private posts in the six countries studied, as well as to officials of the

Organization of American States and the U.S. government, who gave so generously of their time and knowledge to the authors.

United Fruit has been a factor of varying influence in the economic life of several friendly, but small, republics in Central America. At times its banana operations in some of these countries have been brought to public attention, and not always in a laudatory way. The National Planning Association received full encouragement from the company in giving adequate coverage of United Fruit's principal business—bananas—and in extending its inquiry beyond the formula utilized in this series up to now. The authors in this study have related much more than a story of a rough road to success—they also provide a painstaking economic and social analysis of the banana business in the Western Hemisphere.

Eugene W. Burgess

Eugene W. Burgess
Director of Research

May 1958

★

THE

UNITED FRUIT COMPANY

IN LATIN AMERICA

by

Stacy May and *Galo Plaza*

★

I.

Brief History: Evolution of the Business

THIS IS the story of how, over a relatively short period of time, a highly perishable tropical fruit has become an important item in world trade. It is the story of how an implausible product, which was being introduced into the United States as a curiosity a little over 80 years ago, is today carried by the millions of stems, on more than a hundred fast refrigerated ships, from farms in the tropics to markets in the United States, Canada, and Europe, to become a common foodstuff in almost every household.

Our study concerns primarily the United Fruit Company as a producer and exporter of bananas. It explores the world banana market, the basic economics of banana growing and distribution. It focuses particularly on the role of United Fruit in the banana industry, its impact on producing countries, its problems and future trends, not only with respect to production and marketing of the fruit, but also

1

in its relations with governments, its labor force, and with public opinion, both in the United States and Latin America.

The study concentrates on what has happened since 1950. But in order to better visualize the company's present activities, one must look back and examine how the banana came to occupy its present important place in international commerce and how United came to exercise its present predominantly important place in the world trade of bananas and, particularly, in the American trade. It is not a simple success story from the beginning; it is more than that. It is a story of dreams and ambitions, of struggle and despair, of misunderstanding and even of hatred, of trial and error; all of this against the backdrop of sodden humidity, heat nightmares, tropical rains, hurricanes, and murderous yellow fever, dysentery, and malaria. It is also the story of improvement through experience; it is the saga of the rise of stout-hearted men, big as Ulysses in their achievements. It could be written as a romance, its pages bathed in the clean salt spray of the tropical seas as flying fish scatter before the bows of graceful Yankee clipper ships. But our task is the more prosaic one of recording facts as we found them.

No one has summed up more forcefully the contrast between past and present attitudes of those responsible for the banana industry than Samuel Zemurray. This was in a statement attributed to him shortly after he first became associated with the United Fruit Company as Managing Director in 1932 after a long career as one of the most colorful banana pioneers and one of United's most formidable rivals. In his reference to the past he clearly was speaking of banana pioneers generally rather than of the company he had just joined when he said: "I feel guilty about some of the things we did . . . all we cared about was dividends. Well, you can't do business that way today. We have learned that what's best for the countries we operate in is best for the company. Maybe we can't make the people love us, but we can make ourselves so useful to them, that they will want us to stay." This frank and deeply felt expression of attitude is still dominant today. Through mutual understanding between the company and the people and their governments, a new, clear and mutually profitable relationship is evolving.

HISTORY OF THE BANANA

THE BANANA'S HISTORY goes back thousands of years. Rumphius, who has been called the greatest botanist before Lin-

2

naeus, in his *Herbarium Amboinense,* written in shadowy antiquity, mentions that the banana even then was of venerable lineage. It is a recognized fact that man has used the banana as a food staple for thousands of years. It was one of the first fruits grown by primitive agricultural peoples.

The banana is often referred to in ancient Hindu, Chinese, Greek, and Roman literature. Mention of the banana is found in various sacred texts of oriental people. Chief of these writings are two Hindu epics, the *Mahabharata,* the work of an unknown author, and the *Ramayana* of the poet Valmiki, and there also are references in certain sacred Buddhist texts. These chronicles describe a beverage derived from bananas which Buddhist monks are allowed to drink. Yang Fu, a Chinese official in the second century A.D., wrote an *Encyclopedia of Rare Things,* in which he describes the banana plant. This possibly is the first mention made of the banana in Chinese texts. The Greek naturalist philosopher Theophrastus wrote a book on plants in the fourth century B.C. in which he describes the banana. His book is considered the first scientific botanical work extant. The Roman naturalist Pliny the Elder describes the banana plant in his *Historia Naturalis* written in 77 A.D. He mentions Theophrastus as his source of information. Modern archeologists have found the banana depicted in ancient ruins such as the Buddhist temple of Bharhut dating from the second century B.C. and the Javanese monument to Buddha erected in Borobodur in the year 850 A.D.

The exact origin of the banana is not entirely clear. Dr. Herbert Spinden[1], anthropologist, wrote: "The first home of the edible banana was in all probability the humid tropical region of Southern Asia, which includes Northeast India, Burma, Cambodia and parts of Southern China, as well as the large islands of Sumatra, Java, Borneo, the Philippines and Formosa. Here, the seedless varieties of the true domestic banana are commonly found growing wild, although perhaps they have merely escaped from cultivation." From the East the banana was most likely introduced to Egypt and Africa by early eastern traders. The banana variety that predominates in contemporary world trade, the Gros Michel, was probably first brought to the New World by a French botanist, François Pouat, around 1836. The old Spanish chroniclers state that upon the arrival of the Conquistadores in the New World's tropics, they found platanos or cooking bananas as early as 1504, the date the city of Santo Domingo, the first capital of Spanish America, was founded on the island of Hispaniola.

---

[1] Quoted in Charles Morrow Wilson, *Empire in Green and Gold,* Henry Holt & Co., Inc., New York, 1947, p. 13.

Oviedo in his *Historia General e Natural de Indias* assigns to Friar Tomas de Berlanga, Bishop of Panama and discoverer of the Galapagos Islands, credit for introducing the first plantings of true fruit banana types from the Canary Islands to Santo Domingo in 1516: "There is a fruit here, called platanos, but in truth they are not . . . nor did they used to be in the Indies, but were brought hither. One hears on all sides that this special kind was brought from the islands of Grand Canaria in the year 1516 by the Reverend Friar Tomas de Berlanga of the Order of Predicadores to this city of Santo Domingo, whence they spread to the other settlements of this island and to all other islands peopled by Christians and they had even been carried to the mainland and in every port they have flourished . . . ."

THE BANANA TRADE

FOOD HAS BEEN a major commodity in world trade for a long time. Grain and fish were traded for pottery and jewelry among the Greeks, the Phoenicians, and other early settlers of the Mediterranean. As civilizations matured, and palates became epicurean, foreign foods were in high demand. The ancient Romans, at the height of their civilization, imported jars of salted fish from the Black Seas at high prices, causing old Senator Cato to complain in a speech to the Senate that "Rome was the only city in the world where such a jar of fish cost more than a yoke of oxen."

The banana, until the year 1866, was virtually unknown in Western Europe and the United States. The first bananas were brought to the States in the early nineteenth century by sea captains who, on returning from voyages to tropical America had loaded as extraordinary cargo bunches of the strange yellow tropical fruit. Carl B. Frank started importing bananas from Colon to New York in 1866 from plantations near the present Canal Zone. At the Philadelphia Centennial Exposition of American Independence in 1876, bananas wrapped in tinfoil were sold to intrigued buyers at 10¢ apiece. Yet, today, less than a century later, the banana is a staple in almost every home.

The banana trade, in its infant evolution, was hazardous and unpredictable. Pioneering in the pestilent jungle lowlands, where bananas grow, was heartbreaking because the jungle fights to reclaim its terrain and only the strong survive. Lack of roads and transportation made it doubly difficult. In Central America there was not even regular shipping service to the north before 1855.

In 1870, Captain Lorenzo Dow Baker, commander of the fishing schooner *Telegraph* out of Wellfleet, Massachusetts, loaded as extra cargo 160 bunches of bananas purchased for a shilling a bunch at Port Antonio, Jamaica. Eleven days after the date of purchase the *Telegraph* docked in Jersey City, where the bananas sold at two dollars a bunch. Captain Baker's profitable sale in Jersey City led him to believe that he could capture the consumer's taste with good tropical fruit in the same way the fruit had caught his fancy on the wharfs at Port Antonio. So he continued to carry bananas as extra cargo from Jamaica, unloading in the larger port of Boston. In Boston, Andrew Preston, an agent of the small but respected produce firm, Seaverns & Co., sold the bananas at a commission. Banana sales in Boston were uniformly successful. Both Baker and Preston thought that increased shipping and selling of bananas would prove a profitable independent business. In 1876, Baker was a prosperous shipper and partner in the Standard Steam Navigation Company. He persuaded Andrew Preston and nine of his partners to form an independent fruit agency. So, in 1885, the Boston Fruit Company was founded.

Captain Baker settled in Jamaica where he supervised the shipping and freighting of bananas to Boston on Standard Steam Navigation Company ships. Preston, as Boston's sales manager, found new markets for the increasing influx of bananas from Jamaica. The Boston Fruit Company prospered, more ships were added to the fleets, more markets were developed.

FORMATION OF THE UNITED FRUIT COMPANY

To MEET INCREASING DEMANDS for bananas in the States, Baker and Preston realized they would have to look farther abroad than Jamaica, Cuba, and Santo Domingo for their fruit supply. They had heard of Minor Keith, a railroad builder in Costa Rica, whose companies—the Tropical Trading and Transport Company, the Colombia Land Company, and Snyder Banana Company—had been shipping bananas from Colombia, Costa Rica, Panama, and Nicaragua to New Orleans.

The demand for bananas was growing steadily. By 1898, the total importation of bananas from the American tropics was 16 million stems. No more were imported only because this was the total product available. Over a hundred firms were engaged in the importation of bananas to the United States before 1899. During the early years, when small cargoes were easily disposed of at ships' sides for high prices, it was possible to operate at a profit even with the crudest and most wasteful methods. As the demand grew and the marketing of bananas expanded beyond the ports of entry, most of the small inefficient firms, that had enjoyed temporary success, fell by the wayside. At the time the United Fruit Company was founded, about 22 firms remained in business, including the Boston Fruit Company, which served the northeastern sector of the United States, and the Keith interests that operated out of New Orleans.

Minor Keith, who had borrowed heavily on short terms from New York and London financing companies in order to further railroad construction in Costa Rica, ran into difficulties in meeting his obligations. Matters were further complicated when the firm of Hoadley & Company of New Orleans, which had been his distributor for years, failed, involving Mr. Keith in a loss of $1.5 million. Because of the failure of his agent, Keith was compelled to make new arrangements for the distribution of his fruit and entered into negotiations with Preston, President of the Boston Fruit Company. The Fruit Dispatch Company, which had recently been formed by Boston Fruit for the purpose of expanding and expediting the distribution and sales of bananas, took over the handling of some of Keith's fruit.

This business relationship grew into a consolidation of the interests of the Boston Fruit Company and the companies controlled by Keith. The motivation of the merger was not to eliminate competition. The Boston Fruit Company, with production in the Caribbean islands and marketing organizations in the northeastern United States, served an entirely different sector of the country than that covered by Keith. The latter's fruit came from Central America and Colombia and was marketed throughout the South from New Orleans and Mobile. However, both saw the need for expanding production and a more efficient system of marketing. Both had been victims of floods, drought, blowdowns, and political upheavals. They realized that a more constant and reliable flow of fruit from the tropics could only be obtained by spreading their production base to a number of areas so that any local disaster could be counterbalanced by a good crop elsewhere. These were the obvious and logical reasons why these two noncompeting groups of banana companies concluded negotiations and were consolidated into a single entity, the United Fruit Company.

Incorporated on March 30, 1899, under the laws of the State of New Jersey, United Fruit had an authorized capital of $20 million. At the first offering, only $1,650,000 was invested by the public, but within one year a total of $11,230,000 had been subscribed. The company was authorized under its charter to acquire by purchase or development banana and other properties. Under this charter, United purchased the property, business, and shares of the Boston Fruit Company and its associated companies for $5,200,000, and from Keith and his associates all the properties owned by the Tropical Trading and Transport Company, Ltd., the Colombia Land Company, Ltd., and the Snyder Banana Company for about $4 million.

The following were the first officers and directors of the new company:

President and Director. . . . Andrew W. Preston, Brookline, Mass.
First Vice President
    and Director . . . . Minor C. Keith, Brooklyn, N. Y.
Second Vice President
    and Director . . . . Lamont G. Burnham, Boston, Mass.
Director . . . . .T. Jefferson Coolidge, Jr., Manchester, Mass.
Director . . . . .Kenneth K. McLeren, Jersey City, N.J.
Secretary . . . . .Bradley W. Palmer, Boston, Mass.
Treasurer . . . . .Charles A. Hubbard, Boston, Mass.

The organization of the United Fruit Company marked the end of the era of pioneering, of risks and hardships, easy profits as well as total failures, and the beginning of a new era that converted the highly perishable tropical banana into an important item of world trade.

The new United Fruit Company had 112 miles of railroad; 212,394 acres of land, of which 61,263 acres were in production; and a capital of $11,230,000. After formation of United, the young organization began developing and expanding other sources of supply. It bought lands in Santo Domingo, Honduras, Guatemala, Panama, and Cuba, and additional acreage in Nicaragua, Jamaica, and Colombia. By 1930, its capital had increased to $215 million. Land was exceedingly cheap in the vast undeveloped lowlands, and eager governments made available large tracts of jungle territories for the prospect of getting them opened to profitable development through an enterprise that would supply basic railroad and port facilities that could be furnished in no other way.

On the home front, Preston developed additional markets in Boston and surrounding areas. He established outlets in other ports along the East Coast—Baltimore, Philadelphia, and New York. More ships were added to the fleets and the company looked to Europe as another market ground. By 1910, United was shipping its bananas to Europe. Today, United Fruit is the major banana concern in the world, and in 1956 it sold almost 39 million stems in North America and Europe.

RAILROADS AND THE BANANA INDUSTRY

UNITED FRUIT PROBABLY would not hold its present position as the major banana company in the world had it not been for the ingenuity of Minor Keith. His uncle, Henry Meiggs, in the 1850's had pioneered in the railroad industry in Chile and Peru. Tomas Guardia, President of Costa Rica, in 1870 contracted with Meiggs and Keith to build a national railroad from Port Limón on the Caribbean to the mountain town of San Jose, the country's capital.

The construction of the railroad through the tropical jungles of Costa Rica met with one disaster after another. Dysentery, malaria, and other tropical diseases constantly cut down manpower. Meiggs died of yellow fever; so did three of Keith's brothers, and Keith was left to carry out the construction. Besides the ever-present toll of disease, food supplies often spoiled before reaching workers on inland plantations, and shiploads of construction materials coming from overseas were nearly always delayed by storms at sea or lost on reefs and shoals in the hazardous harbor of Port Limón. Minor Keith had married the daughter of an ex-President of Costa Rica; he had an engaging personality and made many friends. He was a good organizer and a man with considerable financial experience; his ambition was to build a railroad system through all of Central America. At his death, his German biographer, Herman W. Bitter, referred to Keith as "the uncrowned King of Central America."

Keith had completed only 60 miles of the railroad when he ran out of funds. He was forced to find another source of income so that construction could be carried on. Experimentally, he planted bananas in the Zent Valley, back of Limón, for he had heard that the tropical fruit had a market in the United States. He shipped the first harvest of Zent Valley bananas via his railroad to Port Limón and from there they were taken to New Orleans where they were promptly sold for a profit. Highly encouraged, Keith began expanding his banana planting and shipping, and in 1883 was supplying shipping companies in Costa Rica, Panama, Nicaragua, and Colombia with bananas. With additional capital from banana sales, Keith pushed the railroad to completion in 1890.

Completion of the Costa Rican railroad, despite man-killing diseases and swampy lands, may be compared to the engineering marvel of the two North American Harmon brothers in constructing the Quito-Guayaquil railroad in Ecuador. Keith looked to Panama as his next railroad site, and United viewed Panama as another potential banana development. Planting and railroad building in Panama were successful. Soon Panama was producing millions of banana stems for export by United Fruit. In Guatemala and Honduras, the company also investigated possibilities and found in the Caribbean lowlands of the two countries additional banana lands.

It is interesting to observe the close relationship between railroads in Central America and the development of banana production. All the Central American republics, at one time or another, dreamed of building ocean-to-ocean railroads, taking advantage of the narrowness of the continent in Central America. The immense financial success of the Panama railroad, built in 1850, was an added incentive.

Some major railroads had been started before United Fruit came into existence, but the roads were not completed and the dreams of transcontinental railroads never came true. The fast-growing banana business furnished abundant cargo for these railroads whenever they traversed banana country and in some cases the revenues from the transportation of bananas saved the railroads from bankruptcy. Also, United and other fruit companies built railroads for the handling of bananas, freight, and people required for the banana industry. Thus, economic reasons explain why most of the railroads' mileage in the Central American countries is to be found on the coastal plains, where bananas are grown, and why the banana industry has been closely related with the operation of railroads in that area.

The construction of railroads was an indispensable and integral part of the development of banana plantations in areas not previously served by any form of land transportation. The United Fruit Company was interested in building railroads for the service of its banana operations; the lines would logically follow the shortest good route from the port or connecting line to the banana plantation. These railroads were of utmost importance to the countries in tropical America because they opened up undeveloped land and made possible its transformation into banana plantations, which contributed substantially to the national wealth in countries where mineral resources have not been developed and agriculture is the chief source of income. Notably, bananas contribute a large part of that income.

In Costa Rica, Keith built part of the international railroad, but when banana growing overshadowed interest in railroad building across the continent, he concentrated his efforts on rail construction in the lowlands back of Port Limón. Early in the century, United Fruit built the Northern Railway to serve its banana operations on the Atlantic Coast. Later it acquired the right to operate the lines of the Costa Rican Railway which then extended from Port Limón to San Jose. The company has disposed of its interests in the Northern and Costa Rican railways on the Atlantic Coast, and now has only local banana railroads on the Pacific Coast.

Honduras also had high hopes of a transcontinental railroad as a means to encourage the setting up of a federation of Central American republics and to cash in on the growing traffic from the East to the California gold fields. An attempt was made to float a loan for this purpose as far back as 1853, but not much resulted from these efforts until 1867-70, when a 50-mile road was built from Puerto Cortez on the Caribbean Coast toward the interior. Banana interests, during the Bonilla regime, obtained authorization to set up the TELA Railroad Company and the Trujillo Railroad Company, and in compensation received government land. In 1924, out of some 400,000 acres of land controlled by United in Honduras, about 175,000 had been obtained as compensation for railroad construction. Land grants of this type were ordinary procedure, and in addition national governments granted exemptions of port duties and other concessions in order to hasten the construction of rail lines. Several attempts were made to continue construction of the national railroad toward the Pacific, but nothing ever materialized. The line never went further inland than San Pedro Sula. The fact is that to this date, although there are over 900 miles of railroad in Honduras, all are within the rich banana lands of the North Coast. The capital city, Tegucigalpa, and other major towns still lack rail communication.

In Guatemala, railroads came long before bananas, and in this country many of the major towns are connected by rail to the sea. Before 1885, 20 miles were built from the capital, Guatemala City, toward the Atlantic. During the decade from 1880 to 1890, American contractors built the Central Railroad of Guatemala, which connects the capital with San Jose on the Pacific Coast, and the Western Railway, which connects with Puerto Champerico, also on the Pacific. Later on, 136 miles were constructed from Puerto Barrios on the Atlantic toward the capital.

In 1904, Keith and William C. van Horn contracted for the construction of the Northern Railroad. A company was formed, called the Guatemala Railroad Company, and was incorporated under the laws of the State of New Jersey with a capital of $40 million. The new company took over the 136 miles in operation from Puerto Barrios and constructed the remaining 61 miles over the mountains to Guatemala City. In 1912, this company changed its name to International Railways of Central America, and the Western Railroad with 200 miles of track was taken over. This system of railroads which extended from Guatemala into El Salvador, grew over the years. In 1930, International Railways operated about 887 miles of track. Although Keith's dream of connecting the Central American republics with Mexico to the north and Panama to the south never came true, his contribution to the building of railroads in the Caribbean region was extraordinary.

International Railways, with too little traffic to support its expenses, had been on the verge of bankruptcy and in the hope of solving its financial difficulties it approached United Fruit and reached an understanding that became effective in 1936. Previous to this, United had signed a contract with the government of Guatemala which granted the company the right to develop a large banana plantation at Tiquisate on the Pacific Coast and bound it to build, at its own expense, a rail line from Tiquisate to an open roadstead on the Pacific at Concepción del Mar. According to the contract, it was to be a port open to all shippers. Had this port been built, International Railways inevitably would have lost much of its profitable long-haul traffic from the West Coast to Puerto Barrios on the Atlantic. Most of that traffic, notably export coffee, would have moved out via the West Coast port instead.

In this situation, under pressure to help solve the railroad's financial difficulties, United Fruit agreed in 1936 not to build a port at all on the Pacific Coast near which its Tiquisate plantations were located. Instead, it made a traffic rights agreement with International Railways which enabled it to ship all its Pacific Coast bananas over that company's lines to Puerto Barrios, some 288 miles away on the Atlantic. The agreement, originally covering a period of 25 years, was subsequently extended until 1968. Under its terms, United made substantial capital contributions in cash and equipment to International Railways and was afforded preferential rates on its freight carriage. To enter into these arrangements, United had to persuade the government of Guatemala to release it from its obligation to build the port. After considerable negotiation, the government agreed in March 1936 that the building of the port should be optional rather than obligatory. The modification of United's original plan with respect to its Pacific Coast operations and its subsequent relationships with International Railways have been among the major sources of criticism against the company in Guatemala. (A more extended discussion of the specific issues in dispute is set forth in Chapter VI.)

In Colombia, the Santa Marta Railroad was originally started in 1881 for the exportation of sugar. After Keith became manager of the Colombia Land Company, Ltd., the Santa Marta Railroad Company started to develop transportation of bananas. In 1925, it operated 176 miles of track, 91 of which constituted the main line to Fundación, and 81 miles of branch lines within the plantations. Long years of friction between the railroad company controlled by United Fruit and the Colombian government ended when, in 1932, the company transferred the railway to the government. The government, in turn, leased the railway to United for a 30-year period, and gave the company the right to surrender the lease at an earlier date. The company exercised this option in 1947, and the railroad has since been operated as the Magdalena Division of the National Railways of Colombia.

Although railroad building preceded the development of the banana industry in Panama, the operation of railroads in the banana-growing regions of this country is intimately associated with United Fruit. Early in the century, United built railway lines connecting its plantations with the port of Bocas del Toro on the Atlantic Coast. In 1927, the government completed its railway from interior points to Puerto Armuelles on the Pacific. United Fruit then built a network of lines connecting with the government railway to provide transportation for bananas from its farms on the Pacific side to this port.

Railroads were vital to the banana enterprise. If the banana interests had not provided them, railroad service for the scantily populated lowlands in Central America would have been delayed for many decades. But the banana companies did not provide a railway network ideally suited to serve the overall economic needs of the several national economies. That was not their business. Nevertheless, historically railroads and bananas have become so closely associated in the minds of people in the area, that the banana companies more often have been censured for their failure to provide fully for all railway needs, than credited for their considerable contributions to this important field.

UNITED FRUIT'S COMPETITION

THROUGHOUT ITS GROWTH, United Fruit has had competition. In early years, the Boston Fruit Company had supplied bananas for the city of Boston and surrounding areas, but as successful sales brought in money, Boston Fruit began to consider the possibility of developing markets in New York, Baltimore, Philadelphia, Mobile, and New Orleans. In general, Boston Fruit had been more lucky than other early banana companies. The banana lands of Jamaica had not been struck by the sudden hurricanes that had wiped out so many of the banana lands held by other small enterprises. Boston Fruit, because of its consistent policy of maintaining several sources of supply, was a stable and respectable little company with enough capital to look after its interests. But both Preston and Baker knew that to insure their business they had to expand both banana supplies and markets.

Boston Fruit proceeded cautiously and wisely. Wherever it was financially advantageous, it bought out small companies in ports along the East Coast. Later, union with Keith's Tropical Trading & Transport Company and the formation of United Fruit gave the Boston firm additional banana supplies and markets along the East Coast and in New Orleans. After the Boston and Keith groups joined forces, the United Fruit Company emerged as the largest enterprise servicing the world banana trade. From 1900 until 1910, its average yearly business accounted for well over three-quarters of total stems imported by the North American and European markets combined. In 1900, there were about 20 competing companies operating in these markets, but less than one-quarter of the total trade was divided between them.

United's relative position declined steadily subsequent to this first decade of its existence. The inherent hazards of the business have contributed to a high incidence of business casualties among those who have attempted to enter into this precarious vocation. The risks have not prevented many from trying, and an ever-increasing number has met with success. Today, there are about 160 importing firms servicing the North American market alone. The largest of these, after United Fruit, is the Standard Fruit and Steamship Company, which imports about 30 percent of the stem volume handled by United Fruit in this market.

Between 1910 and 1930, United Fruit's competitors made steady inroads upon its overall position in the two great import markets. A number of additional mergers, or rather purchases of going companies, were effected by United during this period, but only one was of major importance. The portion of the whole trade handled by its competitors increased rather than diminished. On the average, United handled about 60 percent of the total trade over this 20-year period as against 77 percent in its first decade of operations.

November 1929 marked the last important merger transaction in United Fruit's history. That was the date when it purchased the Cuyamel Fruit Company. The president of Cuyamel, and the creative brain that had built it to important stature, was Samuel Zemurray. The name is one that assumes sufficient importance in United Fruit's subsequent fortunes to warrant here a review of the transaction's background. But first, to round out the theme under discussion, it is appropriate to note that the acquisition of Cuyamel did not appreciably halt the steady encroachment of United Fruit's competitors upon its position in the world market. That position continued to decline, until today the company's share in the world banana trade is of the order of

Chart I
United Fruit's Share of the Combined North American and European Banana Market Has Steadily Declined

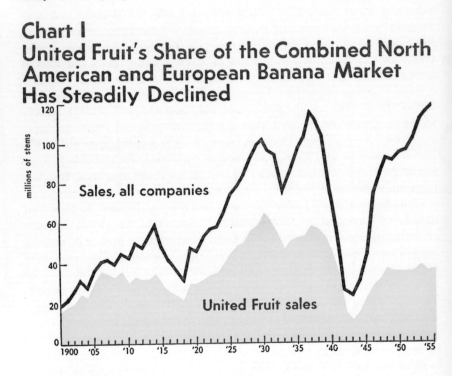

28 percent. In the past 10 years, Ecuador has emerged from a very minor status in the trade to become, since 1951, the largest exporter of bananas in the world. All but a small fraction of this increase has been accounted for by competitors of the United Fruit Company, a number of whom have outstripped United in numbers of stems produced in that country and exported from it. In Colombia, also, there has been a very considerable increase in banana production and export by local producers unaffiliated with United Fruit. They have overcome the inherent disadvantages of relatively small-scale independent oper-

ation by organizing two cooperatives through which their production is marketed.

It has been stated that the present-day United Fruit Company represents the merged businesses of some 21 banana concerns that once operated independently. The inference is drawn that by acquiring rival business interests it has succeeded in eliminating serious competitors and increasing its own stature. The record fails to bear this out. It shows that over the years there has been a marked growth both in the numbers of its competitors and the weight of their competition. Since the earliest days of its formative infancy, the record shows no acquisitions of going businesses by United that were of significant size individually or in combination other than that of the Zemurray interests. And Cuyamel, itself, appears to have increased United Fruit's relative position in even the North American market by a very scant margin.

SAMUEL ZEMURRAY AND CUYAMEL

THE SON OF A POOR BESSARABIAN FARMER, Zemurray came to the United States in 1892. At the age of 15 he helped his uncle and aunt run a little country store in Selma, Alabama. One day he ran into a banana jobber who was closing a deal with a grocer and at once saw the possibility of making a profit by selling in nearby communities ripe bananas, which sold at a discount on the docks in Mobile, before they spoiled completely. Successful in this venture, he expanded his area by shipping bananas to inland cities by rail. Next he merged with small competing companies in Mobile, Ashbel Hubbard and Thatcher Brothers Steamship Company. In 1905, he went to Honduras, then a country of constantly changing governments and recurrent revolutions. Zemurray had been purchasing bananas in the area, but then he bought land along the Cuyamel River with the idea of building a railway and growing his own fruit. However, Zemurray felt that if his venture were to pay, he would have to have certain government concessions—a guarantee against increased taxes, permission to build a railroad, and above all customs-free importation of needed construction materials upon which he considered the import duties prohibitive.

The President of Honduras at the end of 1910 was Miguel Davila. As the story is told in the March 1933 issue of *Fortune* magazine, at the same time that Zemurray was wondering how he could obtain the necessary government concessions for his Cuyamel Company, Davila was negotiating with bankers in the United States for a loan to save the country from bankruptcy. The banking interests agreed to lend Honduras the money, but only upon the stipulation that they be allowed to name their own agent, who would have control of Honduran customs collections to assure that the obligated payments of interest and principal amortization on their loan would be met. Zemurray realized that if Davila were to sign the papers for the loan, the New York banking interests might balk at any transaction that proposed even minor cuts in the existing schedule of import duties.

Needless to say, the prospect of mortgaging customs revenues to foreign banking control was not popular with many elements in Honduras. One dissenter was General Manuel Bonilla, an ex-President of Honduras living in exile in the United States and anxious to return to power. Upon the basis of a common interest in blocking the proposed loan, Bonilla went to New Orleans, sought out Zemurray, and obtained from him a loan sufficient to purchase the yacht *Hornet* that had been used for a period by the U. S. Navy. Zemurray financed also the purchase of a case of rifles with ammunition and a machine gun. On Zemurray's own power launch, Bonilla and two soldier-of-fortune cohorts were carried out to the *Hornet* and loaded aboard with their guns, thus eluding U. S. Secret Service men who were assigned to prevent the coup of which Washington had heard rumors. Zemurray himself waved the adventurers good-bye as the *Hornet* sailed from Biloxi for Honduras. The revolutionary trio disembarked in Puerto Cortez, gathered enough Bonilla sympathizers to oust Davila, and Bonilla was quickly reinstated as President. The loan agreement that Davila had hastily signed was repudiated by the Honduran Congress, and Zemurray was given every concession he had sought. The United Fruit Company, of course, was in no way involved in this incident, which occurred 20 years before it bought out Samuel Zemurray's interest in Cuyamel.

Zemurray's boundless energy, engaging personality, and many good friends in Honduras pushed him ahead in his new activity as a grower of bananas. He proved to be a good farmer. He risked millions in large-scale irrigation, on selective pruning, on propping trees with bamboo poles to keep the fruit from falling to the ground and bruising. He let the floods overflow in inferior lowlands and when later the water was permitted to drain away, a deep layer of rich alluvial soil was left on which bigger and better bananas grew. Through these practices, Zemurray was shipping to northern markets bananas of equal or better quality than those shipped by United Fruit. He had a further advantage in that he had his headquarters in the tropics and gave his banana growing personal attention. United Fruit managers had to follow directions from far-off Boston. Zemurray had become a very serious competitor; his Cuyamel Company sold more and more bananas and the quotations of its stock rose steadily.

In 1915, Cuyamel had begun to expand into the Motagua Valley region along the Honduran-Guatemalan border, for which it had been granted a concession by Honduras. The political jurisdiction of the area had been in dispute between the two governments for more than 65 years. United Fruit had a well-established interest in the area based upon the territorial claims of Guatemala. Both Guatemalan and Honduran troops were sent into the area and a few minor skirmishes took place. The incident is mentioned here because it frequently has been cited as an example of the close involvement of the early banana pioneers in Latin American politics.

In common with a number of parallel situations involving other foreign corporations that have occurred in various Latin American countries and elsewhere, opinions differ on this case. Some feel that this typifies a situation in which political frictions were brought to a head by the efforts of rival business corporations to enlist governmental support of their interests. Others feel it was more a matter of governments seeking to use such influence as important foreign corporations might bring to bear in support of their respective political claims. We have no firm basis for forming a judgment upon this issue. It can be stated that the U. S. State Department offered its services in mediation of this dispute, which was not settled until after the Cuyamel Fruit Company had ceased to exist.

In November 1929, Zemurray sold his interest for 300,000 shares of United Fruit stock worth $31,500,000, which made him the company's largest single stockholder. Now a man of great wealth, Zemurray retired to his home in New Orleans, but as soon as the depression took hold, he found that his wealth was shrinking alarmingly. United Fruit stock that he had acquired dropped to a record low of 10¼ a share, which reduced the value of his holdings by $27 million. In 1920, the company's profit had reached a high of $44.6 million; in 1932, profits dropped to $6.2 million.

As a large stockholder, Zemurray demanded to be heard in Boston and after a short struggle with his fellow directors, he took over complete control of Latin American activities under the impressive title of Managing Director in Charge of Operations. United Fruit stock climbed back to 26 in a matter of weeks on the strength of his prestige alone. He moved down to the tropics, established personal contacts with his old associates, gave local managers a freer hand, and overhauled operations all around. He had to face the serious menace of the rapid spread of sigatoka and of other serious banana plant diseases, which if left unchecked could have wiped out the industry.

SHIPPING, COMMUNICATIONS, AND MARKETING

IN THE EARLY DAYS, United shipped its fruit on the small vessels of the New Orleans, Belize, Royal Mail and Central American Steamship Company and of the Bluefields Steamship Company, which it controlled. In 1904, the Tropical Fruit Steamship Company, Ltd., was organized and three ships commissioned for the banana trade sailed under the British flag.

Andrew Preston created United's Great White Fleet. He saw a profit in passenger traffic and in 1899 chartered four new ships (the *Admiral Dewey, Admiral Schley, Admiral Sampson,* and the *Farragut*), that originally had been built for the Navy. Each carried 53 passengers and 35,000 bunches of bananas, which assured a fast and efficient service from the tropics to U. S. ports. In 1903, the *Venus,* owned by the Weinbergers of New Orleans and chartered by United, was rigged up for refrigeration, and as the first successful refrigerated ship started a new era in ocean transportation. Preston contracted for the building of three almost identical ships, the *San Jose, Limón,* and *Esparta,* the nucleus of the White Fleet which grew to 95 ships by 1933.

Fast, refrigerated ships alone could not assure the efficient movement of bananas from the tropics to the United States. The profitable handling of bananas also involves rapid communication of directives and information between domestic offices and the remote plantations. Telephone and telegraph services between the United States and areas of United's tropical operations were hopelessly inadequate. As early as 1903, Preston and Keith became interested in radio. Pioneering in wireless communication was expensive and not always successful. Static and tropical storms were a constant problem. In 1904, United was first to put commercial radio on shipboard. At last in 1910, thanks to Preston's vision and tenacity, uninterrupted radio communication between the United States and Central America was formally established. For the first time commercial international broadcasting became trustworthy. In 1913, Tropical Radio Telegraph Company was incorporated as a subsidiary of United Fruit.

Fast transportation from the tropics and an efficient communication system helped, but much more was needed to assure the proper marketing of the fruit. The pioneer banana trade was the acme of disorder.

18

The almost complete lack of quality standards severely handicapped reliability in merchandising. Not much fruit was moving to interior markets, and an efficient and rapid distribution system had to be established if such markets were to be adequately supplied. For this purpose, Fruit Dispatch was organized by the Boston Fruit Company in Boston and New York and then expanded throughout the United States. It was maintained as a separate subsidiary by United Fruit. Success in the banana trade depends not only on growing large and healthy stems of bananas, but on the integrated operation of producing the fruit in the American tropics coordinated with efficient transportation and distribution throughout the marketing areas.

THE COMPANY IN PERSPECTIVE

TO EVALUATE EVENTS of half a century or more ago in the light of present-day standards and practices is to invite distortion and commit injustice. Past events can be better weighed and understood in the light of their own time and scene. The days of banana pioneering were rough times in Central American politics. Countries and factions within countries were chronically at war with each other. A president was no sooner inaugurated than overthrown. Strong men took over and ran the countries as if they were their own personal properties until they stopped a bullet or until stronger men succeeded. International relationships reflected this dismal state of affairs. Seen through U. S. State Department eyes, tropical America was a convulsive, unstable region that needed watching and protection. Looked at from below, the actions and attitudes of the United States were symbolized by the image of Uncle Sam forwarding his self-interest with the benefit of a big stick.

The banana-producing countries were poor; few mineral resources had been developed; they depended almost entirely on the agriculture of their cool, high, inland valleys. Their coastal lowlands were covered by virgin jungles; the few so-called "ports" that served to maintain tenuous contact with the outside world were pestholes. No wonder the governments were eager to attract those enterprising Americans that had found a use for their wastelands and were willing to invest unheard-of amounts of dollars in clearing the jungle and building railways for the growing of bananas. This explains why national governments were willing to sign contracts and grant concessions on terms that today would be considered grossly unfavorable. But, at that time, such arrangements represented to the governments an oppor-

19

tunity for opening up to civilization without cost great tracts of land that were valueless to them as they stood, and with no other hope for increasing their value in sight. To the foreign investors, the terms did not appear to be unreasonably cheap, in view of what they conceived the risks to be—a judgment that has been vindicated by time. Even from the vantage point of hindsight, it is difficult to say whether or not, if the producing countries had set harder terms, the job would have got done. It did, and most of the modern ports in Central America are there because banana pioneers built them.

The early contracts made by United Fruit in tropical countries fixed low export taxes on bananas for a period of years and granted certain tax exemptions. Among these were exemption from import duty on heavy equipment and materials for the construction and operation of railroads, wharves, electric plants, communication facilities, and in some instances exemption for materials and supplies for irrigation and drainage works. Its contract of 1900 with Costa Rica, for example, remitted export taxes entirely for a period of 10 years, and for the following 20 years set the banana export tax at 1¢ per stem. In 1930, this tax was raised to 2¢ per stem. Its original contract in Guatemala called for payments to the central government of $14,000 per year plus an export tax of 1¢ per stem. The company, however, remained liable for other taxes payable by local enterprises—such as property taxes, consular fees, and import duties on all articles except those specifically exempted.

At the time United Fruit started its tropical operations, there was no income tax either in the United States or in any of the tropical countries. When the United States established its income tax in 1914, the income of U. S. companies from operations abroad was made subject to income tax here with a credit for income taxes paid abroad. When the tropical countries, in turn, began enacting income taxes, it was found that some of the contracts under which United was operating stipulated that the company was not subject to any taxes beyond those specifically listed. In all such cases, United Fruit amended these contracts to accept liability to income taxes in the countries in which it operates. Costa Rica took the initiative and deserves major credit for bargaining through the pattern that now applies throughout the Central American area. This change has greatly increased the revenue of tropical countries from the operations of United Fruit. From the detailed accounting of the company's operations in later chapters, it will be seen that its overall tax contributions to the producing countries currently run at a level that by no stretch of the imagination could be held to place it in a preferential position.

20

The very existence of special contracts between foreign corporations and sovereign governments is something that grates upon Latin American sensibilities, regardless of whether or not the terms are equitable. It is only fair to point out, however, that because of the character of the company's operations in developing jungle areas, some form of contract with the local government was mandatory. United had to construct such important works as railways, wharves, electric plants, radio stations, and other works of a similar character, which is not permissible without government authorization in the form of a franchise or contract. Furthermore, rightly or wrongly, foreign investors generally have been reluctant to commit to relatively immature economies large amounts of capital in this class of development, without having assurance in explicit contract terms that the burdens on its works and operations would not be radically increased for a period of years.

Foreign companies necessarily have to deal with existing governments. In countries in which there are frequent changes in the governing establishments and where political passions run high, it is inevitable that recriminations will be hurled—both for having dealt with the deposed and for dealing with those who replace them. United Fruit, as a foreign corporation conspicuous for its size, has been a particularly eligible target for such double-barreled attacks. Another source of fear and suspicion has been the comparatively giant size of the company in a number of the Latin American countries in which it operates. It frequently is baited by some of the Latin American press which often refers to it as *el pulpo* (the octopus), and sometimes accuses it of installing and deposing governments, bribing officials, and throwing its weight around in order to obtain advantages.

Although our study did not sift the detailed record of the early turbulent years and therefore we are not qualified to establish the degree of historic truth or falsehood behind these charges, we can say that they have little relevance to its behavior record of recent times. Most of the responsible public officials whom we systematically interviewed spoke in generally favorable terms of the company's current standard of conduct. In searching for an explanation of what is undoubtedly a lingering residue of bitter feeling in certain quarters, it seems likely that the historic setting may have been a contributing factor. In its formative years at the turn of the century, United may have been seized upon as a present and therefore tangible symbol of widespread Latin American discontent with the U. S. government for what was considered high-handed practice in its policy toward Latin America.

21

What no one has criticized is the way the company developed the land. Once they fell into United Fruit hands, tropical swamps and jungles soon blossomed into immense plots of luscious green banana plants, set out in rows, on well-drained, properly fertilized, and irrigated soil. Progressive agriculture practices, never heard of before, in connection with silting, flooding, and spraying in a never-ending fight against plant disease, produced millions of stems of the golden fruit for export. Whole communities sprang up almost overnight; workers came from afar attracted by the high wages—the highest paid to rural workers in the tropics. In addition, the company had free housing for its agricultural labor, free hospitals, schools, and labor clubs. Extensive programs of sanitation were carried out to eradicate tropical disease, swamps drained, sewer and potable water systems put in. Cost of food was kept to a minimum in company commissaries where other goods also could be obtained at bargain prices.

In these well-organized agricultural enterprises, every eight banana farms constituted a district, and four districts a division. Usually each division was served by a modern port where spotlessly white, refrigerated ships would stand at the docks loading stems of bananas. The carefully handled bunches moved by the tens of thousands from the farms over the extensive railroad network.

The growth of United Fruit in a period of less than 60 years has been remarkable. It is not a particularly large corporation by standards in the United States, but it is by Central American terms of reference. (The comparative size of its economic role in its small host countries is detailed in Chapter VI.) For example, in Honduras, the company's taxes, wage payments, and other expenditures are the largest for any single economic unit in the country. At one time in Costa Rica, the national budget was not as large as that of the company. Things that are conspicuously strange are often resented, and for all of its long residence in the Caribbean, the United Fruit Company is marked as foreign and, therefore, strange. Things that are large are often feared and, in the eyes of Central America, the company is a very large representative of an awesomely large neighbor to the north. It is not surprising, then, that the image of the United Fruit Company as reflected in Central American minds should be partially clouded by resentment and fear. In Ecuador and Colombia, on the other hand, where the company's roles are of comparatively modest dimension in the overall economies, its general reputation is blurred by few misgivings or doubts.

What is surprising is that, shadowed or serene, the images of what the company's activities mean to the areas of its foreign operation

22

bear so little resemblance to what the actual record shows. Preconceptions about foreign private investments generally, and about United Fruit in particular; are so strong that people, both north and south of the border, tend to see what they expect to see rather than what is there.

It is probable that the United Fruit Company might have done more than it has to present a clearer accounting of its complex operations, and to correct inaccurate statements by others before misconceptions had time to take root. It is certain that scholars concerned with the development field have done far too little to provide a clearly understandable frame of reference through which the significant effects of various types of development investments might be appraised in comparative terms.

The chapters that follow will develop such a framework for measuring the particular case under study in objective terms that have general meaning. The operations of one company will be analyzed in a way that we hope will add significantly to an understanding of the important field of direct private investments of international scope—a field that has scarcely been touched by quantitative investigation.

But the findings of the particular case are of significance, too. For the United Fruit Company is surely one of the most important examples extant of international investment based on agriculture. It can be viewed either as a corporate colossus of exceptional stature and resources or as an average-sized representative of U. S. business of international scope by looking through a single lens of narrow sectional perspective. It has been our endeavor to look at the record through two-lensed spectacles. Clearly the interests of United Fruit are rooted in both halves of the Western Hemisphere, and its future depends upon the economic progress of both. Just as clearly, its operations are of importance to both, though the weighting here is significantly greater to the south than to the north.

All of us, in this hemisphere, will have to develop vision that understandingly spans the gap between the cultures of the two Americas, a myopia that has persisted too long and stretched too wide in a period of world history that is driving our interests ever closer together. We hope and we believe that the record of the United Fruit Company is one that will serve to cement mutual understanding and respect on the part of those who have the patience to read our findings as set forth in the pages that follow.

II.

The World Banana Market

THE PRESENT STUDY is directed neither toward justification
nor criticism of the United Fruit Company's operations over the
more than half century of its history. We feel that it would be an
essentially sterile exercise to attempt to disentangle the skein of events
since 1899. Since then, a banana industry of sufficient size to assume
importance in international commerce literally has been created by
imaginative traders, with the United Fruit Company exercising a
dominant role in the process. To reconstruct and appraise the historical record in a way that would allow recriminations to be balanced against solid accomplishments would call for an omniscient
judgment that we do not feel we possess.

Rather, we have set ourselves the much more modest, though still
not unambitious, task of attempting to contribute toward an understanding of what the banana industry is, of who benefits from it and
by how much, and to appraise the record of the United Fruit Company in the industry as it operates today. Our perspective, then, is
contemporary rather than historic. Most of our field work was completed in 1956, and our major concentration is upon operations in the
year 1955, the latest year for which national accounts data for the
several banana-producing countries were available in relatively complete form.

We are acutely conscious of the fact that our study deals with a
field in which the ideas of most people are colored by strongly held
preconceptions based upon an interpretation of past events rather
than upon an examination of the current record. It has seemed to us
that a useful service could be performed by describing the present
organization and procedure of banana production and marketing, by
measuring what can be measured, and by limiting subjective judgments to matters not susceptible to appraisal in objective terms.
Where we are forced to make value judgments, it is our hope that at
least relative objectivity may be achieved through the circumstance
of a joint authorship that combines North American with Latin American outlooks.

More particularly, our interest in the United Fruit Company record
is focused upon its impact upon the economic development process

in the six Latin American republics selected for intensive study—Guatemala, Honduras, Costa Rica, Panama, Colombia, and Ecuador. These were singled out because their combined banana shipments represent close to 60 percent of the tonnage weight of world banana exports, and because about 95 percent of the bananas handled by the United Fruit Company in 1955 was produced in or purchased from these six sources. Through this sampling procedure, we could limit our field work to supportable dimension, and still cover the bulk of the world banana production for export, and a preponderant portion of United's banana procurement operations.

In concentrating upon United Fruit's contributions to economic development in these six countries, we are guided by our conviction that the widest possible diffusion of vigorous economic growth is one of the most important concerns of the contemporary free world. We are convinced that adherence to and strengthening of democratic institutions in the less developed countries of the world depends in large measure upon the demonstration that aspirations for general economic progress can be realized under free institutions. And we believe that the flow of investment capital from the capital-generating nations of high industrial development to the capital-poor countries is a major instrument for helping to stimulate balanced growth in the latter.

We start with the premise that investment capital, private or public, will not continue to flow unless it receives a return judged to be adequate. Therefore we shall examine the profitability of United Fruit investments in the six republics upon this criterion. But it seems equally clear to us that continuing hospitality for foreign private investment ventures cannot be expected to endure unless there is clear evidence that it is contributing to the development of the host nations to a degree that would not be realizable without it. Accordingly, we shall examine the United Fruit record to see whether or not its operations present convincing evidence of satisfactory performance upon this score.

Before we embark upon such an examination of the operations of the company, it is requisite that we establish a frame of reference, by presenting a picture of the world banana market as a whole.

WORLD BANANA PRODUCTION AND CONSUMPTION

THE FOOD AND AGRICULTURE ORGANIZATION of the United Nations estimates world banana production in 1955 at 11.6

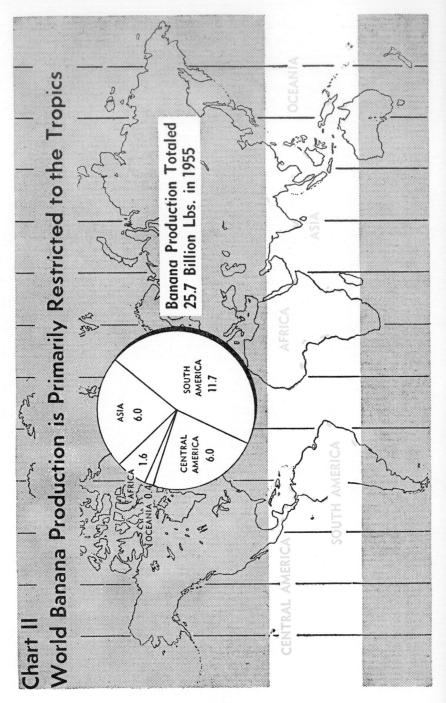

Chart II
World Banana Production is Primarily Restricted to the Tropics

Banana Production Totaled
25.7 Billion Lbs. in 1955

ASIA
6.0

SOUTH
AMERICA
11.7

CENTRAL
AMERICA
6.0

AFRICA
1.6

OCEANIA 0.4

OCEANIA

ASIA

AFRICA

CENTRAL AMERICA

SOUTH AMERICA

26

million metric tons or about 25.7 billion pounds. It apportions about 46 percent of this to South America, 23 percent to Central America, 23 percent to Asia, 6.5 percent to Africa[1], and 1.5 percent to Oceania. As such, the banana crop is the fourth largest of the world's reported fruit crops, exceeded in tonnage production only by grapes (88.0 billion pounds), by citrus fruit (39.2 billion pounds), and by apples (29.1 billion pounds). If the portion of the grape crop produced for making wine (71.4 billion pounds) rather than for consumption as fruit is deducted, and that of apples produced for cider (8.8 billion pounds), bananas displace both grapes and apples and are second only to citrus among the world's fruit crops consumed directly as food. Excluding grapes, citrus, and apples, the tonnage of bananas exceeds by a considerable margin the combined weight of the remaining important fruit crops of the world—pears, pineapples, dates, and figs (17.2 billion pounds, combined, for 1955).

Table 1 | **1955 World Banana Production**

Producing area	Million Pounds	% of total
Central America.	5,950	23.2
South America.	11,700	45.6
Asia.	5,950	23.2
Africa.	1,650	6.4
Oceania.	400	1.6
World total.	26,650	100.0

Source: *Agricultural and Economic Statistics,* monthly bulletin of FAO, July-August 1957. (Corrected by assigning Canary Island production to Africa rather than to Europe.)

Table 1 covers a world population for 1955 estimated at 2,490 million persons. On this basis, the average consumption of bananas by each man, woman, and child was 10.3 pounds in 1955 on a stem-weight basis.[2] Only the subcategory of citrus fruits, comprising oranges, tan-

---

[1] In the FAO accounting the banana production of the Canary Islands is attributed to Spain. It has seemed to us more appropriate to attribute this banana production to Africa since the Canaries, while a Spanish possession, lie off the African Coast well south of the European boundaries.

[2] The actual weight of bananas reaching consumers averages about 15 percent less, and the wastage factor on other fruits varies. Throughout this chapter production weights are used for comparisons given.

gerines, and clementines shows a larger per capita consumption, 12.6 pounds; and only apples, 8.1 pounds, and grapes, 6.6 pounds, were serious rivals of the banana among the world's consumption fruits.

It is, of course, obvious that such blanket averages have little relationship to the actual pattern of fruit consumption by the world's populace. Banana production is restricted to the tropics and more particularly to humid tropic areas. For successful growth, most varieties require a temperature range between 55° and 105° F., and almost all suffer severe damage when temperatures drop below 50° to 52° F. Since the banana cannot be grown as a seasonal crop—its cycle of development ranges from 12 to 15 months from planting to harvest—its range of cultivation is restricted to the zones in which year-round temperatures are within these extremes. It is further restricted to areas that can provide its exceptionally high moisture requirements (four to five inches monthly or 60 inches annually as a minimum) through heavy and evenly spaced rainfall or generous water supplies for irrigation.

The banana thrives best in alluvial, well-drained soils, though it will tolerate clay soils of friable consistency. Since its stalk is merely a tightly rolled cylinder of leaf sheaves, it is particularly vulnerable to blowdowns or uprooting by floods when heavy with fruit. Even relatively mild winds can seriously injure the fruit by shredding the protecting leaf structure upon which healthy fruit production depends. The areas that can grow bananas successfully upon a commercial basis must therefore provide the necessary environmental factors of temperature, moisture, soil characteristics, and freedom from damaging wind and flood recurrence.

In general, the areas that can provide a hospitable environment for banana culture are found in low-lying, high-precipitation lands between 20° North and 24° South latitude, with the extremes set by 24° North and 30° South latitude. The range of actual banana production is indicated by the areas listed in Table 1. The major Latin American areas in which bananas are produced for export are shown in the map on page ii.

It might be assumed that the areas of important production would be the areas of major consumption. Yet, as indicated in Table 2, some of the broad areas of banana production are heavy banana consumers as well, while others are not. On a per capita basis, the highest level of consumption in 1955 was in South America, 80 pounds per capita; while Central America (including Mexico and islands of the West Atlantic) consumed about 52 pounds per capita; Asia less than 7 pounds; Africa about 1.5 pounds; and Oceania, 27 pounds. In the

United States and Canada combined consumption of bananas was 20
pounds per capita, and for Europe it was 9 pounds—an average of
almost 13.5 pounds per capita for the two combined.

Table 2	Banana Production and Consumption (Stem-weight basis)			
	Production		Consumption[a]	
Area	Billion lbs.	Percent	Billion lbs.	Percent
Central America	6.0	23	3.0	12
South America	11.7	46	9.9	38
Asia	6.0	23	6.0	23
Africa	1.6	6	0.3	1
Europe	—	—	2.5	10
Oceania	0.4	2	0.4	2
North America	—	—	3.6	14
Total	25.6	100	25.6	100

[a] Derived by subtracting exports and adding imports as reported by the U. S.
Department of Agriculture from FAO data on production. Again, Canary
Island production has been assigned to Africa rather than Europe.

Thus, up to the present time, it is fair to say that bananas have
assumed as important a place in the average diet in the two major
industrialized areas of the temperate zone as for the vast majority
of the people living in what we regard as tropical areas. In India,
for example, the apparent annual per capita consumption of bananas
is only about 11 pounds. Since there is so little inter-country trade
in bananas within the tropic zones, it follows that there is an extraordinarily high annual per capita consumption in some of the major
producing countries, while in other tropical countries the consumption
rate of bananas is very low. For 1955, on the basis of *reported* production minus export figures, Brazilians consumed something like
150 pounds per capita; Costa Ricans, 350 pounds; Panamanians, 380
pounds; and Ecuadorians a fantastic 500 to 600 pounds per capita.
Even allowing for apparent inflation in some of the reported production figures and for the known fact that there is considerable feeding
of bananas to livestock in some of these countries, the human consumption of bananas where they are grown in profusion clearly reaches
heroic proportions.

OF THE ESTIMATED 25.7 billion pounds of bananas produced for commercial sale in 1955, something over 25 percent was exported in international trade.

The breakdown by areas of export and import, given in the Appendix Table, is adapted from figures compiled by the U. S. Department of Agriculture. We have adjusted the North American import weights slightly upward upon the basis of evidence that the official estimates of the Department of Agriculture do not give sufficient allowance to the increases in average stem weight in recent years. This has the effect of raising the world total of 1955 imports from the Department's estimate of about 6.6 billion to 6.7 billion pounds. It is probable that, on the export side, there is a comparable degree of understatement of weights for fruit going to North America but we have not attempted to make this adjustment in the data presented. The discrepancy is not large enough to alter substantially the proportionate shipments as reported by broad area. Reported import and export figures never are in exact balance because of inevitable inaccuracies in accounting and because, due to time consumed in ocean transport, there are always some shipments credited as exports at the end of one year that only show up as imports when delivered at the beginning of the following year.

On the export side, the data show that almost 80 percent of all reported banana exports in 1955 were shipped from Middle America, including Mexico and the islands of the West Atlantic, and from the three South American banana exporters—Ecuador, Colombia, and Brazil. Africa accounted for about 20 percent; Asia (entirely from Taiwan) for a bit more than 1 percent; and Oceania for less than 1 percent. It is clear, then, that Latin America is the dominant banana-exporting area of the world, and that the West Coast of Africa (in which the tabulation includes the Canary Islands) is the only other major area that plays a significant exporting role, and that a relatively minor one, in the overall picture.

On the import side, North America (United States and Canada) and Western Europe, neither of which produces any bananas on a commercial scale, are the outlets for over 90 percent of world banana trade. Argentina, Chile, and Uruguay are the principal Latin American importers, with Brazil and Ecuador as sources of supply. The breakdown of world banana imports for 1955 is shown below.

Of the North American imports, about 92 percent went to the United States and a little more than 8 percent to Canada, most of

Chart III
North America and Europe Are Major Banana Importers . . .
Central and South America Are Chief Exporters

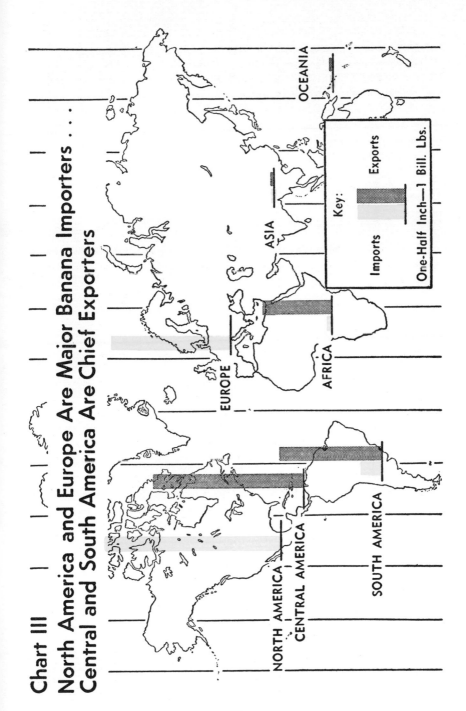

Key:

Imports

Exports

One-Half Inch—1 Bill. Lbs.

OCEANIA

ASIA

EUROPE

AFRICA

NORTH AMERICA

CENTRAL AMERICA

SOUTH AMERICA

the latter transshipped in bond from U. S. ports. Of the three South American importing countries, Argentina takes more than 80 percent of the total. African imports are divided among the Union of South Africa, Algeria, French Morocco, Southern Rhodesia, and Tunisia in the order of their importance as banana importers. Japan is the only listed Asian importer, with about 54 million pounds imported in 1955; and New Zealand the sole importer in Oceania at a slightly lower level than Japan.

Table 3 | **World Imports of Bananas, 1955**

Importing area	Billion lbs. imported	% of world imports
United States and Canada	3.60	53.8
Europe	2.47	36.9
South America	.43	6.4
Africa, Asia, Oceania	.20	2.9
Total	6.70	100.0

It now can be seen that this remarkable tropical fruit, originating in the Far East and for thousands of years rarely even listed in the learned chronicles of the West, has undergone a dramatic metamorphosis—largely within the last century. Almost in the manner of historic glacial drifts, it has crept from its original domicile in the East into western zones, until today of all bananas grown, the roots of 70 percent thrust down in the soil of the Western Hemisphere. Another 5 percent grows along the African shores that rim the Atlantic. Considered in marketing terms, within the short span of the past 60 years this exotic fruit has burst the containing bounds of its central tropic environment, and has moved northward, and to a lesser extent to the south, to find a place in the fruit bowls of temperate zone tables from the Yukon to California, from Scandinavia to Austria and Italy, and from Chile to Uruguay.

Agriculturally, bananas are chained to the tropics. Commercially, about one-fourth of all that are produced find a market outside the temperature zones in which they thrive. And nine-tenths of this fourth find their way to the industrial heart of the western world—to North America and Western Europe, whose inhabitants a century ago scarcely knew what a banana was, except for the scholarly few who read the works of Pliny the Elder or of the Swedish botanist Linnaeus. An important part of our story is concerned with how this remarkable change came to be. It is the more remarkable in that it is a phenomenon that has occurred on a comparable scale with respect to no other delicately perishable, definitely tropical fruit.

The general picture of major world fruit exports, presented in Table 4 as the average exports in metric tons, 1951-53, is adapted from a study by Erik Mortenson, entitled "Trends in Production and Consumption of Fruit and Vegetables," in the September 1955 issue of the FAO publication, *Agricultural Economics and Statistics*. The

Table 4 — **Major World Fruit Exports** [a]

Type of fruit	Export 1951-53 average (1,000 metric tons)	% of fresh fruit	% of total
Fresh fruit:			
Bananas............................	2,552	40.7	36.4
Oranges and tangerines..............	2,060	32.8	29.4
Lemons and limes...................	261	4.2	3.7
Grapefruit.........................	127	2.0	1.8
Apples, table......................	714	11.4	10.2
Pears, table.......................	186	3.0	2.7
Grapes, table [b]...................	218	3.5	3.1
Pineapple [c]......................	154	2.4	2.2
Total..............................	6,272	100.0	89.5
Dried fruit:			
Dates..............................	343		4.9
Raisins [d]........................	285		4.0
Prunes [e].........................	49		0.7
Dried figs.........................	48		0.7
Other dried fruit [f]..............	12		0.2
Total dried fruit..................	737		10.5
Total all fruit...................	7,009		100.0

[a] Excluding China and the U.S.S.R. [b] Grapes sold for fresh consumption.
[c] Including fresh equivalent of canned pineapple. [d] Including currants.
[e] Excluding Bulgaria and Romania. [f] Apricots, peaches, apples, and pears.

table, which was evidently compiled on the basis of official FAO trade statistics, would appear to give a reasonable basis for comparing the relative magnitudes of the reported trade in the several fruits that bulk large in international commerce.

On this accounting, the trade in bananas for 1951-53 accounted for over 36 percent of all world commerce in fruit and for more than 40 percent of world trade in fresh fruits. Oranges and tangerines make up the only other fruit category that is of even proximate importance as a world trade item upon a weight basis, and the amount of bananas traded is about 25 percent larger. Citrus fruit, however, hardly classifies as a tropical fruit. Again using FAO figures, the 1954 record shows that almost two-thirds of commercially produced oranges and tangerines were grown in temperate zone areas, more than 50 percent in the United States and Western Europe alone. Temperate zone countries furnish 70 percent of all exports. Over 85 percent of commercial grapefruit culture is restricted to the United States, and three-quarters of all commercially grown lemons and limes are produced in the United States, Europe, Japan, Argentina, and Uruguay. Aside from the fact that citrus fruit is far easier to ship than bananas, the striking fact is that all citrus shipments from *tropical areas* amount to only about one-quarter, by weight, of banana shipments, all of which originate in tropical areas.

Pineapples qualify as a tropical fruit crop, but the FOA figures show that only about 10 percent of total production is exported in world trade, and the great bulk of this was shipped in canned rather than fresh fruit form. Canned pineapples are included in the fresh fruit category upon the basis of the equivalent fresh fruit content.

Dates are preponderantly a tropical area crop, and about one-fifth of reported production is exported internationally. But the big export is in dry rather than fresh fruit form and, in 1954, world trade in dates amounted to less than one-ninth that of bananas on a tonnage basis. Figs are the other entry on the list that in most people's minds would fall into the classification of tropical fruit. Actually, FAO figures assign considerably over half of commercial fig culture to Western Europe and the United States, and total fig exports, again with shipments preponderantly in dried form, account for less than 1 percent of world fruit trade.

How did it come about that the banana (which is technically a herbaceous vegetable) should have become the one tropical "fruit" that has become a major item in the diet of North Americans and Europeans? Why the banana among the literally scores of fruits that are native to the tropics? Why not the mangosteen of which poet-gourmets have written in ecstatic terms, or the luscious mango, the peptic papaya, or the delicately flavored naranjilla? It is certainly not because of special qualities that make the banana easy to grow or to transport.

34

Chart IV
World Trade in Bananas Averages 40% of World Trade in Fresh Fruit

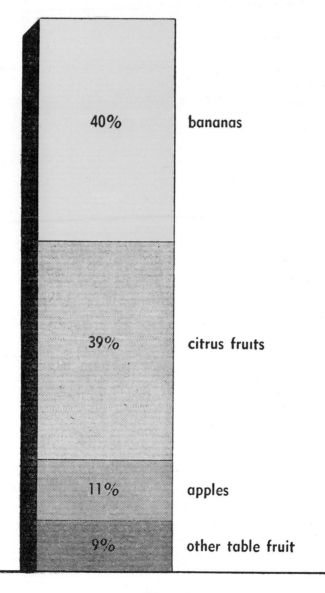

40%   bananas

39%   citrus fruits

11%   apples

9%   other table fruit

We already have pointed out that the banana is singularly demanding with respect to the temperature, soil, precipitation, drainage, and wind conditions of its environment. The areas that can offer an even proximate optimum of all of these factors are relatively limited. As we shall see, bananas are subject to blights of devastating intensity for which it is tantalizingly difficult and formidably expensive to find adequate controls. This is virtually a seedless plant, with new cultivations established by planting large pseudobulbs or rhizomes, and there is no wood stalk to permit grafting. Thus, there has been no success to date in developing, through the genetic approach, man-made strains that would combine the disease-resistant characteristics of certain varieties with the better qualities for handling and ripening inherent in others that are vulnerable to disease. In addition to disease blights, insect pests that destroy plant and fruit abound wherever bananas are grown.

The banana is a bulky fruit, shipped attached to a stem that accounts for about 7 to 8 percent of worthless weight, from which the fruit fingers protrude in a fashion that invites crushing and bruising under anything less than the tenderest handling. It must be cut in a green state, before full maturity—how long before depends upon the length of haulage to ultimate market—and the permissible time span between cutting and eating by the consumer is limited to not more than 21 to 25 days. Yet, bananas regularly travel from 2,000 to 6,000 miles by water and up to 1,500 additional miles by rail and truck to reach their ultimate markets. Any accumulation of dust or gravel before or during transit, any roughness or cramping in stowing or carriage, even fingering by customers on the retailer's shelves shows up in marring discoloration of the delicate, golden skin of the ripened fruit and depreciates its marketability. Strict temperature controls have to be maintained from the time of loading aboard ship to delivery to retailer, and the latter is under strong compulsion to sell his fruit to customers within 24 hours after receipt.

Every stage, from plantation to retail sale, requires meticulous planning and coordination, upon a time schedule far more precise than pertains to any other major commodity of world trade. Supply in every market must be geared to a demand that, in turn, is affected by the availabilities of competitive fruits. The cutting by maturity grade, the transport to shipping port, the stowing, the ocean carriage, the unloading, the sorting (by size, condition, and degree of ripeness), the shipment by truck or rail to distribution centers, the operations in the jobbers' ripening rooms, the trucking to retailers, and the sale to customers—every one of these stages is a tailored process with minimal tolerances for departure from a schedule that has to be calculated from its beginning. Even small divergences from the rigid timetable and handling requirements result in losses; whereas major departures would spell a total loss for the shipments involved.

If Captain Lorenzo Baker, Minor Keith, Thomas Hart, Andrew Preston, and even the imaginative Sam Zemurray had been able to visualize the complications that were to beset the production and marketing of bananas as a large-scale item in world trade, it is improbable that they would have had the fortitude to launch and expand the United Fruit Company. But if they had not made the start, it is probable that this thoroughly implausible commodity—implausible in the sense of its inherent lack of adaptability to the hazards of world marketing—would have bulked no larger in temperate zone food economies than do pineapples, or figs, or dates today. Happily, for the North American and European consumer, and for the Latin American banana-producing economies as well, the vision of these pioneers was too limited to foresee the involvements or, at least, too sanguine to sense the formidable impediments that were to arise. So they built the foundations of today's giant trade, largely unaware of the whirling windmill blades before which even a Don Quixote might have quailed.

The Valuation of the World Banana Market

The money value of bananas that enter into world trade, to the best of our knowledge, has had no systematic study. Values are commonly attributed to exports on an f.o.b. basis, and to imports on a c.i.f. basis. Such reporting is generally made by applying to the number of stems involved in either case a formula price that usually grossly understates the prices at which sales are actually made. Accordingly, the reported export valuation for a given country as shown in its annual trade account figures often represents 50 percent, or even less, of what it actually receives upon its adjusted accounts. The International Monetary Fund, in its work of keeping track of international balance of payment flows, has been forced to make radical adjustments in reported banana trade figures to avoid untenably large distortions in the accounts of the major banana exporting countries. But the Fund only makes its adjustments for those countries in which banana exports account for a major portion of foreign exchange revenues.

The authors of this study, in attempting to put valuation figures on the world banana trade as a whole, have started with the North American market about which a good deal is known and which represented 54 percent of the world's total banana imports in 1955. We have less complete data on the European marketing structure, which represented 37 percent of 1955 imports by weight, but there is sufficient evidence to indicate that an extrapolation of the American cost structure to that segment will not give any upward bias to the whole. The costs per pound of European bananas are consistently higher from original purchase in the producing areas on through the transportation and distribution chain. The remaining segment of world trade in bananas is too small to importantly distort the whole structure.

Our estimating base, combining relatively complete North American marketing data with the very detailed information made available by the United Fruit Company on all phases of its operations, is indicated in Table 5.

Table 5 | **United Fruit's Share of the World Banana Market 1955**

Importing area	United Fruit Million stems	United Fruit Million pounds	Competitors Million stems	Competitors Million pounds	Total Million stems	Total Million pounds
United States and Canada............	29.5	2,333	20.4[a]	1,271[b]	49.9	3,604[a]
Europe...............	7.1[c]	339	62.9[a]	2,129[b]	70.0	2,468[d]
South America........	—	—	8.6[e]	429	8.6[e]	429[d]
Africa, Asia, Oceania...	—	—	3.9[e]	196	3.9[e]	196[d]
Total.................	36.6	2,672	95.8	4,025	132.4	6,697

[a] Estimated.
[b] Residual, i.e., total minus United Fruit's share.
[c] 5.5 million stems from Central America and 1.6 million from the Cameroons.
[d] From U. S. Department of Agriculture count bunch data.
[e] 50-pound count bunches.

On a stem basis, the United Fruit Company accounted for 59 percent of North American imports, for 10 percent of European and for 28 percent of the world total. But on a weight basis—and bananas are sold by weight in markets of distribution—there are indications that the percentages of United Fruit's shipments are somewhat higher

38

Chart V
United Fruit's Share of the World Banana Market

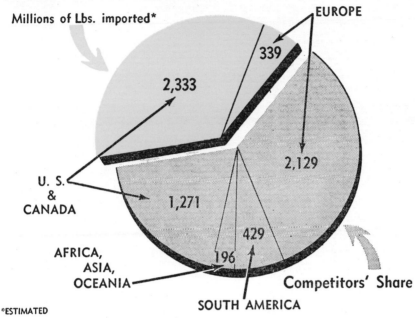

Millions of Lbs. imported*

EUROPE

339

2,333

U. S.
&
CANADA

2,129

1,271

AFRICA,
ASIA,
OCEANIA

429

196

Competitors' Share

SOUTH AMERICA

*ESTIMATED

in each case, since the stem weight of the company's shipments generally runs above market averages.

Our specific data gleaned from the United Fruit Company's records furnished a far more precise base for the portion of the field that it covered than anything available in published studies. To this we added everything that could be furnished by public officials and private banana operators in the six countries in which we made detailed field surveys. As has been noted, these six, between them, produced about 60 percent of the bananas shipped in international trade in 1955. In sum, while our global estimates have been pieced together from these sources, and then blown up to represent the whole market as revealed by world trade and production statistics, we believe that our findings reasonably represent the general magnitudes of a field in which there has been no previous basis for any general appraisal.

In Chapter III, we shall present in some detail the procedures through which we arrived at an estimate of how much consumers spend for bananas in the United States and Canada and how the consumer's dollar is broken down in this market to cover the costs and profits of the several services involved in making them available from the time when they are put aboard ships to the time when they are slipped into the housewife's shopping bag. In Chapter IV, we shall trace the consumer's dollar back through its apportionment among the several operations required to produce the fruit and arrange for stowage aboard ship for consignment to export markets, leaning heavily on data gleaned from our six-country survey. Here, however, it appears appropriate to anticipate a few of the major findings presented in these forthcoming chapters, in order to round out our world market picture by assigning money values to the tonnage data given above.

It is our finding that, in 1955, North American consumers spent about $527 million for bananas—3,063 million pounds consumption weight; 3,604 million pounds stem weight—at an average retail price of 17.2¢ per pound. We know that Europeans paid a somewhat higher price per pound than Americans, and that other importing areas paid somewhat less. Taking the North American price as average, and knowing that this area accounted for 54 percent of all imports, we can estimate the world retail expenditure for *imported* bananas at approximately $976 million.

We have seen earlier that about three-quarters of the reported world commercial production of bananas is consumed in the countries where they are produced. We have no overall reporting of what consumers paid for bananas in the producing countries, but we have some data on this for our six-country sample. In these countries, bananas sold on the local market for from one-fifth to one-tenth of what they brought when sold as export stems. It is certainly conservative to estimate that the totality of fruit grown for local markets throughout the world, although almost three times as great in quantity, has less than one-half and perhaps not more than a third the value of that committed to export markets. It is probably safe to estimate the total retail value of the 1955 world's commercial banana crop at between $1.3 billion and $1.5 billion.

We are able to make a reasonably proximate estimate of the value in 1955 of world banana exports f.o.b. vessels at ports of embarkation. On the basis of our North American consumer dollar analysis that follows, it will be seen that about 27¢ out of each such dollar spent on bananas represents the return actually realized by producing countries. Hence, of the estimated $976 million sales at retail, $263 million can be assigned as the share of the producing countries from their banana exports. This general dimension will be confirmed in Chapter IV as well, where it will be shown that our six countries actually realized about $157 million from their banana sales in 1955— which accords with their 60 percent share in the total tonnage of that year's world banana shipments.

III.

The Consumer's Banana Dollar
in the United States and Canada

As OF MID-1955, there were just under 181 million inhabitants in the United States and Canada combined. The peoples of these two countries consumed a trifle under 300 billion pounds of food in that year—or about 1,660 pounds per capita. Banana consumption for the area totaled 3,063 million pounds[1] or 17 pounds[2] per capita of population. Thus, upon a weight basis, the banana, an exotic fruit every pound of which had to be imported from tropical areas, accounted for a full 1 percent of North American diets.

It would be reasonable to expect that this food item, with its inherent perishability and its necessarily long carriage by sea, rail, and truck under constant temperature controls, would qualify as a luxury food product of relatively high price. This is far from being the case. The total combined food bill for the United States and Canada in 1955 is estimated at over $60 billion. The banana bill of North American consumers for the same year was about $527 million. The average price of 17.2¢ for bananas was well under the average of 20¢ per pound paid for food of all classes.

This relatively low retail cost has put bananas financially within the reach of practically all North American consumers. These consumers can afford to include more fruit in their diets than can be afforded in most parts of the world and the banana has fitted well into the assortment they choose to eat. Not only is it palatable to most tastes, but it also has characteristics of flavor and texture sufficiently different from other fruits to enable it to contribute significantly to the variety in eating satisfactions which people naturally desire. When we add to this the fact that the banana is nutritional, we can begin to understand how this implausible commodity has come to occupy the place it does in the food consumption pattern of this continent.

---

[1] Although 3,604 million pounds was the stem weight of imported bananas, the actual weight of fruit consumed is about 15 percent less.
[2] This is equivalent to about 20 pounds per capita on a stem-weight basis.

In the market lists for low-cost, moderate-cost, and liberal meals drawn up by the Bureau of Human Nutrition and Home Economics of the U. S. Department of Agriculture bananas are specifically included in the category of "other vegetables and fruits." This classification reflects the varied nutrient content of this fruit as distinguished from the citrus fruits which are recommended specifically for their high content of Vitamin C. With respect to the 10 other nutrients considered important enough by the Bureau to be itemized in its published tables bananas outrank oranges in all except two. In a list of 20 fruits they rank second in carbohydrates, third in thiamine, fourth in protein, fifth in riboflavin, sixth in niacin, seventh in Vitamin A, eighth in phosphorus, and ninth in iron. In terms of food energy they rank fourth in the list of 20, being surpassed only by avacados, grapes, and blueberries. As purchased by the housewife, each pound has an energy content of 264 calories, which compares with 300 in dressed fish, 312 in fresh whole milk, and 325 in potatoes. Because of their high content of sugar, vitamins, and minerals and because they are easily digestible, bananas are recommended for children and are popular with this important group of consumers. They satisfy hunger remarkably well in spite of their low fat content and have proved an acceptable element in the diets of those who have to limit their overall intake of food. They are convenient for inclusion in lunch-box meals and can be eaten sanitarily regardless of the surroundings or the cleanliness of the eater's hands.

Nutritional research has demonstrated that the inclusion of bananas in the diets of normal children stimulates the retention of mineral elements contained in the various foods they eat and tends to increase their growth rates. The giving of bananas as the first solid food of all infants entering the New York Foundling Hospital was made routine practice more than 25 years ago. For all who suffer from celiac disease the banana is literally a necessity of life. The digestive systems of those afflicted with this disease cannot use carbohydrates obtained from cereals, sugars, and potatoes, since such foods produce diarrhea. Fortunately, however, carbohydrates in the form of ripe bananas appear to be tolerated perfectly and thus make possible the eventual cure of the trouble in almost all cases. Although other fruits may be substituted before the cure is completed, the banana has been found to be the most satisfactory and the only safe food for use in the early stages of the treatment now customarily prescribed for this disease.

It is the purpose of the present chapter to explain the genuinely extraordinary phenomenon of how this foreign-produced food, which now accounts for almost 10 percent of all fruit—fresh, processed, dried, and frozen—eaten in North America, comes into our market and to describe and put a price tag on the various stages of its transport and merchandising.

We start with the bananas loaded aboard ship in the six countries in which we made a first-hand study of production methods. In 1955, these countries shipped about 4 billion pounds, the equivalent of approximately 3.4 billion pounds of retailed fruit after allowing for 15 percent shrinkage in weight of stems and damaged fruit discarded in the distribution process. As we shall see in the following chapter, the six countries realized about $157 million for their 1955 banana shipments, or 3.93¢ per pound for bananas on the stem and 4.62¢ per pound of merchantable bananas at retail level.

OCEAN TRANSPORTATION

OUR PRESENT STARTING POINT, then, is the banana fleet, with hatches battened down upon a cargo of bananas owned by North American distributors. In 1955, the United Fruit Company, the major North American distributor, operated a fleet of 62 vessels. Fifty of these were fully refrigerated fruit carriers, ranging from about 3,000 to over 7,000 gross tons, which handled all but about 120 million pounds (sold directly at port to European importers supplying their own shipping) of United's 2,672 million pounds of banana consignments. During 1955, this fleet completed 982 voyages of about 5.2 million nautical miles, the great bulk of which was determined by the demands of the company's banana distribution. About 90 percent of all United's banana consignments went to the North American market, and since 95 percent of all its banana shipments originated in our six-country sample, we can derive from a study of its shipping operations a representative picture of the ocean link in the chain of banana distribution between areas of supply and the U. S.-Canadian market.

At last count, there were over 160 importers of bananas into the United States, but most of them are quite small. United Fruit imported about 59 percent of the stems entering the North American market. As we have noted, its percentage on a weight basis was probably somewhat higher, although there is no accurate record of the weight of its competitors' imports. Importers normally purchase the fruit in the countries where it is produced or themselves produce an important share of the stems imported—as is the case with United

44

and its principal competitor in the Western Hemisphere, the Standard Fruit and Steamship Company. United Fruit, in 1955, produced on its own plantations about 70 percent of its North American shipments, while Standard depended to a somewhat larger extent on purchased fruit.

From about 1875 to 1900, bananas traveled as deck cargo on sailing vessels and steamships from Central America and the West Indies into U. S. ports. Gradually, ventilated cargo ships were introduced, with simple equipment to keep a constant flow of air over bananas stowed in closed holds. Beginning in the early 1900's the refrigerator ship or "reefer" has increasingly taken over, until today this type of vessel carries most bananas shipped in the North American and European trades, although a few "ventilators" are still in use. The modern banana reefer is a highly specialized instrument devised for this particular use, although it can be, and is sometimes, used for shipping other fruits, dairy products, and meat products.

Bananas are always loaded green—the degree of maturity determined by the length of the voyage envisaged—but the ripening process proceeds inexorably day by day. In the course of ripening, a great amount of heat is generated as well as carbon dioxide, ethylene, and other gases. Both heat and ethylene gas hasten the ripening process and they must be dispelled or the cargo will be overly ripe before reaching its destination. The reefer is equipped to exhaust the gases in each stowage compartment of every carrying hold. It must have ample refrigerating capacity to precool each compartment to a sufficiently low temperature to rapidly lower the pulp temperature of fruit loaded in tropic heat to 53° or 54° F. And the refrigeration must be sufficiently flexible to keep the subsequent temperatures in each compartment at between 55° and 60° F. (depending upon the variety and maturity of the fruit carried) for the duration of the voyage. Obviously, heating facilities are required also as cargoes move into northern winter climates. A given ship may have from as few as six to as many as 14 compartments and up to nine or 10 separate cooler units. The space served by an individual refrigerating unit must be completely insulated to minimize the damage done if one or more coolers should break down.

In addition to the ventilating and cooling systems, banana ships require other special fittings. The floor of each stowage deck is covered with a wooden grating that allows constant circulation of air, under as well as over and through the stowed fruit. Each compartment is subdivided by movable, vertical bin boards to prevent the cargo from damage through shifting caused by the roll or pitch of the ship in heavy seas. Within each bin, the banana stems are carefully stowed by highly skilled men who must gauge with fine precision the degree of compactness that will prevent shifting or rubbing without bruising or crushing the fruit fingers. The bottom layer of stems is always stowed vertically, butt end down, with the second tier either flat or vertical with either butt or tip end down, and if there is a third tier, it is stowed flat on top of the vertical tiers.

The hatches of banana ships must be ample to accommodate the automatic loading and discharging elevators that are used in efficient ports to hasten these processes. It is of course important to ship-use efficiency to shorten the time that the ship is held at dockside, but even more urgent is the necessity for moving the bananas on a minimal time schedule. For in the banana trade, as in few others, time is money. Every hour of schedule delay means increased loss through spoilage; every hour that must be added to the planned scheduling means that the fruit must be cut at a less mature stage and therefore entails loss in the weight of merchantable fruit produced or purchased.

The importer has three choices. He can own and operate his own reefer fleet; he can charter his required tonnage of refrigerator ships from independent ship operators, thus shifting a heavy capital investment requirement to other shoulders; or he can combine the two alternatives. In practice, all three methods are in use in both the North American and the European banana trades. Banana shipping costs, over a period of time, have varied little among the three procedures. But since reefers, with slight shift-over costs, can be used for other fresh produce moving in world trade, the demand for banana space may be greater or less than the available reefer supply at any given time. Chartering rates move up and down accordingly, and the banana importer may or may not be able to arrange charters at a tenable price when competitive demand for reefers is heavy. Direct ownership of a major portion of his reefer requirements eliminates these short-run risks. Accordingly, United, Standard, and others of the larger importers have found it desirable to become ship proprietors and operators on a considerable scale.

For several reasons it is not practical to describe the banana movement to North America in 1955 with precise particularity. The ships that serviced the North American banana trade that year varied widely in size, speed, and operating efficiency; there were numerous new entries and withdrawals during the year; and we have an accurate record only for United Fruit shipping operations. From the United record, however, we can construct a hypothetical picture that gives an adequate notion of the entire movement.

North American imports in 1955 amounted to just about 50 million stems. From United Fruit experience in this trade, we find that the average round-trip voyage (for 1953 and 1955) was 4,147 miles. Therefore, although bananas are carried for only half of the round-trip distance, it is proper to compute the stem mileage requirements at 4,147 x 50 million stems, a total of 207,350 million stem miles.

An ideal fleet for this carriage would be apportioned between ships ranging from about 3,700 gross tons to about 8,000 gross tons, with actual maintained speeds of from under 15 knots per hour to well over 17 (360 to 420 miles per 24-hour day), and carrying anywhere from 27,000 to perhaps 61,000 stems on each voyage. Such flexibility in the size, speed, and carrying capacity of the banana fleet is dictated by the wide variations in the length of voyages between the several major embarkation and debarkation ports serving North American markets. They range from a little over 1,800 nautical miles for the round trip between Honduras and Mobile or New Orleans to something over 7,500 nautical miles between the west coasts of Costa Rica or Panama and Seattle. Also, flexibility is required because there is a great deal of variation in the quantities of fruit available for shipment between different producing centers or even in the receiving capacity of a given debarkation port from time to time. Experience shows that, allowing for loading and discharge time in ports and layups for repairs or cargo inavailability, 255 days per year of actual steaming is a reasonable average for each ship.

On this basis, the shipping complement needed to accommodate North American banana imports from Latin American producing areas would be represented by 43 modern reefer ships, *averaging* about 5,800 gross tons, maintaining average speeds of 16.5 miles per hour on both northern and southern voyages, and averaging 255 sea-days in the year, with each carrying 47,755 stems per voyage upon 24.35 round-trip voyages. Performance standards of this hypothetical, uniform fleet may be set forth in the following terms:

(a) 16.5 miles per hour x 24 hours = 396 miles per ship per day.

(b) 255 steaming days x 396 miles = 100,980 miles per ship per year.

(c) 43 ships x 100,980 miles = 4,342,000 *fleet* miles per year.

(d) 4,342,000 fleet miles ÷ 4,147 miles per round trip = 1,047 voyages.

(e) 50,000,000 stems ÷ 1,047 voyages = 47,755 stems per voyage.

(f) 100,980 miles per ship per year $\div$ 4,147 miles per voyage = 24.35 round trips per ship per year.

(g) 255 steaming days $\div$ 24.35 round trips = a shade less than 10.5 days of running time per voyage.

(h) $\frac{1}{2}$ of 10.5 days = 5.25 days average running time each way.

Again, basing our estimates upon actual experience in banana ship acquisitions, the current reproduction cost of efficient banana reefers—in European yards where construction costs are markedly lower than in the United States—works out to $3,667 for each 1,000 stems of carriage in the North American trade. A fleet capable of carrying 50 million stems would cost something over $183 million at current reproduction costs (50,000 x $3,667 = $183,350,000). Actually, since the working components of a fleet are continuously being retired and replaced, with depreciation being taken on allowable estimates of the degree of obsolescence accrued to each unit, it is appropriate to assume that the effective valuation of a going fleet at any given time would be about half of the current reproduction cost—or between $91 and $92 million ($\frac{1}{2}$ of $183,350,000 = $91,675,000).

We are able to check this estimate against the actual accounting figures of the United Fruit Company's fleet. Since this company carried 59 percent of the North American stem imports in 1955, the theoretical value of its fleet on this trade would be about $54.5 million. The company's entire fleet, at the end of 1955, had a book value of $52.7 million, although some slight deduction should be made from this to cover the 8 percent of its banana carriage for which the company's own fleet serviced the European trade, and for a small proportion of fleet investment in other than fruit-carrying vessels. However, the major part of the discrepancy reflects the fact that the average age and quality of vessels of the company's banana fleet in 1955 was somewhat poorer than the theoretical ideal. On a 50 percent depreciated basis against actual cost, the value of its banana-carrying tonnage at the end of 1955 comes to $54.2 million. Our overall estimate of something over $90 million as a realistic investment figure for ships servicing the entire North American banana trade is thus verified.

Upon the basis of United Fruit operations, the average charge for banana shipments between port of embarkation and discharge in North American ports was 1.51¢ per pound for weight of stems imported. This charge is representative of the going commercial rate charged by independent fleet operators performing a similar service. Allowing for the fact that it was necessary to import 1.1764 pounds stem weight for each pound of bananas reaching the consumer, this amounts to 1.78¢ per pound of actual fruit consumed. Applying this to the total 1955 banana trade for North America (3.063 billion pounds consumption basis x 1.78¢), we get a total ocean carriage charge of about $54.5 million on the year's trade.

It is obvious that if this were the only ship earnings, it would be insufficient to pay fleet operating costs, depreciation, and return on a $90 million investment. All of the banana ships in the North American trade, including those of the United Fruit Company, carry return cargo, generally at established Conference rates, to earn additional revenue.

We now have our fruit alongside the dock in one of the North American entry ports. The ship bringing them in has been notified in advance of temperatures at the port. If they are very low, the temperature of the stowage compartments aboard ship will have been raised some 12 hours before arrival to protect the delicate fruit pulp from undue chilling in the unloading process. *It is ready for discharge at a cost averaging 6.40¢ per consumption pound (4.62¢ cost in country of origin plus 1.78¢ ocean freight.)*[3]

IMPORTERS' HANDLING AND MARGIN

As a BANANA SHIP noses alongside the pier at, say, Weehawken near the Jersey end of New York City's Lincoln Tunnel or at New Orleans, a highly intricate mechanized procedure is set in motion. By the time the lines have been made fast, the ship's hatches have been removed. There are four hatches on each of the larger reefers. A giant elevator crane wheels into position on the dock opposite each hatch, its top reaching well over the side of the ship and its arm thrusting across deck and deep into the ship's carrying holds. The crane is really an endless belt conveyor to which are affixed at regular, closely spaced intervals horizontal canvas pockets, rubberized and padded, each of which can cradle even the largest stems that weigh more than a hundred pounds each.

As the pocketed belts revolve, men of the longshore crew pick the stems from their firmly stacked rows in the stowage compartments and swing them onto the shoulder pad of another worker who walks his stem over to the conveyor and places it on its side in one of the

[3] On a stem-weight basis the equivalent charges would be 5.44¢ per stem-weight pound (3.93¢ in country of origin plus 1.51¢ ocean freight).

belt pockets, and then returns for another. This process goes on simultaneously in several compartments at a time on each deck level, so that a good proportion of the pockets on the conveyor serving each hatch are filled as they move on their upward journey. The conveyor carries the stems of green fruit up into the daylight, across the ship's deck and down its side to the dock level. The chain of pockets passes an electric "eye" which tallies accurately the number of stems of fruit discharged.

The elevator crane conveyors automatically, and very gently, deposit the stems on horizontal conveyors which run in an intricate pattern along the pier from shipside to railway sidetracks and truck-loading ports. All stems ride on foam rubber cradles attached to the horizontal conveyors. At convenient stations along each conveyor line men are located whose job it is to grade and classify each stem as it passes. The grader sings out his appraisal and an assistant marks the call by pasting a small paper tab to the stem, its color designating the classification made. This color code varies from port to port. On the New York-Weehawken piers of United, green signifies Heavy Nines (stems having more than nine hands of well developed fruit); red marks Light Nines; white, eight-hand stems; and pink, seven-hand stems, the lightest that are normally imported to this market. Other colors signify quality, appearance, or condition classifications. A black label signifies that some of the fingers are beginning to turn yellow and a gray label that the stem as a whole is too nearly ripe to stand shipment. Such stems must be disposed of in the local market, generally at a sacrifice price. A purple label means that the stem, because of faulty appearance, crushing or bruising of some fingers, or stem breakage is rejected for sale. Such stems are pulled off the conveyors at a given point, the salvagable fruit cut off and boxed for donation to charitable institutions that make regular calls at the banana piers to collect this perfectly wholesome but nonmerchantable fruit. A yellow label denotes that stems have been classified as "Specials," or substandard for any of a variety of reasons such as undersized stems or fingers, marred fruit, or other flaws that dictate its downgrading, and a brown label indicates that the stem is not to be sold but reserved for experimental ripening or other testing.

The job of accurately classifying stems of fruit as they whirl by on the conveyor belt at the pace of a brisk walk calls for a high degree of skill that is born of long experience. The reputation of the importer depends upon his delivery to the jobber of the size and type of fruit that the latter has ordered in a condition that meets requirements. The importer's representatives, at a given port, have advance notice of the size, source, and general composition by grade and condition of each cargo, and its precise arrival schedule. This sales force tries to dispose of the complete cargo through advance orders from jobbers throughout its distribution area. Fruit arriving in Weehawken may be sold in the New York metropolitan area or be consigned to New England, to Buffalo or Rochester in northern New York State, or to Montreal. Shipments to New Orleans or Mobile fan out through Louisiana and Texas and move northward to cover the entire central area of the United States and Canada. Charleston, Miami, and Tampa generally service the southeastern section of the United States; Baltimore the Middle Atlantic States; Los Angeles and San Francisco the Far West, Southwest, and Mountain States; and Seattle the Northwestern States and Western Canadian provinces. Fruit that has not been sold in advance may be consigned as "rollers" to sub-distribution stations along the line, and the importers' sales forces in these areas are alerted to see that customers are found before it arrives.

The horizontal conveyors carry the tagged fruit along the piers— covered piers in northern ports where winter temperatures are low, for the fruit must be protected from chilling even in the brief interval of discharge and dispatch—to the freight cars and trucks assembled to carry the product to points of predetermined destination.

As the fruit arrives opposite the car or truck to be loaded, workers along the line pick off the stems bearing the appropriate colored label—Heavy or Light Nines, Eights, or Sevens according to what the jobber has ordered, carry it a few steps to the waiting railway car or truck, and hoist it aboard, stepping on a tally indicator that records each stem loaded. Stowage on railway cars or trucks follows much the same pattern as stowage in the ship's holds, always with punctilious care to assure firm packing, bracing, and tying to prevent rubbing in carriage or crushing or bruising that would mar the fruit. Each car carries about 300 stems, so that 250 to 275 railway cars may be required to discharge a large reefer's cargo. The standard railway refrigerator car—and there are now more than 100,000 of them on North American service—has been carefully engineered to serve banana haulage requirements. It is light-weight, refrigerated, heavily insulated, mechanically ventilated, and carries charcoal or portable alcohol heaters when outside temperatures are low. It is equipped with inside thermometers to register in-transit temperatures, and frequent inspection is made along the line with re-icing or refueling of heaters provided at way points to assure that the proper temperatures are maintained throughout each haul.

51

The large trailer trucks that are employed for the shorter hauls are similarly equipped. Each truck has been weighed on a big platform scale before loading and the process is repeated after loading to record the weight of its banana stem cargo. In a remarkably few hours, the fruit has passed from the custody of the importer to that of the jobber who, except in the case of "rollers," takes over when it is loaded on the internal transport vehicle.

There appear to be no published data covering importers' investments, operating costs, sales organization, and mark-ups, but from the United Fruit records we can reconstruct a pattern that is reasonably representative of the North American market as a whole. Behind the discharge operations that have been briefly described here, there is an elaborate network of activities that the importer must maintain. In the case of United Fruit, at least, this includes promotion and advertising through newspapers, magazines, radio, and television to keep the product continuously in the public consciousness in order that it may hold its important place against competing food items in the American diet. It includes sustained research effort on the banana's nutritional qualities and on all phases of its handling, with the view of progressive improvement of the condition and attractiveness of the fruit made available to the ultimate consumer. To this end, there is intensive cooperation with medical groups, dietitians, institutional food purchasers, newspaper and magazine departments and publishers dealing in food and cookery advice and information, as well as with the restaurant, confectioner, and ice cream industries. The sales force, through a network of subdepots covering all of United States and Canada, systematically keeps in touch with jobbers throughout the country, and the inspection force similarly covers the fruit in transit to assure correct handling by the carriers.

Since the operation of the major importers is not restricted to distribution alone, but involves also the growing of fruit in centers of production, the purchase of additional fruit from independents, its transport to points of embarkation, provision of ocean carriage, and discharge and sale at ports of entry, it is extremely difficult to apportion accurately the amount of importers' capital that is invested in this phase of North American banana distribution. The problem is accentuated by the fact that of the 160 North American importers, only the United Fruit Company issues annual statements in sufficient particularity to furnish even an approximate breakdown of the detail of its operations.

From United Fruit's generous access to its operations accounts, we are able to derive a very complete picture of its integrated opera-

52

tions. From these, we find that of the $390 million of total assets at the end of 1955, $300.7 million may properly be assigned to those activities of the company directly related to the production, purchase, distribution, and sale of the bananas it handles. Since a fraction over 87 percent of its banana shipments in 1955 went to North America, its total banana capital for the North American trade can be estimated at about $262 million. If the other importers had a comparably heavy investment, the total could amount to as much as $440 million. But the next largest importer, Standard Fruit, reported total assets of only $42 million. This is about 16 percent of the banana assets attributed to United Fruit's integrated North American operations, although Standard imported almost 30 percent as many stems to the North American market as did United. And the other importers —supplying perhaps 23 percent of North American stem imports— probably had proportionately less capital invested than Standard. *Altogether, the integrated investment of North American importers in 1955 probably amounted to somewhere in the neighborhood of $335 million, including the estimated $90 million ship investment and perhaps $12 to $13 million in importer-owned elevator cranes, conveyor equipment, and other installations in the North American ports.*

Again using United Fruit accounting, we can estimate the importers' direct costs of handling and sales in North America at 0.57¢ per pound of fruit imported on the stem basis and at about 0.67¢ per pound of saleable fruit at retail level.

On top of these direct costs, there is the importer's margin, which must cover the return on all phases of his investment in what we have seen to be a highly integrated operation, as well as the major item of taxes in the United States. We estimate this margin to have amounted in 1955 to 1.41¢ per pound on a stem basis, or 1.66¢ per consumption pound.

Since about 3.063 billion pounds of bananas were consumed in North America in 1955, the total yield from a margin of a 1.66¢ per pound comes to $50.85 million, which would amount to a 15 percent return before U. S. income taxes on a $335 million investment. At current corporate income tax rates, this amounts to from 8 to 10 percent as a final return.

THE JOBBERS

A VARIETY OF COSTS must be met by the jobber after payment for the banana stem. These include inland transportation charges, losses from shrinkage in weight, costs for ripening rooms, delivery to retailers, and so on. *In 1955, North American banana jobbers paid an average of 7.42¢ per pound for bananas on a stem-weight basis, the equivalent of 8.73¢ per pound of fruit available for sale to retailers.*

Inland Transportation

Since the jobber generally takes title to the fruit when it is loaded onto the railway refrigerator car at port of entry, he has to pay the cost of inland transport by rail before the operations that are under his direct control commence. We have estimated that perhaps 84 percent of the fruit coming into North American ports of entry is forwarded to subdepots of distribution through rail shipments. The remaining 16 percent is picked up directly by the trucks of those jobbers serving zones sufficiently close to ports of entry to make rail shipment to sub-distribution points unnecessary. The lowest transportation cost for any jobber, then, may be estimated at about 0.35¢ per pound (0.3¢ per pound stem-weight basis) for average local pickup cost. This applies whether the pickup occurs at the ship or at subdepots on railway lines at interior points.

But the great bulk of the fruit moving from importer to jobber moves by rail to subdepots from which the jobbers' trucks take delivery. The task of arriving at an exact *average* railway carriage cost for all bananas moving by that medium is exceedingly complex. We have made a computation for the U. S. and Canadian markets involving individual freight rates between normal shipping and distribution centers and arrived at an average by weighting the quantities of shipments over each. The mathematical computations are far too intricate to warrant detailed presentation here, but the range of charges in 1955 over the literally hundreds of routes may be defined as running between 0.6¢ per pound (from Weehawken to nearby New England points) to over 2.6¢ per pound from Seattle to points in interior Western Canada. *On a weighted average basis, we have computed 1955 transportation charges paid by the jobber, including his local pickup charges, at 1.34¢ per pound of bananas that he sells to retailers.*

Adding this 1.34¢ to the 8.73¢ per pound that the jobbers paid the importers (the 7.42¢ per stem-weight pound, plus 1.31¢ for shrinkage of weight that the jobber absorbs in cutting the fruit from the stems and culling substandard or damaged hands and fingers), we arrive at an average cost to the jobber of 10.07¢ per pound of saleable fruit.

There is no clean-cut method for arriving at the capital value of railway and truck facilities that service the North American banana trade. However, we do have figures of railway revenue derived from banana haulage which amount to 0.375 percent of total railway revenue. Applying this ratio to the approximately $30 billion of total capital assets of the U. S. railroad system gives a figure of $112,500,000 that might reasonably be assigned as the value of railway assets devoted to banana haulage in the United States. If we add to this a proportionate amount of the Canadian railroad investments, plus an allowance for trucking facilities and something for the port facilities that are generally owned by municipalities, *we can estimate that something like $135 million is invested in the internal carriage of bananas in the North American market.*

Jobbers' Facilities, Procedures, and Markups

There are perhaps 1,800 banana jobbers in North America, of which about 150 are in Canada. They represent the essential middle link in the distribution chain between the importer and the retailer. In their hands is the essential process of ripening. They also absorb the major 15 percent shrinkage in weight, when the fruit is cut from the stems, is finally culled, and sold to retailers in a form suitable for final sale to consumers. They provide delivery service to the local retailers, often extend credit facilities, and carry the burden of maintaining inventories to balance out fluctuations in the week-to-week demands of the retailers.

Very few of the North American jobbers deal exclusively with one importer. The jobber must know the quantity, size, condition, and type of fruit that the retailers in his area want, and see that it is furnished. They buy from whatever importer can fill this demand at the most advantageous price. The first choice of the North American market is for the variety of banana known as the Gros Michel. This type of banana has certain advantages over all others in size and general shipping qualities. The fingers hug the stem rather than protrude, and thus suffer less from crushing and abrasion in transit, and its thicker stems provide a lower incidence of breakage. Gros Michels have a further advantage over other types in that they tend to ripen in a more uniform fashion under normal handling. The United Fruit Company imports nothing but Gros Michel bananas in its North American trade. Other types of bananas known as "varieties," however, are imported to North America and are even more prevalent in the European trade. These include Cavendish, Lacatan,

Bout Rond, and others. To insure uniform ripening of the fingers, it is the general practice with the varieties to introduce ethylene gas from portable containers into the ripening rooms in which the variety fruit is hung. With Gros Michels, this is unnecessary unless the supply-demand situation necessitates a shortening of the standard ripening cycle.

In addition to specifying the variety of fruit wanted, the jobber is interested in and keeps close track of the seasonal and cyclical qualities of fruit from specific areas. Thus, he may find at a given time that Santa Marta fruit from Colombia, Fortuna (United Fruit) or Frico (Standard Fruit) from Honduras, Chiriqui or Colón from Panama, Golfito from Costa Rica, or Pacific from Ecuador comes closest in size and condition of fingers, weight of stems, and quality of fruit to meeting his customers' demands. Or he may find it advantageous, because of the price differential, to purchase Standard Fruit's Golden Beauty—Cavendish or Bout Rond varieties—from Honduras.

To the housewife in North America, a banana is a banana. Not one in a million knows the difference between a Gros Michel and a Cavendish or Lacatan banana, nor are the differences in flavor or nutritional qualities of any material importance. The general preference for the Gros Michel banana in the North American market rests upon the size, appearance, and handling qualities that make it easier to present this type of banana to the housewife in a way that will make her pause at the banana display and make a purchase rather than pass it by. From the firsthand testimony of many jobbers and retailers, we can record that sales volume responds with extraordinary sensitivity to attractiveness of the fruit displayed, and there is general consensus that the Gros Michel meets this specification better than any of its rivals. It is both easier for the jobber to handle and ripen, and it has a generally longer life on the retailer's counter before deterioration of appearance sets in to prejudice consumer acceptance.

The jobbers with whom we have talked are acutely conscious of three factors as major determinants of the profitability of their operations. The first is quality and appearance of the fruit. There seems to be general agreement that their volume of sales in North American markets goes up when they can deliver to retailers bananas of attractive appearance, uniform ripeness, and with a holding life on retailers' display shelves of from one to two days.

Second, they are keenly aware of the shrinkage factor. We have used a 15 percent shrinkage incidence as an average, but the actual jobbers' shrinkage varies widely on individual consignments (from between 10 or 12 percent to 21 percent or even higher) depending upon the number of bananas that he must discard as unsaleable in addition to the inevitable 7 or 8 percent loss represented by the weight of the central stem to which the hands are attached. Naturally, the jobbers' profits are importantly influenced by the ratio of the weight of fruit purchased on a stem basis, and the weight of merchantable fruit that he can sell to the retailer. Again, the Gros Michel has advantage over other varieties in this respect, but here there are wide divergencies in the shrinkage factor between Gros Michel bananas originating in the several producing areas, or even those from a given area at different seasons of the year.

Ecuadorean bananas, for example, because they are generally less carefully handled than Central American fruit, consistently show a high shrinkage incidence. Jobbers generally testify that the grime acquired by Ecuadorean fruit under current practices of interior shipment results in more scarring and abrasion in transit, which increases the percentages that must be discarded. Also, it has a comparatively high seasonal variation in quality because of the fact that much of it is grown without irrigation in areas that afford too little moisture from natural rainfall during three-quarters of the year. Hence, jobbers generally pay from half to one cent less for Ecuadorean than for Central American fruit, and a number state that they do not handle it at all if they can obtain what they need from other sources.

The third factor—and it is significant that it was rated third rather than first by the jobbers we consulted—is the question of price. Obviously, the jobber will not pay a higher price to one importer than to another for fruit that he judges to be of comparable quality, appearance, condition, and net saleable weight. In most, if not all, North American areas, jobbers have access to fruit offered by more than one of the importing companies. The testimony is singularly unanimous, however, upon the point that an adequate supply of fruit of the highest quality is more important in determining the level of consumer demand upon which jobber volume ultimately depends than minor fluctuations of a cent or two in the retail price level. Accordingly, jobbers generally are swayed to a greater extent by their judgments as to the comparative quality and shrinkage factors in the fruit offered to them than by minor price concessions linked to what they regard as compromises in these key factors.

The jobbers in North America vary widely in size and operating procedure. There are numbers of small firms in this business, each of which serves a limited group of retailer customers. At the other extreme are large operators servicing some hundreds of retail stores within a radius that may extend up to 150 miles. A few of these large jobbers also sell to smaller regional wholesalers or subjobbers, who in turn maintain delivery routes over a more limited area. Many of the large jobbers, in addition to operating their storage and ripening facilities, extend short-term credit to their customers. An increasing number of the large-scale operators are owned by the large food-store chains and supply only their affiliated outlets.

Between 15 and 20 percent of the banana jobbers in the United States are banana specialists and handle no other produce. This group embraces some of the oldest and largest firms in the business. Many of them are family owned, and are now in the third generation of such family management. More typically, the banana jobber also handles other fresh fruits and vegetables—citrus fruits, apples, potatoes, onions, and a variety of seasonal fresh fruits and vegetables. But generally the special handling and ripening facilities required for bananas and the fact that this is a year-round business make banana merchandising the core of the operation to which other distribution is an adjunct.

The Jobber's Plant

The heart of the jobber's establishment is the ripening room. At the end of 1955, the 1,800 banana jobbers in the United States and Canada were maintaining collectively over 8,000 ripening rooms or on an average, about 4.5 to each jobber. Among them were many small one-room establishments, with others ranging in size up to those maintaining 10 ripening rooms in active operation. We can best visualize the jobber's role through describing the facilities of a "typical" four-room jobbing establishment, and following the operations through which it serves the retailers in its orbit of distribution.

A plant with four ripening rooms would have cost about $200,000 to reproduce at the 1955 level of construction and equipment costs. The great bulk of this represents the cost of housing and equipping the ripening room facilities, with a small amount added for the provision of trucks and office space and other facilities necessary to the operation.

In a modern plant, there are provisions for the indoor discharge of trucks bringing in the stems of fruit and for the loading of the fruit to be delivered to retailers after it has been properly ripened, severed from the stems, and packed in box containers that now are pretty generally standardized at a capacity of 40 pounds. The stems may be discharged from the incoming trucks and carried to the ripening rooms

58

on a belt conveyor system of the general type described in connection with the movement of fruit from shipside to railway cars or trucks. More generally, the stems are lifted from the trucks, hung by a cord loop to the hooks of an overhead monorail conveyor, or of wheeled pipe-rack trucks that may be pushed by hand from the truck ports to the ripening rooms. In all cases, there is a premium on moving the received green stems into the ripening rooms with a minimum of lost time.

The ripening room itself is a well-insulated refrigeration chamber in which from 250 to over 500 stems, weighing 24,000 to 40,000 pounds, may be hung under rigorously controlled conditions of temperature and humidity. Glass panels, thermometers, and humidity gauges allow accurate readings of conditions inside the chamber and frequent inspection of the fruit without the disturbance of intermittent opening and closing of the doors.

Since there are inevitable differences in the size, pulp temperature, moisture content, condition, and degree of fruit maturity in every consignment, the job of ripening bananas efficiently requires a high degree of judgment, skill, and experience. It would be quite unfeasible, for example, to attempt to handle Gros Michel and "variety" bananas in the same ripening chamber at the same time. Even with a given type of banana, the jobber's task is made much easier if his chamber can be loaded with fruit of a high degree of uniformity in all its characteristics.

His job is to bring the fruit to the exact classification of ripeness or "color" that will best satisfy the specifications of his retailers when delivered at the time when it is wanted. There are eight color specifications in common usage and, by varying the temperature-humidity controls in his ripening chambers, the jobber can speed up or hold back the normal five-day or six-day ripening process to produce the required color within from three to 10 days. When there is need to accelerate ripening or to counteract the tendency of the variety bananas toward "wild ripening" (the uneven ripening of the hands or individual fingers on a given stem), the jobber commonly introduces a charge of ethylene gas into the chamber as a corrective measure. At the beginning of the ripening cycle, a relatively high degree of temperature and humidity is normally employed. For the first 24 hours, sprayers may be turned on to raise humidity to over 90 percent under 70° F. temperature, with a gradual reduction to 68°, 66°, and finally to 56°-50° on successive days.

When the green fruit has ripened to the required yellow color classification—lighter in summer when high outside temperatures will shorten the permissible holding time on the retailers' shelves and deeper in winter—the fruit is moved out of the ripening rooms by conveyor or pipetrack truck to the cutting tables.

Here the hands are severed from the stems by cutters, and the hands themselves are subdivided into units that each retailer to be served finds most acceptable to fill his customers' needs. Usually, the dealer requires an assortment of unit sizes, varying from three to four banana fingers to six, eight, or even a dozen. The units are carefully nested in the 40-pound boxes or cartons, with shredded paper, or sometimes the polyethylene bags in which the stems have been sheathed for protection in transport, as padding. The boxes may be either one-trip cardboard containers that the retailer discards, or returnable wooden or aluminum trays for which the retailer normally pays a deposit refundable when returned to the jobber's truck drivers at the time when he makes new deliveries.

These practices of fruit delivery are developments of the last 30 years. Formerly, all fruit was delivered to the retailer on the stem which he hung in his store and from which his clerks cut hands or portions of hands to the customer's requirements. Modern retail merchandising methods have made this procedure prohibitively time-consuming and expensive, and over 95 percent of all bananas are now delivered to retailers in the manner described.

To an increasing degree, jobbers are prepackaging the fruit for the retailer by banding each cluster unit with tape on which the retailer may record weight and price for his customers' convenience and to minimize the handling by clerks and customers that tends to mar the delicate skins of ripened fruit. A further refinement is for the jobber to pack each cluster in "cello-trays"—one or more standard sizes of cardboard boxes with transparent cellophane tops through which the fingers inside may be clearly seen without any touching of the fruit after it leaves the jobber's establishment. This form of packaging has many advantages, in addition to the protection it affords: The package retains the fruit moisture and makes for attractive display. The cartons generally have printed instructions telling the consumer how to recognize the deep yellow shade with a speckling of small brown dots that signifies the stage when the banana may be eaten with maximum enjoyment and nutrition, as well as giving recipe suggestions for its use in cooking, in salads, or with cereals. This, together with other merchandising and advertising themes, reflects the position of bananas as competitors for the consumer's favor not only with other fresh fruits but with a considerable range of alternate food products.

The Accountancy of Banana Jobbing

Allowing about 300 stems to the average-sized ripening room and one week as the average ripening cycle, the 8,000 rooms operated by North American jobbers have the theoretical capacity to turn over as much as 125 million stems per year. Since North American consumption in recent years has been averaging only slightly more than 50 million stems annually, it is clear that there is a considerable margin of surplus capacity. But in this business, as in many others, fluctuations in seasonal demand, the incidence of holidays, and other factors call for peak capacities considerably larger than would be necessary to service perfectly distributed requirements.

The current reproduction cost of North American jobbers' establishments may be estimated at around $400 million (8,000 rooms at $50,000 per room). Upon the reasonable assumption that half of the value of existing plants has been depreciated, it would be fair to estimate the current book value of these facilities at about $200 million.

In addition to their investments in handling facilities, jobbers must provide working capital to cover their inventory requirements, payrolls, credit extended to retailers, and other current expenses. A reasonable allowance for this would average $10,000 per jobber, an $18 million total for the 1,800 North American jobbers. *Thus we arrive at an overall estimate of $218 million as the depreciated value of capital invested in 1955 by jobbers to service the North American banana trade.* This is a very considerable sum (even if substantially less than what it would have required to reproduce the same facilities at 1955 construction and equipment costs). It represents an average investment of about $121,000 per jobber, although hundreds of the smaller establishments had no more than $30,000 to $60,000 invested in this business in 1955, while the investments of some of the larger jobbers ranged up to half a million dollars.

A composite 1955 operations account per pound of fruit handled by a jobber located in an area where inland freight charges happened to approximate the North American average—in Central Texas, Oregon, or Northern New England, for example—was about as shown in the table which appears below.

The jobber's margin of 1.1 cents per pound would have yielded, in 1955, a total return before taxes of $33,693,000 on total sales of 3,063 billion pounds of fruit. On a total investment of $218 million, this would have provided a gross return before income taxes of something less than 15.5 percent, or about the same as that estimated for the integrated operations of the importer group.

Purchase cost (green, stem basis)	7.42
Inland transport (including local pickup cost)	1.34
Shrinkage at 15 percent of pound cost on stem basis	1.31
Cost to jobber per pound of saleable fruit	10.07
Ripening room costs per pound of saleable fruit	.92
Delivery costs per pound of saleable fruit	.81
Total jobber costs per pound of saleable fruit...........	11.80
Jobbers' margin	1.10
Jobbers' selling price	12.90

OPERATION OF THE RETAILER

THE FINAL LINK in the marketing chain is the vast array of retail stores which provide direct contact with the ultimate consumer. We have seen that, in 1955, these stores paid an average of 12.9 cents for each pound of bananas delivered to them by the jobbers.

Food retailing in the United States and Canada is now dominated by large unit stores. These are not necessarily units owned by large chains. It is the costs and the resulting prices set by these large units which determine the overall costs of retail distribution. As the pace-setters, their operations are of primary interest. The concept of a large food unit has come to be defined in current usage (and in statistical analysis) as a unit having annual sales of $375,000 or more. This is now the accepted definition of the term supermarket. Some such large stores are owned and operated as a single unit by one owner-operator. Many others are owned in small groups of two to 10 stores, all located in single communities or metropolitan areas. They are thus not chain stores since that term carries the implication of widely dispersed operations over broad regional areas. A currently accepted, though arbitrary, definition by the U. S. Department of Commerce is that these large stores are called "independent" if the units under single ownership do not exceed 10 in number. Thus, groups of one to 10 stores owned and managed by a single owner are not chains. Groups of 11 or more, by this same arbitrary convention, are to be called chains.

Fairly elaborate efforts are constantly being made in the United States, both by private and governmental research agencies, to determine the shares of different types of stores in the total sales volume, and the numbers of each type in operation. The results can be summarized as follows:

1. Total U. S. food-store sales in 1955 have been estimated as $45.97 billion by the Department of Commerce. This total is exclusive of food purchased by hotels, restaurants, the military establishment, and a variety of institutions. Of this food-store total, specialty stores (delicatessens, bakeries, small meat stores, general stores, health food outlets, etc.) did $6.55 billion. The remaining $39.42 billion sales volume was in the hands of the true food stores. But all food stores sell some nonfood items: drugs, household supplies, books and stationery, clothing. Statistically, it is as yet not known accurately what is the exact nonfood percentage. Estimates of 4 percent to 5 percent of the dollar total are often used. This would bring the total food-sale volume down from $46 billion to about $44 billion. Including Canada, the North American total would be about $48.5 billion. About 1 percent of this represented banana sales, since a small part of the estimated $527 million banana consumption in North America was dispensed through restaurants and institutions rather than sold by food stores.

2. From a study of food marketing in the United States, it appears that supermarkets accounted for 59.7 percent, or nearly $24 billion, of the $39.4 billion total attributed to food stores proper in 1955. Their dominance in the field is thus clear. There were about 21,450 units of this size in operation, of which only 11,140 were owned by chain stores, now defined as 11 or more units under one ownership. A medium-sized group (coming to be known in marketing parlance as "superettes"), having sales of between $75,000 and $375,000 per unit annually, account for another 26.4 percent of the total. The remaining small stores having less than $75,000 annual volume, of which there are still 272,000 in operation in the United States alone, did the residual 13.9 percent of 1955 volume, again exclusive of the specialty store category.

The pace-setters in prices and operating methods are clearly the supermarkets. Within this category, the leaders in North American food retailing today are the independently owned supermarket units owning only one store in some cases, and not over 10 at most; they have forged ahead most rapidly in the past decade. It is the efficiency of these local leaders and of some, though by no means all, the larger chain managements which symbolizes the efficiency and operating skill of U. S. and Canadian retailing.

Such stores sell packaged grocery items at the amazingly low margin of about 16¢ out of each $1.00 of sales. This was unheard of in 1900 or 1910—when grocery stores took a comfortable 25¢ or 30¢ for such easy-to-sell items. In the severe depression years, when the supermarket method of retailing suddenly grew to maturity, this margin fell as low as 10¢ to 12¢ on each sales dollar. The average margin has crept up since 1940, but the operating performance of these typically American units in the face of rising labor and real estate costs is still spectacular.

But their performance in selling fresh fruits and vegetables is not at comparably low margins. In the elaborate statistical testing that is currently conducted by trade organizations or publications connected with retail food merchandising, attention has been drawn to the differences in performance, and reasons for them. Two clear-cut indicators of the higher expense involved in handling fresh fruit and vegetables show up in current analyses of operations. Careful accounting methods and analyses of their own operations are important hallmarks of successful management in the leading stores.

First, retail selling of fresh fruits and vegetables requires more floor space per sales dollar. In one cross-section sample survey, it was shown that they required 17.4 percent of space in stores, while contributing only 12.8 percent of sales volume. Secondly, they require more man-hours of employees' time. In the same survey, fruit and vegetable items contributed only $17.05 of sales per man-hour, while grocery items contributed $34.12 per man-hour. Expert management recognizes these handicaps by setting gross margins much higher on produce items than on packaged groceries. Thus, the computed margins used to set prices show that grocery items were set at 15.68¢ per $1.00 of sales, and produce items at 26.38¢. The produce category, logically, has to contribute a margin 70 percent higher than that required for the staple grocery lines, a differential recognizing the higher space and man-hour requirements involved. Another survey using a somewhat different sample of stores (but again chosen from the more efficient leaders) confirms these basic causes for the higher margins required to handle produce. The third major category of food sales, meat, falls between the two others, with an average established margin of 20.18¢.

There has been in the past few years much less detailed analysis of the margins set by leading stores on individual products within these broad categories. But such studies as have been made indicate that, in addition to the factors of space cost and employee time, the setting of margins also reflects such factors as wastage and spoilage, the

64

necessity for daily re-handling of particular products (such as night-and-morning removal of material off display counters and into controlled-temperature storage space), and the necessity for additional cleanup and sanitation efforts. Thus, indicated margins on some seasonal fruits and vegetables run as high as 35¢ to 38¢ on each dollar of sales. In other cases, rapid sales turnover, ease of handling, and small bulk permit margins below 20¢. From the scattered evidence available, bananas fall into about the middle of the range in one or two studies where as many as 40 items have been analyzed.

In one local study made in Seattle in 1948 for 40 stores, the margin on bananas was found to average 21.6¢ per dollar of sales. In another study, made in January 1950, the banana margin was 23.1¢. A leading publication in the food retailing field, in an advisory survey for operators, has suggested that bananas along with a number of other fruits and vegetables should be placed at a basic 25 percent margin level. If consideration is taken of the fact that any actual data secured for a single product are nearly always from the more efficient stores, and do not take into account the wider margins applied by small independents and by the specialty stores (such as delicatessens), this margin of 25 percent for bananas probably reflects the North American average of retail food store practice. Were it not for the constant pressure from the efficient leader stores, however, the average level would be much higher—perhaps 35 percent.

Since there is a factor of loss from waste and spoilage included in the pricing of nearly all items in this category of fresh produce, no separate allowance needs to be made for this factor. It is considered by authorities to be in the range of 2 percent to 3 percent in the case of bananas, but considerably higher in some other fruits and a few vegetables. The actual margins used by stores include within themselves such necessary allowance for this source of higher cost.

It must be remembered that bananas are sold in a great majority of the 350,000 or more retail food outlets of the country. An exact computation of the actual margin would require a very large and expensive sampling survey, and one that would also reflect conditions at several different times of the year. No such comprehensive survey has ever been made. Fortunately, we have an entirely independent check that verifies that the 25 percent margin is the one that actually applied on 1955 banana sales at retail. The Bureau of Labor Statistics, in connection with its consumers' price index, tabulates monthly the actual retail sales prices of a wide variety of items that are considered representative in the shopping lists of consumers, from centers carefully selected to give an accurate cross-section for the United States as a whole. Bananas are among the items so sampled.

For 1955, the average price paid by U. S. consumers for bananas, as shown by the Bureau's sampling, averaged 17¢ per pound. When allowance is made for the 8 percent of Canadian sales, estimated to be almost 4¢ per pound higher because of the higher freight rates for the longer hauls involved, and for minor adjustments to cover sales in areas not covered by the survey and direct sales to institutions, we calculate an average sales price for North America in 1955 of 17.2¢ for the two countries combined. Twenty-five percent of 17.2¢ is 4.3¢ which, subtracted from 17.2¢, gives us the 12.9¢ figure which we built up in our separate and independent calculation as the average jobbers' selling price to the North American retail trade.

Investment in food retailing stores is, of course, not specifically allocable to any one item sold, such as bananas. But it is of interest to place a valuation on what may be termed a "second-level" investment in the marketing chain for bananas. This is in contrast with the direct, or "first-level" investment in plantations, refrigerated ships, dock and handling facilities, and in jobbers' ripening and storage plants.

As an overall average, food retailing requires capital of about 17.5¢ for each $1.00 of sales. The ratio would be higher but for the fact that the vast majority of food stores are located on leased land, and almost as large a proportion use rented or leased buildings. Some large chains have a higher investment-sales ratio; but many small stores and individual units are below this figure. The land and buildings so leased are, in a vague sense, part of the necessary capital required—but this relationship is a tenuous one for our analysis. Much of food retailers' investment is in working capital, that is, inventory and cash on hand, plus some fixed investment in warehouses, trucks, and store fixtures.

The ratio of 17.5¢ investment per $1.00 of sales would indicate a rough total of $8.5 billion as the directly identifiable investment associated with retailing $48.5 billion in food. For bananas, which account for about 1 percent of the sales volume, the roughly proportionate sum of $85 million is the second-level share of that item in a somewhat uncertain total. We can note that the 4.3¢ retail markup per pound yielded all North American food retailers approximately $131 million in revenue, but we know of no accurate way of appraising the particular cost of banana sales and the resulting net revenue. We can say, however, that the supermarkets, the dominant class among food retailers, in their overall operations realized about 12 percent to 13 percent of profits before taxes on their invested capital.

Summary of the Consumer's Banana Dollar

FROM THESE COMPUTATIONS, then, we can offer the following summary of how each dollar spent by consumers in the United States and Canada was distributed among the several links in the distribution chain through which it traveled on its long route to the North American larder:

	Share of banana dollar	Costs per pound consumption basis
North American consumer expenditure	$1.00[a]	17.20¢
The retailers' costs and margin...	.25	4.30
Jobber's selling price to retailer..	.75	12.90
The jobber's margin	.06	1.10
The jobber's handling costs	.10	1.73
Inland transportation (including jobber's pickup)	.08	1.34
Importers' selling price to jobber	.51	8.73
Importers' margin	.10	1.66
Importers' costs at point of sale	.41	7.07
Importers' distribution and sales expense	.04	.67
Importers' landed cost	.37	6.40
Ocean freight	.10	1.78
Amount realized by producing countries	.27	4.62

[a] In 1955, at an average North American retail price of 17.2¢ per pound, $1.00 purchased a shade above 5.8 pounds of bananas.

In translating the costs and margins of each step in the distribution process into the equivalent share of the consumer's dollar, it is, of course, possible to read the figures in the first column as percentage

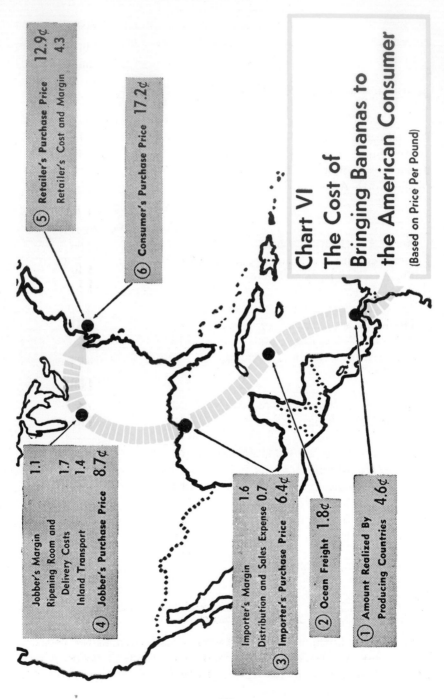

⑤ Retailer's Purchase Price 12.9¢
Retailer's Cost and Margin 4.3

⑥ Consumer's Purchase Price 17.2¢

Chart VI
The Cost of
Bringing Bananas to
the American Consumer

(Based on Price Per Pound)

Jobber's Margin 1.1
Ripening Room and
Delivery Costs 1.7
Inland Transport 1.4
④ Jobber's Purchase Price 8.7¢

Importer's Margin 1.6
Distribution and Sales Expense 0.7
③ Importer's Purchase Price 6.4¢

② Ocean Freight 1.8¢

① Amount Realized By
Producing Countries 4.6¢

68

Chart VII
Of Each Dollar Spent for Bananas—

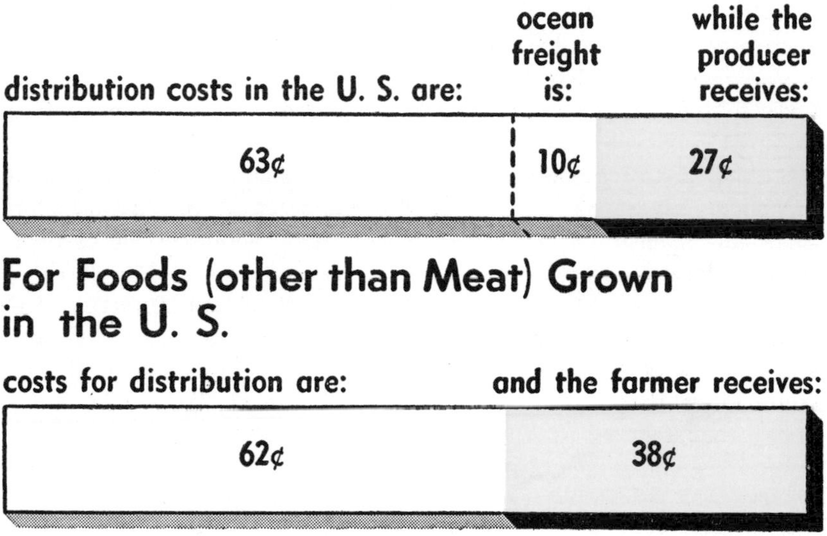

distribution costs in the U. S. are:	ocean freight is:	while the producer receives:
63¢	10¢	27¢

For Foods (other than Meat) Grown in the U. S.

costs for distribution are:	and the farmer receives:
62¢	38¢

shares that accrue to each link in the distribution chain—27 percent to the countries of origin, 24 percent for importers' costs of ocean carriage and subsequent distribution and the return on their complete investment of capital and effort, 24 percent for jobber's costs and margins, and 25 percent for retailers.

Two explanatory comments would seem to be in order.

First, in apportioning the share assignable to the importer's margin, we have taken into consideration the realistic fact that close to 80 percent on a stem-count basis and over 80 percent on a weight basis of all North American banana imports are handled by integrated operators. Such operators produce a large portion of the fruit they handle, provide extensive services to many of the independent producers from whom they purchase fruit, operate extensive transportation systems in the countries of procurement, and own and operate a large proportion of the fleet of ocean carriers that bring it in. Hence, our importer's margin in this accounting is related to the integrated operations of North American importers, rather than exclusively to that part of their operations that actually takes place in North America as such. One of the main purposes of our exercise is to arrive at an accurate estimate of the return realized by the countries of production. Therefore, in our accounting here and in the next chapter, we have adopted the procedure of accounting for all steps up to the importers' margin at estimated actual cost. Accordingly, our listing of the importers' margin of 10 percent includes estimated return on the complete *integrated operation* of North American importers, deducting only income taxes that the importer pays to the countries of production, but including the income taxes that he pays in the United States and Canada.

Second, the 27 percent return from the consumer's dollar that our accounting shows as accruing to the countries of production represents an accurate appraisal of what those countries actually receive and retain from their banana exports. If we add to it the 10 percent represented by cost of ocean transport, it will be seen that the landed cost of bananas at 37 percent of retail value closely approximates the 37 percent or 38 percent share of the retail value of all foodstuffs other than meat produced and consumed within the United States that accrued to American farmers in 1955.

We have ended this chapter, then, by giving a final table that summarizes the estimated capital investments in the North American distributive system that have been presented piecemeal in earlier pages.

We make no pretense of precise accuracy for the figures set forth in Table 6. They are admittedly estimates, derived by methods that have been explained in this chapter, but we believe that they represent reasonable orders of magnitude for the North American banana trade as a whole. As such, they serve to dramatize the formidably large North American investment—more than three-quarters of a billion dollars —that has been required to develop and sustain the market for bananas in this area at something over an annual level of a half-billion dollars.

If foreign investment had not been forthcoming, there is no ground for believing that the present North American trade in this commodity would have developed into anything larger than the trade in other tropical fruits, none of which represents more than a trickle compared to the flood of banana commerce. Since the United States pioneered in banana trade development, it is not even clear that without this initiative the remaining 46 percent of the world banana trade would have grown to anything like its present magnitude. If the market had not thus been created, whatever benefit has been derived by

Chart VIII
North American Investment Supporting
Banana Supply is Estimated at . . .

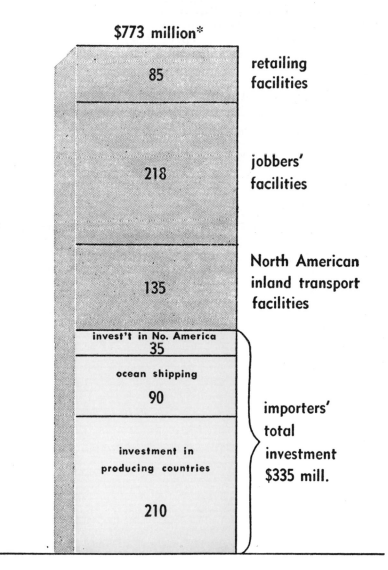

$773 million*

85	retailing facilities
218	jobbers' facilities
135	North American inland transport facilities
invest't in No. America 35	importers' total investment $335 mill.
ocean shipping 90	
investment in producing countries 210	

*Depreciated book value basis.

the countries that produce bananas would never have been realized. The appraisal of just how much the producing countries have benefited from their banana exports is the subject of the chapter that follows.

Table 6 | Approximate Capital Investment in Banana Distribution United States and Canada Book Value (Depreciated) Basis (In U. S. dollars)

Cost element	First-level investment	Second-level investment
1. Ocean transportation facilities..........	$ 90,000,000	
2. Distributor-owned port discharge facilities.	12,500,000	
3. Other distributor investment...........	232,500,000 [a]	
4. Inland transportation facilities..........		$135,000,000
5. Banana jobbers' investment............	218,000,000	
6. Food retailers' facilities...............		85,000,000
7. Total North American banana investment.	$553,000,000 [a]	$220,000,000

[a] We know that all but a small fraction of United Fruit's total banana investments, other than investment in shipping facilities, are located in the tropical producing areas from which its imports are derived. It is reasonable to assume that this applies equally in the case of other North American banana importers. Therefore, something like 90 percent of Item 3 in Table 6, represents investment of North American importers in countries of origin rather than in the United States or Canada. To arrive at a rough estimate of the total first-level banana investment actually located in North America, one would have to reduce the $553 million estimate in the first column under Item 7 by subtracting 90 percent of Item 3, leaving about $344 million. However, since our calculation of importers' margin covers the entire realization of North American investment *wherever located*, deducting only income taxes actually paid in countries of origin, the estimates as presented in Table 6 are appropriate to the accounting method employed for our consumer dollar breakdown.

72

IV.

Banana Production and Producers' Revenue

THE MOVEMENT OF BANANAS over the oceans to North American entry ports and from St. John, New York, Baltimore, Charleston, Mobile, New Orleans, Los Angeles, San Francisco, and Seattle to consumers throughout the United States and Canada has been described. We broke down the average consumer's price of 17.2¢ a pound in 1955 among the several main steps in the distribution chain. In doing so, we found that the f.o.b. value to countries of shipment amounted to a little under 53 percent of the importer's selling price of 8.73¢ in North America, and to about 27 percent of the consumer's banana dollar.

In general, Latin American bananas consigned to Europe were worth about 1.35¢ more per pound than North American shipments upon an f.o.b. basis, largely because the European fruit must be cut at a lighter, less mature stage in order to survive the longer sea voyage. Yet the cost of growing and handling these light stems is virtually the same as that of the heavier stems consigned to the North American market. Thus we have estimated the average weight per stem of all North American imports in 1955 at a trifle over 72 pounds against an average weight per stem for European imports of 35 pounds.[1] Much of this weight disparity results from Europe's heavy dependence upon supply areas where bananas are grown under conditions and agricultural practices far inferior to those in Latin America. A better measure of the distance-from-market factor upon weight is found in the record of United Fruit Company shipments to the two markets. In 1955, United's shipments from Latin American countries to North America averaged 79.1 pounds per stem, while its European shipments from the same area averaged 49.7 pounds per stem, or about 37 percent lighter. Most, though not all, of this is attributable to the differences in the maturity stage of the fruit cut for the respective markets.

THE PRODUCING COUNTRIES

PRODUCTION OPERATIONS will be examined on the basis largely of our firsthand study of banana culture in the six coun-

---

[1] Based on data given in Table 5, Chapter II.

tries—Guatemala, Honduras, Costa Rica, Panama, Colombia, and Ecuador—which collectively produced about 60 percent of the 1955 banana tonnage that entered world trade, and about 92 percent of North American imports.

A parenthetical statement about these six countries may be in order. They have only two conspicuous common attributes that lend themselves to safe generalization: All are Spanish-speaking countries, at least in the sense that in each Spanish is the official language. All grow bananas for export on low-lying, humid lands in the American tropics that have been cleared of their tangled rain-forest cover, or on swampland that has been drained and silted over for this purpose. On almost every other count their differences are at least as striking as their similarities. Their combined populations in 1955 totaled something over 23 million, of which Colombia alone, with about 13 million, had well over half, Ecuador and Guatemala between 3 and 4 million each, Honduras about 1.7 million, and Costa Rica and Panama less than 1 million each. Colombia has more than 60 percent of the total land area of the six republics. Three of the six, Guatemala, Honduras, and Costa Rica are Central American countries; two—Colombia and Ecuador—are South American. Panama is ambiguously perched between the two. It is Central American in location but since historically it was once a part of Colombia, it regards itself as one of the South American republics.

There are very wide divergences among the six in ethnic composition. In Ecuador and Guatemala the indigenous Indian cultures are very dominant; in Costa Rica they have all but disappeared; while in the others there have been varying degrees of admixture between the Indian and white, Indian and Negro, and Negro-white inhabitants. There are marked differences also in the degree of literacy, the relative political stability, the cultural and economic patterns, and the levels of economic accomplishments among these six republics. Although the data for such comparisons are far from satisfactory, it is probable that the levels of per capita income are almost twice as high in Panama, Colombia, and Costa Rica as in Ecuador, Honduras, and Guatemala. Colombia, with its much larger population and area has carried industrial development further than any of the others. In Panama, as might be expected, the operation of the Canal has importantly influenced the national economic trends.

It is obvious that even with respect to the common economic interest that all of the six countries share—the growing of bananas for export —the impact of this endeavor upon their several economies varies widely. There is a correspondingly wide divergence in the relative

74

importance of the United Fruit Company operations in the banana production and export business of the six republics. Accordingly, detailed analysis of these two factors must await the country-by-country examination that will be set forth in chapters to follow. Table 7, however, will serve to dramatize both of these points. It will be seen from this tabulation that while bananas accounted for 20 percent of the total value of 1955 exports of the six countries, the incidence varied widely among them. For Panama, bananas earned 74 percent of all export revenue, for Ecuador 55 percent, Honduras 50 per cent, Costa Rica 41 percent, Guatemala 18 percent, while for Colombia they accounted for only 4 percent of export earnings.[2]

For the six countries combined, coffee exports brought in more than three times as much revenue as banana exports—$631 million against $192 million from bananas. But the great magnitude of the discrepancy was almost completely accounted for by the huge coffee export of Colombia. The year's foreign exchange earnings from coffee were considerably higher than banana earnings in Guatemala, and slightly higher in Costa Rica as well, but bananas were more important than coffee in each of the other three countries. Panama exported no coffee at all. The combined banana exports of the five republics other than Colombia exceeded their combined coffee exports by about 15 percent.

The United Fruit Company marketed 60 percent by value of all bananas exported from the combined area, but again the incidence of its importance was very different from country to country. Its shipments accounted for virtually all of Costa Rica's banana export earnings,[3] 93 percent of Panama's, 75 percent of Guatemala's, 69 percent in the case of Honduras, 58 percent for Colombia, and only 19 percent with respect to Ecuador's banana shipments. It should be noted that Ecuador's shipments, even on a value basis, exceeded the combined exports of its two closest rivals in the banana trade, and accounted for about 33 percent of the total banana exports of the six countries.

One additional comment will add useful perspective on how the pattern of United Fruit Company's banana operations varied from

---

[2] It is worthy of note that in Panama, largely because of revenues from the Panama Canal, exports play a far less decisive role in the overall balance-of-payments position than in the other five republics. In 1955, Panama's merchandise exports accounted for only about 25 percent of its total foreign exchange earnings upon current account, as compared with 85 percent for Costa Rica and more than 90 percent in each of the other four countries.

[3] This situation may be expected to change substantially over the next few years. Standard Fruit has just started to plant variety bananas, highly resistant to Panama disease, on a large area in the Atlantic Zone where the United Fruit Company formerly grew Gros Michels, but which it abandoned many years ago because the soil had become infested with the fusaria of Panama disease.

Table 7 | Relative Importance of Total Banana Exports And United Fruit Banana Exports In the Six Countries, 1955 (Value figures in thousand U.S. dollars)

Country	Value of total exports	Value of banana exports	% Banana exports to total exports	United Fruit banana exports		United Fruit shipments[a]		National coffee exports	
				Value	% of total banana exports	% Produced	% Purchased	Value	% of total exports
Colombia..........	579,600	24,200	4	13,973	58	30	70	484,100	84
Costa Rica........	80,900	33,210	41	32,843	99	88	12	37,360	46
Ecuador..........	113,900	62,300	55	11,594	19	25	75	23,100	20
Guatemala........	109,200	19,900	18	14,943	75	81	19	75,200	69
Honduras.........	50,500	25,500	50	17,577	69	66	34	11,100	22
Panama...........	36,300	27,000	74	25,194	93	100	—	—	—
Total.............	970,400	192,110	20	116,124	60	68	32	630,860	65

[a] On a stem basis.

Chart IX
Importance of Bananas in Six Countries' Total Exports in 1955

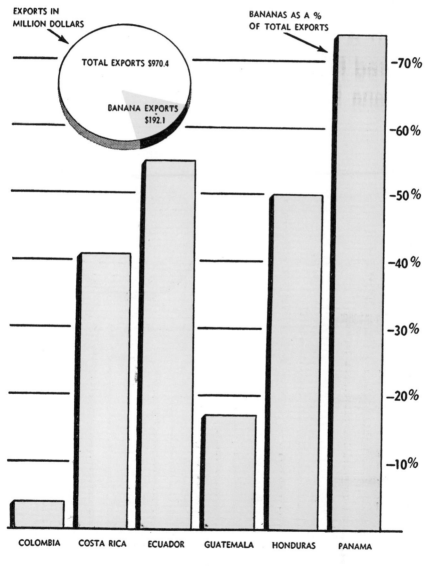

EXPORTS IN
MILLION DOLLARS

BANANAS AS A %
OF TOTAL EXPORTS

TOTAL EXPORTS $970.4

BANANA EXPORTS
$192.1

−70%

−60%

−50%

−40%

−30%

−20%

−10%

COLOMBIA   COSTA RICA   ECUADOR   GUATEMALA   HONDURAS   PANAMA

Chart X
United Fruit's Share of Six Countries' Banana Exports in 1955

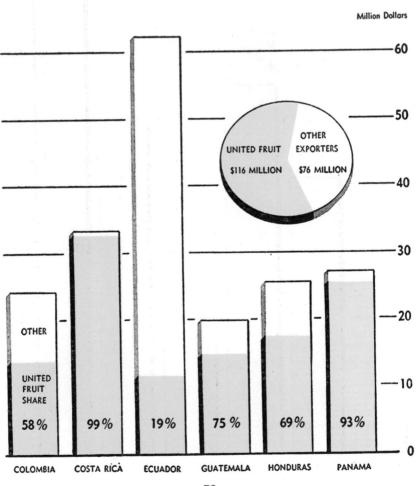

Million Dollars

UNITED FRUIT $116 MILLION

OTHER EXPORTERS $76 MILLION

60

50

40

30

20

OTHER

UNITED FRUIT SHARE

10

0

COLOMBIA	COSTA RICA	ECUADOR	GUATEMALA	HONDURAS	PANAMA
58%	99%	19%	75%	69%	93%

country to country. On an overall basis, the company grew 68 percent of the stems that it shipped from the six countries. From Panama, it shipped only fruit that was grown on its own plantations. In Costa Rica, it grew 88 percent of the bananas it exported and procured the other 12 percent from independent banana farmers. For Guatemala and Honduras, respectively, the percentages were 81 and 66 percent grown versus 19 percent and 34 percent purchased. But the pattern was radically different in both Colombia and Ecuador. In the former, United Fruit produced only 30 percent of its banana shipments. It procured the rest from local independent growers, under contracts calling for a variety of company-provided services including sigatoka control and fertilizer supply. In the case of Ecuador, the company's own plantations provided only 25 percent of its shipped fruit, and in that country almost all of its purchased fruit was procured on the open market, without any contractual relationships with the independents who supplied it. The significance of these variations will be discussed as we review the situation on a country-by-country basis. But first we will follow the production and distribution procedures step by step.

Banana Lands

THE FIRST STEP in banana production is the acquisition of suitable land. Table 8 helps to give some perspective on the relationship of banana lands to total areas and acreage planted to all crops in the six republics as well as upon the weight of United Fruit holdings and banana operations in the overall picture. A number of observations may be drawn from this table.

The term "Banana Republic" has been rather widely and loosely applied to at least all of the countries of the isthmus, but it is clear that banana production is far from monopolizing a large percentage of even that portion of land devoted to crop production. For the six republics collectively, banana culture represented only a trifle over 3.5 percent of total crop acreage. The incidence is highest—12 percent—in Ecuador, which has never been termed a "Banana Republic." It is next highest in Costa Rica where banana acreage amounts to about 7 percent of total crop acreage; in Panama the incidence is on the order of 6 percent; and in Honduras about 4 percent. In Guatemala and Colombia, banana culture takes less than 2 percent of the land planted in crops.

This picture hardly conforms to the general concept conjured up by the term "monoculture"—a label contrived by sociologists and

Table 8	Banana Acreage and Land Use in Six Countries with United Fruit's Share (In thousands of acres)

	Six countries			United Fruit Company			
						Total banana acreage [a]	
Country	Total area	Total croplands	Total banana acreage	Total acreage owned	Acreage owned	Mature acreage owned or controlled	Other crop acreage
Guatemala.....	27,000	3,683	40	461	21	28	31
Honduras......	28,000	1,815	70	325	34	28	91
Costa Rica.....	13,000	875	60	497	35	39	72
Panama........	18,000	650	42	151	27	23	41
Colombia......	256,000	7,200	112	100	7	20	10
Ecuador.......	72,000	2,344	284 [b]	192	9	7	10
Total.........	414,000	16,567	608	1,726	133	145	255

[a] United Fruit banana acreage owned includes acreage planted but not mature; mature acreage owned or controlled shows company-owned producing acreage, plus acreage of independent growers under contract to sell to United Fruit.
[b] Acreage reported for 1954; 1955 acreage figures not available.

frequently attached to at least several of the countries that produce bananas. The total agricultural acreage in the six republics—that is, the cleared land devoted either to crop production or animal grazing— is about seven times as large as their combined crop acreage, and at least a large portion of this could be turned into crop production. Furthermore all six republics have even larger areas of uncleared land that could be put to agricultural use. These facts drive the point home that whatever else may be said about them, bananas are not preempting land that might be better employed.

An additional perspective is offered by the data set forth in Table 8. The United Fruit Company, in 1955, held ownership title to 1,726,000 acres (2,700 square miles) of land in the six republics, a little less than a fourth of which was planted in productive crops. Its banana planting of 133,000 acres, in turn, accounted for just over a third of United Fruit's total crop acreage on its own lands. A brief analysis of these company landholdings may throw some light upon the highly controversial issue of whether or not United Fruit has

THE SETTING

Six Latin American Republics

- Colombia ● Costa Rica ● Ecuador
- Guatemala ● Honduras ● Panama

which were the source in 1955 of 60%
of world banana exports and 92% of
North American banana imports.

The U. S. Business

- United Fruit Company

which grew or bought
in these six republics 95% of
all its banana shipments in 1955.

THE VOLUME OF BANANAS shipped in international trade exceeds that of any other fruit and decisively dwarfs that of other tropical fruits. This is despite the fact that bananas are exceptionally susceptible to diseases, blowdowns, and floods, and to deterioration or complete loss with anything less than tender handling under demanding harvesting, shipping, and marketing schedules.

UNITED FRUIT COMPANY, since its incorporation in 1899, has played a leading role in most developments that have made this trade feasible—from large-scale production through disease-control techniques, land and ocean transport, and sales promotion. The company handled 59% of U. S. and Canadian banana imports in 1955 and 10% of Europe's, or 28% of the world total. In that same year, bananas accounted for 4% of Colombia's total exports, 41% of Costa Rica's, 55% of Ecuador's, 18% of Guatemala's, 50% of Honduras', and 74% of Panama's. United Fruit's share of the total banana exports from these six countries amounted to 60%.

THE PLANTATIONS

Carved out of virgin jungle, the company's banana divisions in all six countries are on low-lying, humid lands.

A VAST AMOUNT of manual labor as well as hydraulic engineering is needed, not only for clearing tangled rain forests, but also for drainage canals, dykes, floodways, and irrigation canals. In addition to banana land, acreage is needed for pasturage and other crops for sale and for food; lumber to supply construction materials and railway ties; facilities and living space for the relatively self-contained communities of 30,000 to 40,000 people who make up the average banana division.

Typically, a 20,000-acre division is divided into over 20 banana farms, each organized as a separate community and producing unit. A checkerboard of roads, ditches, bridges, and large and small pipes covers each farm, and all are interconnected—with each other and the division centers—by roads, tramways or railways, and by power, electric, and telephone lines.

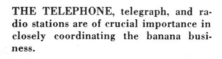

THE TELEPHONE, telegraph, and radio stations are of crucial importance in closely coordinating the banana business.

DIVISION CENTERS, which link the farms to the outside world, are made up of the staff headquarters and community facilities; railway yards, equipment depots, and machine shops; power plants and communications stations; and airstrips and terminals.

GROWING BANANAS

Even before the land is cleared, the farm is staked and lined for planting the banana rhizomes.

ENTIRE "HEADS" are sometimes planted in each hole, but usually they are split into "bits." As young plants emerge, they have to be pruned and surrounding lush growth cleaned out until banana plants are able to provide sufficient shade to inhibit such competition.

IRRIGATION CANAL feeds the pumphouse which in turn drives water through a network of pipes to the banana plants.

Water is a "must" for both overhead and undertree irrigation of banana plants.

THE YOUNG PLANTS, shown at top, are served by undertree irrigation. Each automatic revolving spray nozzle of the overhead irrigation towers, seen above, are watering mature plants for a radius of over three acres. One plant yields a stem (bunch) of fruit—United's weigh anywhere from 75 to over 100 pounds—about 10 to 12 months from planting.

When all goes well, each acre on a well-managed plantation may produce annually 300 or more stems of the Gros Michel bananas grown by United. But this seldom happens. Because of the many hazards to which bananas are subject, marketable yields, year in and year out, are about 25% less.

PANAMA DISEASE has killed banana plants in the dark area of this air view (diagonal white line, running from upper left to right, is a railroad, indicating scale). This fungus disease attacks the rhizome and root system of the plant and results finally in complete destruction. United Fruit has pioneered in flood fallowing to control this major blight—an expensive method, practical only for large-scale operators since it involves moving enormous amounts of earth and pumping water, and requires large reserves of lands for new banana plantings.

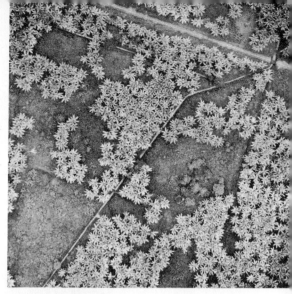

ARTIFICIAL LAKES are part of the flood-fallowing program. Chemical content of flood-fallowed lake is tested, above, to determine whether infection remains. If not, the lake may be drained, and banana growing resumed. Here a plowman cuts lines in flood-fallowed land, indicating where banana rhizomes are to be planted.

SIGATOKA, an air-borne fungus, first causes irregular ripening and cuts down the size of fruit; eventually, it kills the plants. For its control, United Fruit plantations are equipped with central mixing and pumping stations and an elaborate gridwork of small pipes with outlets at frequent intervals to allow workers to spray Bordeaux mixture on every banana plant at regular periods.

FLOODS AND BLOWDOWNS continue despite efforts to ameliorate their effects. Systems of barrage dykes and floodways to carry waters around fields sometimes cover about as great an area as the actual banana plantings. In some areas where winds cause frequent blowdowns, the large-scale planting of trees for windbreaks has been undertaken.

FARM TO RETAILER

Banana cutting has to be arranged on a precise schedule timed to proper maturity, shipcalls at loading ports, and movement to shipside without delays before cooling.

HARVESTING is a year-round operation, with each stem to be cut selected on the basis of maturity appropriate to the distance from its port of consignment. The cutter nicks the stalk just enough so that the bunch rests on the shoulder pad of a waiting courier. He then severs the stem, and the carrier deposits it on a padded cart for transport to the receiving station.

MODERN receiving stations usually are equipped with overhead monorail conveyors on which the "strung" fruit is hung and moved along to large washing vats. After it dries, a clear plastic bag, with holes to assure proper ventilation, is slid over each bunch to prevent scarring and damage.

Farm-to-port haulage of bananas varies greatly among producing areas, but generally it is by rail, and many railways have been built and are operated by banana companies.

SPLIT SHEATHS of banana plants are used as protective padding in cars, which are not refrigerated but are slatted to provide maximum ventilation for the perishable fruit.

LOADING AND HAULING to ports proceeds day and night to preserve the fruit and cut down the ship's time in port. After locomotives pick up loaded cars in the fields, their hauls usually vary from 10 to 75 miles, although some are longer.

THESE MODERN PRACTICES, developed to assure speed and tender handling, are in marked contrast to methods at the turn of the century when the picture at left was taken.

AS UNITED'S SHIP noses up to the pier, the first cars loaded with bananas are already rolling into place parallel to the ship's side. It takes some 160 cars to load the average banana ship, and the entire operation usually takes about 24 to 36 hours.

A GANTRY CRANE with a belt of rubberized canvas pockets swings into place opposite each hatch. Stems are carried from the cars on padded shoulders of dockworkers to slings that carry the bananas over shipside and down into the holds. There, other workers stack them precisely in refrigerator compartments. Temperatures during the subsequent voyages—ranging anywhere from 1,800 to 7,500 nautical miles—must be maintained at 55° to 60° F.

At U. S. piers, unloading machinery moves into high gear. Once off the ship, bananas are carried on conveyors past stations where they are tallied and graded, on to points where faulty stems are disposed of, and then to refrigerated cars and trucks assembled by jobbers to carry the bananas to predetermined destinations.

TENTS OVER HOLDS keep cold winter air from damaging fruit during unloading at Weehawken, New Jersey.

UNLOADING continues into the night at a Mobile, Alabama, pier.

Jobbers, who usually take title to their orders at port of entry, ripen the bananas, cull those that are damaged, and prepare them in the forms which each retailer believes are most appealing to his customers.

Chart XI
Bananas Occupy Only a Fraction
Of All Crop Lands

BANANA CROP LANDS AS
PERCENT OF TOTAL

TOTAL CROP LANDS
AS 100%

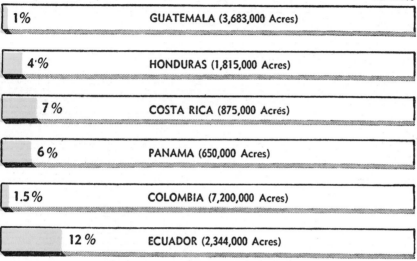

1%	GUATEMALA (3,683,000 Acres)
4·%	HONDURAS (1,815,000 Acres)
7%	COSTA RICA (875,000 Acrés)
6%	PANAMA (650,000 Acres)
1.5%	COLOMBIA (7,200,000 Acres)
12%	ECUADOR (2,344,000 Acres)

monopolized actual and potential banana land in this area to a degree that chokes off the entry of competing producers. Incidentally, it should illuminate some inherent characteristics of banana culture.

The Relative Size of United's Holdings

Certainly, the ownership of more than 1.7 million acres of land in the six republics marks the United Fruit Company as a very large land proprietor by any definition. Yet this vast holding, the great bulk of which was purchased in the form of virgin tropical jungle mostly in completely unopened areas devoid of linkage to settlement centers, amounts to less than four-tenths of 1 percent of their combined land areas. The company's 388,000 acres of land planted to crops accounts for a fraction over 2 percent of all reported croplands in the six republics. In every one of the six countries there still are incomparably larger tracts of virgin forest land as good as or better than the United Fruit holdings for general agricultural purposes. Thus there would seem to be little ground for the claim that the company's landlordship, large though it is, has served as a barrier to agricultural enterprise by others. On the contrary, around almost all of United's divisions (and the same is true of the Standard Fruit Company's Honduran holdings) we saw an extraordinarily large amount of local agricultural and commercial development. This could not have taken root in the absence of the basic port, rail, road, health, education, and communication facilities that the company provided largely at its own cost, or where community provision was made possible by the tax payments from the company operations.

Company-Owned Acreage not in Cropland

Another matter that deserves review concerns the question of why United Fruit should find it necessary to own over four times as much land as it has actually put to use in its plantings of bananas or other crops. Four major points are relevant here:

First, a large-scale banana operation in virgin territory requires far more land than the acreage upon which bananas actually are grown. In carving a banana division out of the wilderness, provision has to be made to house workers, to cultivate food crops to feed them, to provide them with schools, hospitals, churches, and recreational facilities. A network of roads, tramways, and railroads must be established to service the division and to link it with port facilities where sidings, docks, and boat yards also must be established. Pasturage must be provided for a large number of work animals, and for beef and dairy cattle to furnish meat, milk, and butter to feed the workers and their dependents. A very large water supply is needed for the division community and the requisite watershed has to be protected from pollution. Large-scale lumbering operations must be inaugurated to supply railway ties and construction materials. There must be room for machine and railway shops, for pumping stations to supply irrigation water and chemical sprays, for warehouses, commissaries, and power stations. In short, the setting up of a banana division entails the supply of everything needed for a relatively self-contained community of 30,000 to 40,000 people and for its linkage with the outside world.

A second reason why a great deal of land is needed rests on the fact that banana acreage, invariably located in low-lying river valley lands, requires a vast amount of hydraulic engineering. In addition to irrigation facilities, extensive drainage is almost always necessary. In certain divisions, where much of the land is actually lower than the rivers, a network of huge drainage canals must be dug from the plantations to the ocean 10 to 20 miles away. Where seasonal river flooding is a problem, and this is the rule rather than the exception, it is often necessary to build a system of barrage dykes and floodways to carry the flood waters around rather than through the cultivated areas to protect them from destruction. In a number of cases, the area of such floodways rivals the extent of the actual banana plantings. In many areas where wind incidence results in frequent blowdowns, the large-scale planting of trees for windbreaks has been found advisable.

A third factor is important in connection with land acquisition. In each of the six banana-producing countries the large-scale cultivation of bananas involves unrelenting combat with a variety of diseases and insect pests. One of the most serious, sigatoka or leaf spot disease, is an air-borne fungus (Cercospora musae), which developed as a formidable blight in the Far East in the early 1900's, and spread to Latin America in the 1930's. This highly contagious disease destroys banana leaves, which in turn drastically cuts down the size of produced fruit, causes irregular ripening that makes the bananas unsuitable for shipping, and eventually kills off the producing plants. Sigatoka affects all of the variety bananas as well as the Gros Michel, and throughout our six countries systematic control measures now are virtually requisite for successful commercial production. Until very recently, Ecuador was thought to be virtually immune to serious sigatoka infection, but in the last few years this disease has wrought havoc to bananas in Esmeraldas and the upper Guayas River basin and seems to be spreading southward.

Fortunately, sigatoka can be kept under control by regular applications of copper compounds. To this end, the United Fruit Company plantations are now generally equipped with permanent pipe installations through which Bordeaux mixture, prepared in mixing and pumping stations placed throughout its banana cultivations, can be sprayed in water suspension on the plants at regular cycle intervals. Installations for spraying are elaborate and far too expensive for small operators. Only recently, however, successful experiments with a new method of sigatoka control, introduced by missions of the U. S. International Cooperation Administration, have been undertaken in Ecuador; and the new method is beginning to be used in Jamaica, Panama, Guatemala, and Honduras as well. The experiments will be conducted in Colombia early in 1958. Portable equipment is used for applying agricultural oil in the form of a fine mist, either alone or with copper compounds or zinc dithiocarbamate suspended, as a way of controlling sigatoka at less cost for installations and for chemicals. One method, first initiated in Guadalupe by the French, used knapsack sprayers carried on workers' backs, but more recent experiments indicate that helicopter and airplane application will prove more efficient. While results to date are promising, only time will tell whether or not the new methods will make obsolete the permanent installations for Bordeaux spraying.

Panama disease, the second major banana blight, is one that has far greater implications to the question of how much land in addition to current plantings a major banana producer needs. It, also, is a fungus disease caused by a fusarium (Fusarium osysporium f. cubense) that invades the soil and multiplies and spreads at varying rates of speed depending upon soil composition and other factors that, as yet, are imperfectly understood. Panama disease does not spread with the speed of sigatoka, that can wipe out a whole plantation in short order, but it acts more persistently and gradually until it entirely destroys a plantation's usefulness for growing bananas. It has made no inroads to date in the Santa Marta region of northern Colombia, although careful and very intensive research has not been able to determine why this area should have an immunity that is unique in the Western Hemisphere.

This fusarium attacks the rhizome and root system of the banana plant, quickly affects the vascular system through which water and nutrients are fed to the stalk, leaves, and fruit, and results in stunting, leaf withering, and finally in complete destruction. It has no effect on crops, other than the banana, and the Lacatan, Cavendish, and Bout Rond varieties of bananas have demonstrated a high degree of resistance, while the Gros Michel is particularly susceptible. The obvious genetic solution of crossing the resistant characteristics of the Lacatan with the other more desirable qualities of the Gros Michel has so far been unproductive. Since bananas are a virtually seedless crop, and there is no wood structure to make grafting experiments feasible, banana genetics are of an almost unique order of difficulty.

The United Fruit Company has pioneered in seeking a "control" solution through what is known as "flood fallowing." This involves a huge agricultural engineering project of surrounding every field in infected areas with massive dykes, pumping water into the enclosures and holding it at controlled levels for periods varying from four months to a year. Early experiments with flood fallowing were very promising. The water in the man-made lakes seemed effectively to smother the fusaria, and subsequent Gros Michel plantings flourished for as long as seven or eight years before serious reinfection.

Unhappily, as this system has been applied over much wider areas, the results have not been uniformly good. In some instances, the disease has reappeared in virulent form almost immediately, and the span of effective immunity has varied widely even from field to contiguous field in a given division. Obviously, the great expense of the colossal earth-moving operations involved in flood fallowing could not be justified unless the areas so treated could be relied upon to have a productive span of at least five or six years. Even so, this control measure would require larger areas than are actually devoted to banana plantings at any one time, since the system would demand a rotation under which perhaps a fifth or a fourth of a given plantation would always be under water. There is the further consideration that flood fallowing could never be universally applied, since it is applicable only to areas that have adequate water supplies, sufficiently level terrain, and a compact subsoil that will hold the water for the necessary periods of time.

There are, to be sure, certain expedients other than flood fallowing that may be adopted in certain areas to stretch out the productive life of a plantation that is shrinking through the inexorable attrition of soil infection by this dread fusarium. United Fruit and other large operators have employed pump drainage and silting procedures to add to the potential banana acreage swamplands and lands where the soil has been classified as too thin or too barren to support banana cultivation profitably. The procedure for pump drainage is to construct great levees around large swamp areas, to drain the water into sumps at the lowest level in the operation, and to lift it over the levees by siphon pumps for discharge into drainage canals that will carry it to points downstream on the river or out to the sea. Silting is accomplished through hydraulic engineering operations that divert silt-loaded rivers at flood stage from their normal courses through overflow canals allowing their burden of alluvial soil to be deposited in the form of a new topsoil blanket over adjacent low-lying areas.

Obviously, the adaptability of either procedure to a particular locale depends upon whether or not the requisite physical conditions are present. Like flood fallow, the expense of carrying out these two operations, the heavy equipment requirement, and the fact that they are rarely feasible at all unless they can be planned and carried out over a very wide acreage limit their employment to large-scale operators only. To date, there is no practicable means through which an owner of a small plantation can hope to continue banana cultivation when his land is severely infected with Panama disease.

Panama disease has been the greatest single factor in dictating the large-scale banana growers' policy of always maintaining larger holdings of potential banana lands than are put to active use at any given time. It is difficult to see how this can be avoided unless or until a way is found to grow bananas of a type demanded by the dominant North American market under conditions that provide an adequate protection from the ravages of this disease.

In the history of United Fruit operations, according to the company's own account, Panama disease has destroyed and compelled the complete abandonment or suspension of banana-growing operations in the following major divisions: "Almirante Division on the Caribbean Coast of Panama, Trujillo Division on the north coast of Honduras, Limón Division on the east coast of Costa Rica, Quepos Division on the west coast of Costa Rica, the East Coast Nicaraguan Division, the Suriname Division in Dutch Guiana, the British Honduras Division, and practically all of the North Coast Guatemala Division. In infected areas where the disease has spread more slowly, banana farms are continually being destroyed and replaced by planting in other areas." Over a 50-year period, the United Fruit Company alone has been forced to discontinue banana cultivation on about 900,000 acres of land, with Panama disease as the chief reason for abandonment or shifts to other crops.

The impact of the wholesale abandonment of divisions upon local economies and the policies and practical procedures that might cushion such impacts will be reserved for later discussion. The point to be registered here is that until the problem of Panama disease can be resolved, the production of at least Gros Michel bananas will entail moving banana cultivation from acreage that becomes untenably infected to adjacent reserves of virgin acreage sufficiently close to permit use of the huge facilities that make up the apparatus of a modern banana division. The alternative, under present conditions, is the far more drastic and socially more costly procedure of operating a banana division until it no longer can produce enough to warrant continuing operations in bananas, and then to close it up.

There are a variety of other diseases and a host of insect and animal enemies that must be constantly combatted by the banana producer through unrelenting vigilance and expensive control measures. None of these present threats is, as yet, comparably serious to either sigatoka or Panama disease. One bacterial wilt disease, moko (Pseudomonas solanacearum) has recently caused considerable damage in Costa Rica, Honduras, and Colombia, but its spread seemingly can be controlled through rigorous disinfection of machetes as the pruners move from plant to plant, and destruction of all root systems found to be infected.

There is a final point relevant to the fact that United's landholdings are so much larger than the acreage planted in bananas or other crops. Of the 1.7 million acres of land owned by the United Fruit Company in the six republics, it would be a fair estimate that only about a fourth, or something like 450,000 acres, is at all suitable for banana cultivation and not more than half of this can be classified as land upon which it would be feasible to plant Gros Michels as distinguished from the varieties. This means that United is maintaining reserves of some 300,000 acres of potential banana land in addition to its 133,000 acres now under banana cultivation, about half of which could be used only by taking the drastic decision of going into variety production. This does not appear to be an unreasonable margin against the contingencies we have listed.

As to the remaining 1.3 million acres of its landholdings that are not suitable for banana growing, two comments are in order: First, there is a genuine requirement for control of acreage vastly larger than that employed for banana plantings for the purposes that have been cited above, but such requirements fall well below the extent of the company's present holdings.

Second, a large part of United's current holdings were acquired by necessity rather than by design. In order to purchase the potential acreage for growing bananas which it wanted, it was necessary in numerous cases to purchase outright large parcels of land held by private owners who were unwilling to sell only part of their properties. Thus, the company acquired a very large amount of land for which it had no foreseeable use, and which it would be glad to dispose of at nominal price if there were any prospect of anyone's finding productive employment for it. This is evidenced by the fact that, since 1935, the company has reduced its total of owned acreage by about one-third (including considerable acreage of potential banana lands). A great portion of the relinquished area was deeded to central or local governments without compensation. The hard fact is that there is very limited demand for this nonbanana land, even after an area has been opened through the establishment of a banana division, since it is generally surrounded by countless acres of entirely comparable tropical forests that are being put to no productive use.

The Extent of United Fruit Control of Banana Land

There remains the question of the degree of dominance exercised by the United Fruit Company over producing or potential banana land as such. In an antitrust suit complaint filed by the U. S. Department of Justice against United (Civil Action No. 4560, filed July 2, 1954, as amended January 12, 1956) the following is among the allegations made: "With the exception of land in Ecuador, United owns, leases, or otherwise controls 85% of the land in the American tropics suitable for banana cultivation." [4]

If true, this would indicate a degree of dominance sufficient to effectively choke off the entry of other producers on a scale that might offer serious competition. Let us see what evidence on this is presented by the figures given in Table 8, remembering that about 95 percent of all United Fruit's banana shipments in 1955 originated in these six countries, so that this is the area of its major impact. In the first place, the tabulation shows that for the six countries *combined*, United Fruit's owned acreage in bananas was about 22 percent of total reported acreage planted in bananas, and United's producing acreage plus that of independent growers producing under contract with United was about 24 percent of the reported combined total.

But the Attorney General's complaint on this score specifically excepted Ecuador. If Ecuador is disregarded, the total banana acreage of the other five countries is 324,000 acres, of which United's owned acreage accounts for 124,000 acres or about 40 percent. Adding to this acreage of its owned lands that of independent growers producing under contract to United increases the total under company control to 138,000 acres or about 43 percent. This, of course, leaves out the question of how much of the total acreage owned by United in these five countries—a total of 1,534,000 acres—might be classifiable as *potential* banana land. Again the 25 percent proportion cited above is believed to be applicable. Combining both the actual and potential banana land owned by United in the five countries, and adding in the 14,000 acres upon which independents are growing bananas for United under contract, we arrive at a figure of something under 400,000 acres.

Even upon the assumption that the *only* potential banana acreage in the five republics not now under United control was the 186,000 acres actually in production by independents not under contract

---

[4] The attorneys for the government, in a pretrial conference, indicated that its charges regarding land monopoly might not be pressed in this suit.

Early in February 1958, after this study had been completed and was in process of being printed, this antitrust suit was settled through a "consent decree" without judicial determination of the issues presented in the Department of Justice charges. The terms of this decree, accepted by the Department of Justice and approved by United Fruit Company stockholders on April 16, 1958, are set forth in an Appendix note at the end of this report.

While the authors of this study believe that readers should be informed of this agreement and its terms, none of the study's conclusions would have been altered had the decree been entered into before the study was completed.

with United, that company's control would be much less than the 85 percent figure that has been given publicity. But such a comparison is obviously spurious. In response to inquiries that we made on our visits to these five countries, we compiled a listing by specific location and acreage estimation of between 300,000 and 350,000 acres of land that a survey had established as suitable for banana production, but which presently was not being put to use. A study mission recently sent up by the Inter-American Economic and Social Council has estimated that potential acreage suitable for banana plantings but not now put to that use amounts to about 1,600,000 acres in the five countries, with another 580,000 in Mexico.

Much of this potential banana land would, of course, require the same sort of basic facilities that United, Standard, and other large producers had been compelled to install on their divisions. A small fraction of this potential included lands on which bananas had formerly been grown and which had succumbed to Panama disease, so that cultivation of variety bananas rather than Gros Michel would be indicated. Nevertheless, we can state with assurance that United Fruit owns or controls less than a quarter of the actual and potential banana lands in these five countries where its activities are preponderantly concentrated. If the comparison is made on the basis of *the American tropics other than Ecuador,* as in the quoted allegation, it is difficult to see on what reasoning the 85 percent estimate could have been based. Brazil, alone, in which the United Fruit Company does not operate, has a reported 385,000 acres of bananas in production, and Mexico, also outside of United's orbit, reports about 49,000 acres in banana cultivations. These two countries alone have more acreage *presently in banana production* than the total of United Fruit's *potential* banana acreage however generously estimated.

If Ecuador is included in the accounting (and it is difficult to see why it should be excluded since it alone ships about 20 percent of the bananas moving in world trade) the 85 percent claim becomes palpably ridiculous. The United Fruit Company's position, on the objective record, is sufficiently large to raise a host of problems for it and for others in the banana trade. It clearly is one of our tasks to appraise how well or how badly it has exercised the stewardship that is the inevitable burden of those who attain great size. But when we come to our summary of the evidence presented by the complete record, the widely publicized charge that the company maintains a monopolistic control over the major portion of the land areas on which bananas could be produced for the North American market will be given no weight. It is clearly refuted by the facts that have just been cited.

Banana Production

THE ESTABLISHMENT of a modern banana division of, let us say, 20,000 producing acres is a truly monumental job. Depending upon the amount of hydraulic engineering that is necessary, it can easily cost from $20 million to $25 million in initial capital investment, or from $1,000 to $1,250 per banana-producing acre. The number of the world's food crops that have sufficiently high and valuable yields to warrant an investment on this scale can be counted probably upon the fingers of one hand.

Typically, a division of 20,000 acres will be divided into 22 or 23 banana farms, each organized as a separate producing unit with its own workers' and supervisors' housing, equipment complements, commissaries, schools, and dispensaries. Each farm will be crisscrossed with an elaborate gridwork of small pipes with outlets at frequent intervals to allow the sigatoka spray workers to reach every banana plant in every field with the Bordeaux mixture pumped from numerous central mixing and pumping stations appropriately spaced. There will be a similar grid of larger pipe leading to irrigation towers that reach high above the 15- or 20-foot altitude of mature banana plants, and the automatically revolving spray nozzles of these towers throw out great concentric arcs of artificial rain with a radius of over three acres each to cover every inch of the cultivation.

A checkerboard of roads, ditches, and bridges covers each farm, and all farms are interconnected with roads and narrow-gauge tramways or railroads along which steam, diesel, or gasoline powered rolling stock carries in materials, fertilizers, equipment, supplies, and work force, and over which the harvested fruit moves out. All are interconnected, too, by power, electric light, and telephone lines. The transport and communications network binds the several farms to the division center. The center itself is a complex of central offices, staff headquarters, railway yards and shops, equipment depots and machine shops, power plants, commissaries, houses, recreation buildings, baseball and soccer fields, telephone and telegraph stations, schools, hospitals, churches, airstrip and terminal, slaughterhouse and dairy. In short, the farms are linked to a complete small city that is a division headquarters, which in turn maintains its linkages to the outside world.

Almost invariably, private farms, trading centers, and settlements spring up immediately adjacent to the division headquarters, so that the communication system set up by a banana company usually becomes to some extent a public service establishment. Its railways carry general cargo and passengers, its airstrips are used by local airlines, its power stations light noncompany homes, its telegraph or wireless facilities, its hospitals, and even its schools and commissaries commence to serve a generalized community—a community that sprouts, like the suckers from a banana rhizome, from the plantation center that has won a foothold in the jungle.

Clearing and Planting

The first step toward establishing the farm units of a contemplated division is the arduous job of clearing out the tangled mass of trees, brush, and vines on the potential banana land, and establishing the needed drainage system. The former is generally a hand job with the machete, and the latter a heavy machinery job for great drag lines. Even before the heavier bodied trees are felled, the land is staked and lined for planting. The banana rhizomes or pseudobulbs are carted in, and planted in regular rows of a spacing that may vary from two or three to five or six meters (a meter equals 1.0936 yards) between each planting. Botanically, the banana is closely related to the lily, and the banana rhizome is like a giant lily bulb. Sometimes entire "heads" are planted in each hole, but more generally they are split into "bits" weighing from five to 10 pounds each. Care is taken to assure that each bit has one or preferably several buds or eyes from which the sprouts emerge. After the carefully spaced planting has been made, the heavier forest trees are felled. Some are hauled away, but many are allowed to rot in the swiftly destructive moisture of the wet tropics.

As the young plants emerge from the root system or "mat" and push up into the sunlight, excess suckers, and always the "heart" growth, are pruned out so that the most vigorous sucker can develop maximum strength, while from one to several more, appropriately spaced, are allowed to come along to replace the major plant when it is harvested 10 or 12 months later. By that time, the road and path system of the farm has been established, and the disease control and irrigation pipelines laid.

Meticulous cleaning at frequent intervals—more machete work—is required to keep down the lush growth of brush, vine, and weed until the bananas are tall enough and have a sufficiently developed leaf system to furnish enough shade to inhibit such competition. Even then, three or four cleanings each year are required to keep the jungle growth from taking over once more.

After the plants have blossomed, some seven to nine months from their planting, the stalk is required to support the ever-increasing weight of the stem that begins to form. Gros Michel stems from the area average about 79 pounds each when they reach the stage of maturity suitable for North American shipment, but some will weigh from 100 to 130 pounds. The leaf-structure stalk of the banana plant is not well-adapted to carry this weight, particularly when subjected to winds. It is standard procedure, therefore, to prop each stem with one or two bamboo poles or sometimes with guy ropes or wires attached to stakes driven into the ground.

In the case of the Gros Michel and the larger Lacatan varieties, the aim is to produce about 300 or 320 mature plants per acre (750 to 800 per hectare) since experience has shown that more plants than this produce lighter and otherwise inferior stems of fruit. Always, there will be one or two additional suckers to each root system which, ideally, should be ready to flower at about the time that the mature stem is harvested. Thus banana harvesting on a given acreage goes on in a continuous cycle when proper cleaning, pruning, fertilization (chiefly nitrogenous), sigatoka spraying, irrigation, and drainage are provided.

When all goes well, each banana acre of a well-managed plantation may produce 300 or more stems of Gros Michel bananas per year, or about 24,000 pounds of fruit on a stem-weight basis (20,400 pounds consumption basis). In Honduras, the yields per acre of certain well-cared plantings of Cavendish bananas, which may be planted in much closer array than the larger Gros Michel plants, have at times produced as much as 40,000 pounds per acre. But seldom does all go well on banana plantations. Floods, blowdowns, chill, disease, insect damage, and rejects for deficient quality take a toll which, year in and year out, cut down the potential marketable yields by an average of something like 25 percent. Thus, on United Fruit Company plantations, under the most advanced practice, the average yield per acre amounts to about 18,000 pounds of *shipped* fruit, stem-weight basis (15,300 pounds consumption basis). On most banana acreage in the six countries, where farm management standards are far lower than those of the United Fruit Company, the average yields per acre are considerably less.

Disease and Pest Controls

We already have outlined the formidable problems presented by the three most serious banana diseases, Panama, sigatoka, and moko, and the elaborate means that have been devised to combat them. The point that requires emphasis is that the widespread invasion of these diseases in the banana-growing areas has revolutionized the character of this agricultural enterprise. Before their incursion, the raising of bananas was relatively cheap, required limited capital, and called for no more specialized knowledge and discipline in agricultural practice than could be provided by the average small farmer.[5]

Even if substantial success follows from the current experimentation with portable spraying apparatus—some of which is of the knapsack variety that may be carried on a man's back—it is doubtful that the vital matter of keeping under control a blight that can spread across a whole community can be left safely to the initiative of a large number of individual growers. The practice developed by such companies as United and Standard of installing and operating sigatoka control systems for independent growers with whom they maintain purchase contracts is only one of a number of possible patterns through which responsibly centralized supervision might be furnished. It seems quite likely that mist spraying from helicopters or fixed-wing planes will replace pipe-spray installations as the standard procedure.

Panama disease, even more than sigatoka, is likely to be a powerful influence toward centralization and large-scale operations. For, as has been described, the known means for dealing with it entail very large capital expenditures and advanced engineering practices. The great importance of both speed and systematic care in handling and transporting fruit shipments drives in the same direction. Floods and blowdowns—which periodically wipe out a banana crop in an entire area and damage properties to an extent that calls for major expenditures before they can be rehabilitated—make it prohibitively dangerous for even very large producers to confine their operations to one region or even one country.

The United Fruit Company alone is now budgeting over $1 million per year for research, a very large portion of which is related directly or indirectly to solving problems raised by the incidence of banana diseases and insect blights. It maintains field laboratories at La Lima, Honduras, at Coto in Costa Rica, and at Sevilla in Colombia manned by scientists who give full time to this effort. It commissions basic related research at such universities as Cornell, Purdue, and Wis-

[5] When we discuss the current situation in Ecuador, we shall see how the freedom from sigatoka and the low incidence in Panama infestation made it possible for that country to build itself in a short span of less than 10 years into the major banana-exporting country of the world, based largely upon the production of small independent farmers numbering in the thousands. But we shall see, too, how the spread of sigatoka is driving hundreds of these small operators out of business, with the likelihood that Ecuadorian banana exports will finally stabilize at a somewhat lower level, and that production will be consolidated within a much more compact area on the better banana lands in closer proximity to shipping ports, with a centralized rather than an individual supervision over the sigatoka control operations regardless of the unit size of the banana farm proprietorships.

consin in the United States. Standard Fruit also maintains research facilities with particular emphasis on variety bananas. In the absence of such research, the world trade in bananas would long since have withered away to a small fraction of its present size. No serious and sustained research on banana culture has been provided under government auspices except in Trinidad, and this has never been supported on a scale even remotely comparable to that of the United Fruit research program.

Harvesting

When a stem of bananas has matured to the stage appropriate to the market for which it is destined, it must be harvested or it will be lost. On every banana farm, harvesting is a year-round operation. The consumption markets of the world have a limited degree of flexibility—in the short run, at least, they are geared to accept about a given quantity and no more, with seasonal variations depending upon the availability of competing fruits. Furthermore, the reefer fleet equipped for banana carriage has a limited capacity that cannot be quickly expanded and the same is true of the specialized railroad and truck facilities and the ripening room establishments in the great consuming markets. Additionally, at least in the North American trade, which furnishes by far the largest market, it has been demonstrated that moderate differentials in the price of bananas have a relatively minor effect upon short-term demand.

Accordingly, the production, harvesting, and shipment of bananas presents an intricately complex problem in logistics that is unique among any food items that have a comparable importance in world trade. Coffee, tea, cocoa, and grain products of course must be harvested when ripe, but unlike bananas these products may be, and commonly are, stored for indefinite periods when the supply exceeds export demands. Fresh meat products must be shipped promptly, but there is considerable leeway for adjusting slaughtering schedules to market demand. Even with fish and most vegetables and fruits there is generally an alternative between shipment in fresh form or handling through canning or other processing facilities. Dairy products may be turned into butter or cheese that can be stored or turned into powdered or canned milk. But the processing of bananas, to date, has not been developed on a volume basis sufficient to offer any consequential alternative to the requirement for moving bananas when they are ready to be shipped as a fresh fruit item, and future developments along this line are problematic at best.

Banana harvesting, therefore, has to be correlated with market demand and geared to its transport facilities upon unusually close tolerances. Any slippage is almost certain to result in virtually complete loss. Dispositions in the local markets, as we have seen, are both limited and where possible offer a return that is only a minor fraction of their worth on the export market. Banana cutting has to be arranged on a precise schedule timed to ship calls at loading ports that may number two or three each week. The cutting must be scheduled so that bananas move rapidly from the farms to waiting railway cars, or other transportation, which carry them without delays to shipside and stowage under refrigeration. This is another, and one of the strongest factors, in dictating that the trade in this commodity must be organized on a large unit basis if it is to survive at all.

The stems to be cut are carefully selected upon the basis of the maturity classification appropriate to the length of voyage to the port of consignment. The cutter wields a long-handled implement with a chisel-like head with which he nicks the stalk immediately below the bunch just enough to cause the crown with its leaves and fruit stem to bend over gradually until the bunch rests on the shoulder pad of a waiting carrier. The cutter then deftly severs the stem that attaches the bunch to the stalk and the carrier deposits it on a padded cart, trailer, or sometimes on the pack saddles of mules for carriage to the "receiving station."

The receiving station is located on a railway siding or river bank where it is convenient to prepare the fruit bunches for transport by rail or barge to the port of shipment. On modern plantations, the receiving stations are generally covered concrete platforms equipped with overhead monorail conveyors on which the "strung" fruit (heavy cord loops attached to the thin end of the stalk) may be hung, and moved along to large washing vats. Washing is always desirable, and requisite when sigatoka sprays have been used. The strung fruit is dipped into a weak solution of sulfuric or muriatic acid, six or eight immersions to each bunch to remove the sigatoka control chemicals and to kill spiders or other insect hitchhikers. Afterwards it is rinsed in clear water to wash away the acid in which it has been dipped. Then it is carefully stacked on the butt end to dry before loading on railway cars or barges. Again under modern practice, each fruit stem is always bagged before shipment. A transparent bag made of polyethylene, which has holes punched out at intervals to assure proper ventilation, is slid over each bunch so as to prevent possible scarring and damage which might result from the handling of the fruit incident to shipment.

THE HAULAGE OF FRUIT from producing farm to embarkation port varies greatly from country to country and even between producing areas within a given country. Generally, it is hauled on railways, many of them built, equipped, and operated by the large producing companies. In some cases, however, the railways are regularly constituted public utilities, often owned by the government. With the development of highway facilities there is an increasing amount of road haulage by truck, and in some instances the farm to shipside transport is handled by barges. In Ecuador, for example, with its widely scattered pattern of banana production, much of the fruit moves on crude balsa rafts down the Daule, Babahoyo, Balulu, and Guayas rivers, sometimes all the way to Guayaquil and sometimes only to the smaller river mouths where it is loaded on barges for its continuing journey. The great bulk of Ecuadorian fruit moving from the three major shipping ports of Guayaquil, Esmeraldas, and Puerto Bolivar depends upon either raft, barge, and truck haulage, or a combination of the three with some rail haulage added. This multiple handling under less than adequate control procedures has been a major handicap to the condition of Ecuador's bananas upon arrival in consuming markets.

Under the more general system of straight rail carriage that applies in the other five countries, the procedure may be generalized as follows: The haulage between producing farm and port varies from perhaps 10 to 75 miles. There are, however, certain longer hauls. Bananas produced on the west coast of Guatemala, for example, move out through Puerto Barrios on the Atlantic, a rail haul of more than 300 miles. Stowage in railway cars within the countries follows much the same pattern as that prevailing in the United States. The cars, however, are not refrigerated and there is no need for heating. Generally, they are of slatted construction to provide maximum ventilation, and always before the stems are loaded, the floors and sides of the cars are carefully padded with sheaths cut from the banana stalks and with banana leaves to protect the fruit from bruising in transit. Many of them are equipped with special springs to minimize jarring.

Since the average railway car in this service carries about 300 stems, it takes some 160 cars to load a reefer of the 48,000 stem capacity, which is about standard for the banana fleet. From the cutting of the fruit to its final deposit in the holds, there must be meticulous organization and timing not only to reduce the period between cutting and stowing in the ship's refrigeration chambers to a minimum, but also to hold down the ship's time in port to avoid piling up demurrage charges. Ordinarily, the entire loading operation in a port will be accomplished within the span of 24 to 36 hours and the internal transport operation proceeds day and night to make such turnarounds feasible.

At the better embarkation ports the facilities and procedures are much like those described in Chapter III in connection with ship discharge, except that they operate in reverse. As a ship docks, the first cars loaded with fruit are already rolling into place on tracks parallel to the ship's side. Hatches are opened, and a big gantry crane with its endless belt of rubberized canvas pockets swings into place opposite each hatch. Teams of dockworkers lift the stems from the cars, carry them on padded shoulders over to the cranes and place each in one of the slings that lift the stems over shipside, carry them across the deck and down into the stowing holds. There stems are lifted off by other workers who stack them in the refrigerator compartments in the manner already described. As one string of cars is emptied a switch engine shunts it away, and another set of loaded cars is pushed into place. Inspectors note and tally every stem loaded, and those which have been damaged in transit or are judged to be of substandard grade or of the wrong maturity classification are discarded.

At ports like Guayaquil and Esmeraldas in Ecuador, where the banana ships anchor offshore for lack of deep water at dockside, the fruit is barged to shipside and carried through the side ports to the reefer's holds. But the same inspection system is maintained, and many of the reject bunches are thrown into the sea to be washed ashore. We have seen cows on the Esmeraldas beaches that have never seen a meadow, and whose sole fodder is the stems of green bananas wafted unto their white sand pastures as if by miracle over the green-blue waves.

THE BANANA DOLLAR IN THE PRODUCING COUNTRIES

THE ACCOUNTANCY OF OPERATIONS in the producing countries has been left until last. There is really no such thing as a *typical* cost for any of the operations that we have described in generalized terms. The cost of producing a pound of bananas for shipment obviously varies widely from area to area and even upon a given division or farm from year to year.

Where sigatoka control has not been requisite, as in the El Oro district of southwest Ecuador, the cost will be relatively cheap. There are important cost differences, for example, between producing bananas in the Santa Marta area of Colombia that is free of Panama disease and Almirante in Panama. In the latter area a large-scale rehabilitation program is in progress based on flood fallowing that entails earth-moving operations of genuinely awesome scope on a terrain that consists largely of semifluid mire. As this is being written in May 1957, we have just received word of a blowdown on the United Fruit plantations in Honduras that has leveled 5 million stems, including about 3 million stems with fruit sufficiently mature to have been included in the company's estimated 1957 shipments of 8 million stems. If the remaining 5 million stems are harvested and shipped, the cost per pound of produced fruit will have to bear the additional charge for all of the division's costs put into the lost stems together with the costs of replanting.

There is the further question of the applicability of the United Fruit Company's costs to those of other producers who operate without comparable mechanization, and on lower wage scales; who provide far less than large operators like United and Standard in the way of housing, schools, hospitals, and community facilities in general; and whose tax burdens are appreciably lighter. Counterbalancing this is the fact that the yields per acre of the large plantations are generally far above average.

Finally, it is obvious that internal transport charges will vary greatly, depending upon the length and character of hauls from farm to shipside, and how many shifts of cargo must be made in this process from one type of carrier to another.

With all these qualifications, it seems worthwhile to present a table of *average* costs for each step, compiled largely from the record of the United Fruit Company's operations in the six countries for the year 1955. At the least, it will give a good representative sample based on accurate accounting of what is involved in the growing and shipping of bananas in the countries of origin. And it can throw some light on what up to now has been discussed and disputed at great length without benefit of any data to tie it to reality.

A brief interpretation of Table 9 would seem to be in order. First, as we pointed out in Chapter III, the 27 percent of the North American consumers' dollar that accrues to the producing countries is about comparable to what the producers of food in the United States realize from consumers' purchases of domestic produce when the 10 percent cost of ocean shipment is added to the banana realization of the countries of origin.

Second, in our accounting given in this table, we have taken pains

Table 9 — The Breakdown of the Banana Dollar for Six Countries (Accounting for 1955)

	Cents per pound stem basis [a]	Cents per pound consumption basis [a]	Share of the North American consumers' banana dollar (U.S. $ or %)
1. Average farm cost per pound of fruit produced and purchase cost of fruit bought from others.......	1.98	2.33	.14
a. Farm maintenance costs.......	.97	1.14	
b. Disease and insect controls.....	.81	.95	
c. Harvesting costs..............	.20	.24	
2. Inland transportation costs.......	.32	.38	.02
3. Handling costs: loading, unloading, etc............................	.88	1.03	.06
4. Expenditures for property maintenance and disaster repair.........	.45	.53	.03
5. Income taxes paid to producing countries.....................	.28	.33	.02
6. Discrepancy for fruit in transit [b] ..	.02	.02	.00
7. Total realization of producing countries....................	3.93	4.62	.27

[a] All figures in columns 1 and 2 are given in U. S. cents per pound. Since bananas are sold on a stem-weight basis until they reach the jobber, column 1 gives each item upon this basis. Consumers, however, purchase banana fingers by the pound. Since there is an average shrinkage of 15 percent between the weight of shipped stems and the weight of fruit purchased by banana consumers, we have multiplied all figures in column 1 by 1.1764 to arrive at the column 2 figures that conform to the accounting used in Chapter III.
[b] The export and import figures never exactly balance. On the United Fruit accounts for 1955 there was a slight excess of reported stems shipped over stems received, which represents shipped fruit in transit at the year's end not compensated by receipts at beginning of 1955 that were listed as 1954 shipments.

to credit as return to countries of origin only that part of banana export revenue that remained in the country excluding all dividend payments abroad and additions to capital account, either from new capital flows or reinvested earnings. On this accounting, the total average cost of 3.93¢ per pound (stem-weight basis) yielded the six countries a direct revenue of $157 million for 4 billion pounds of stems shipped. This compares with the total value of their banana exports of $192 million as given in Table 7 at the beginning of this chapter. The $35 million difference represents our calculation of the share accruing to the accounts of both foreign and local investors in banana operations within the six countries. It represents their gross return on capital and effort devoted to banana growing, purchase, handling, internal transport, and ship loading in the six countries.

We have not been able to obtain any accurate accounting on the breakdown between foreign and domestic investment within the six countries in the various phases of banana enterprise linked to export trade. Hence, we do not have a firm basis for estimating how this return of $35 million may have been divided between the two. There is a way, however, of arriving at a rough order of magnitude.

From the export figures in Table 7, we can say that 1955 United Fruit shipments from this area amounted to 60 percent of total exports by value. On a depreciated book value basis, the company's investments directly attributable to banana operations in the six countries were about $152 million. If the investment of other operators in the area can be taken as proportionate to that of United, the total investment related to the production and carriage to shipside of export bananas would be $253 million. There are two important considerations that would call for substantial modification of this estimate, but each operates as a counterbalance to the other.

Obviously, the company's investment on purchased fruit would be considerably lighter than on fruit that it both produced and exported. In 1955, almost a third of the fruit that it shipped was purchased from independent producers. This factor would indicate that our estimate of overall banana export investment for the area should be raised. Against this is the consideration that United Fruit's investment in the six countries is proportionately much higher than that of the average domestic producer. Every phase of its procedure that has served as the basis for our description of modern, large-scale banana operations is capital-intensive. On this score, there would be ground for lowering our overall estimate of $253 million. Accordingly, we are impelled to adopt $253 million as our estimate in the absence of anything better, with the frank admission that it is no more than a reasonable appraisal of general magnitude.

To arrive at an estimate of the share of foreign investment in the total, we can add to the figure of $152 million of United Fruit banana capital perhaps $30 million to represent Standard Fruit's banana capital commitment in this area[6] and perhaps $6 million to cover the

---

[6] Standard's 1955 balance sheet shows depreciated book value of tropical lands of $1,265,348; cultivation, railroad, buildings, and equipment in tropics of $32,160,217; and inventories, materials and supplies, advances, etc. (not broken down by location) of $7,451,094. This is a total of over $40 million, the great bulk of which may fairly be attributed to its banana operations within the area of our consideration.

investment of several other large-scale foreign banana operations in Ecuador. Foreign banana investment in the six countries, then, may be calculated at $188 million at least, or over 74 percent of estimated total investment.

On this basis, about $26 million of the estimated gross profit would be credited to foreign operations.[7] and $9 million to locals. *Since the six producing countries get the $157 million of expenditure or cost items as their share of the receipts from banana exports to which we can add our estimate of $9 million profits accruing to locals, their total take for 1955 from banana exports comes to $166 million. In other words, the current income accruing to the producing countries was 86 percent of the value of all bananas shipped—$166 million out of $192 million without any allowance for reinvestment of earnings on the part of the foreign-owned operators.* This certainly is far from an inconsiderable return, particularly when one takes into consideration that the total amount of local capital committed to the enterprise that produced it was probably $65 million (26 percent of $253 million).

The $26 million profits accruing to foreign investors upon their banana operations in the six countries amounted to just under 14 percent of their total estimated capital commitment there, before income tax charges levied upon them outside of this area. In turn, this does not look like an exorbitant deduction when viewed either as a return on $188 million of capital investment or as a subtraction from $192 million of gross foreign exchange earnings that certainly would never have been realized without this foreign capital investment and the entrepreneurship that went with it.

There is a third observation that seems worth making. If to some the 27 percent share of the consumer dollar that was shown to be the amount received by the producing countries seems unduly low, it may be well to remember the elaborate distribution chain described in Chapter III, through which bananas produced in Latin American tropics find their way into the shopping bags of housewives from Tampa to Sacramento, from Boston to Seattle, and from Halifax to Vancouver.

Only 74 percent of the stems shipped from the six producing countries we have been analyzing went to this great North American market. Therefore, only 74 percent of the estimated $65 million of

---

[7] In our accounting procedure we included the income tax paid in the countries of production as a cost item. Accordingly, the estimated profit returns given here would be net for domestic producers, while foreign operators would still have to pay income taxes due in the countries of their incorporation and often in other countries where they carry out distribution functions.

local capital investment in these countries—say $48 million—can be regarded as servicing this trade. This compares with our estimate of $773 million of North American capital committed to all phases of banana production and distribution from farm through retail store facilities.

The 27¢ going to countries of origin out of each dollar spent by North American banana consumers is not small when it is realized that investors in the producing countries have supplied only 6¢ out of each investment dollar required to establish and maintain the trade. Their share of final receipts is four and one-half times as large as their comparative capital contributions.

V.

The United Fruit Company as an Integrated Operation

As A FORERUNNER to detailed analysis of United Fruit's specific operations, we have set forth a description of how the world banana trade is organized, the volume of investment committed to it, the amount of the annual return from the banana exports, and how this return is divided between those responsible for the many steps in the long production-distribution chain. In putting together a picture that seems never before to have been assembled in other than very fragmentary terms, we have been forced to fill in numerous gaps in the existing record by projecting from our firsthand study of the North American market, of the United Fruit Company's accounts, and of banana operations in our six Middle American countries.

Each of these sources of relatively complete and reliable information covers a segment of the world banana trade sufficiently large to assure that estimates of the whole based upon it will not be too wide of the mark. Thus, the North American market provides a sample that in 1955 represented 54 percent of world banana imports for that year. The United Fruit Company handled about 59 percent of the banana stems imported by North America[1] and about 28 percent of all stems reported as moving in world trade. And the six countries in which we made detailed studies of production operations accounted for about 60 percent of the year's world banana exports.

Our accountancy for the overall world trade will be distorted to the degree that the operations on which we could assemble reliable data are not thoroughly representative of the remainder. Although this qualification must be frankly stated, we are confident that the generalized account does represent a substantially accurate picture of the market as a whole. We believe that our samples are sufficiently large and the cross-checks for consistency that we have been able to make sufficiently numerous, both with respect to the data we ourselves gathered and to other published official data, to offer this assurance. At the very least, we can certify that our breakdowns accurately re-

[1] If Canadian imports are segregated, the company's share of U. S. stem imports was slightly lower—about 56 percent.

103

flect the accountancy of that part of the world banana trade that is served by the United Fruit Company.

In this chapter we shall examine in some detail the complete economic record of that company. We have noted previously that its operations are not entirely restricted either to the production and distribution of bananas or, on the production end, to our six-country study area.

THE DIVERSITY OF UNITED FRUIT OPERATIONS

ALTHOUGH BANANAS clearly represent its preponderantly most important activity, and are its essential reason for being, United Fruit produces and sells other commodities as well. Most notable among these are sugar from Cuba and Jamaica; cocoa from Costa Rica, Ecuador, and Panama; and African palm oil from Costa Rica, Honduras, Guatemala, Nicaragua, and Colombia. For a management fee, it acts as agent for the U. S. government in the growing and processing of abaca (Manila hemp) in Guatemala, and formerly did so in Costa Rica, Honduras, and Panama. The abaca installations in Costa Rica and Honduras are being maintained in moth-balled condition. It has plantings of rubber, quinine, essential oils, and a variety of tropical hard and soft woods. In addition to the company's banana production and shipments from the six countries, of which we already have taken account, it produces and ships relatively small quantities from the Dominican Republic and from the British Cameroons in West Africa.

The combined acreage of United Fruit's crop and pasture lands, mainly devoted to the production of food for its 82,000 tropical employees and to the maintenance of its 49,000 cattle and 16,000 horses and mules, is almost as great as its acreage planted in commercial crops. It operates, as has been noted, an extensive system of railways and tramways, and some 62 ships, under both American and foreign flags, that are chiefly ancillary to its banana trade but that also engage in other carriage. It owns and operates the Tropical Radio Telegraph Company, founded in 1904 to service the company's own line of communications for the exacting coordination of banana shipments, but operating now as a regular public utility in the communication field. This radio network spreads between Boston, New York, San Francisco, New Orleans, and Miami in the United States, through Mexico, the West Indies, and all of Central America to Bogotá, Quito, Rio de Janeiro, Asunción, Montevideo, and Buenos Aires in South

104

Table 10 | United Fruit's Improved Acreage and Railways Owned and Operated

| | Acres | | | | | | | Miles | | |
	Bananas	Sugar cane	Cacao	Abaca [a]	Oil palm	Other	Total	Railways (owned)	Railways (operated)	Tramways (owned)
Colombia	6,815				500	9,180	16,495	17.06		1.08
Costa Rica	34,636		23,851			33,333	106,662	309.86		92.73
Cuba		91,521		5,006	9,836	49,934	141,455	327.10		
Dominican Republic	4,067					6,490	10,557	34.57		
Ecuador	9,090		3,328			6,786	19,204			56.48
Guatemala	20,617			4,372	651	25,534	51,174	181.59		35.93
Honduras	34,071			4,913	5,108	80,494	124,586	369.34		4.68
Jamaica	1,863	3,869				909	6,641	11.24	13.13	
Panama	26,600		3,000			38,161	67,761	196.24	14.75	8.91
Other	8,087				1,389	7,807	17,283			65.33
Total	145,846	95,390	30,179	14,291	17,484	258,628	561,818	1447.00	27.88	265.14

Rolling stock:
	Railways (owned)	Tramways (owned)
Locomotives owned	195	47
Cars owned	6,405	771

[a] Operated by United Fruit on an agency contract for General Services Administration of the U. S. government.

America, and extends its coverage to all ships at sea on inter-American routes. A wholly owned United Fruit subsidiary, the Fruit Dispatch Company, operates as distributing agent for all United bananas sold in the United States, and European and Canadian subsidiaries perform similar functions with respect to those areas.

Table 10, taken from the company's 1955 annual report, gives a reasonably complete impression of the production end of its activities by showing its improved acreage and railways owned and operated as of the end of that year, with breakdowns by land use and location.

All of these activities are controlled by the parent organization— the United Fruit Company—which maintains its central offices at 80 Federal Street in Boston, Massachusetts, although the company is incorporated under the statutes of the State of New Jersey. Under federal law, the producing subsidiaries of United Fruit that operate exclusively in Latin American countries qualify for the status of Western Hemisphere Corporation. This means that the federal corporate income tax rate on their profits from operations in Latin American republics is set at 38 percent—14 percentage points below that which applies to U.S. corporations whose business activities are essentially domestic or are concerned with foreign operations outside the boundaries of the Western Hemisphere. Although there is some variation in the pattern that applies from country to country, generally United Fruit pays an income tax of 30 percent, directly to the Latin American countries in which its production operations are organized, upon all profits attributable to the business it conducts there. Again, under U.S. law, these local income tax payments are deductible from the corporate income tax that, in the absence of foreign payments, would be collected by the United States. The U.S. Treasury Department exercises direct supervision over the apportionment of revenues and profits between domestic and foreign transactions in the company's total operations.

The involved corporate structure of the United Fruit Company logically reflects the broad scope—territorially and functionally—of what it does. Nevertheless, the manifest complexity of its organizational pattern, with numerous subsidiaries owned and controlled by a parent company, makes it obligatory for us to present a clear accounting on the *totality of its operations*. It is necessary to examine the consolidated accounts of the company to show whether or not our accounting of its banana operations and the rate of profits indicated in our breakdown of the banana dollar accurately reflect the profitability of that segment of the company's total business. We need a

Table 11

United Fruit Company and Subsidiaries [a]
Consolidated Balance Sheet as of Dec. 31, 1955

Assets

Current assets..		$ 98,493,249
Materials and supplies at average cost................		25,049,522
Planters loans and other loans and receivables........		12,700,492
Insurance fund.......................................		5,979,024
Other assets...		4,705,762
Fixed assets—		
lands, cultivations, bldgs., r.r., etc., at cost:		
Tropical...............................	$329,887,860	
Domestic...............................	20,563,985	
Livestock..................................	3,875,941	
Steamships, at cost........................	99,399,455	
	453,727,241	
Less accumulated depreciation.................	223,593,787	230,133,454
Deferred charges.....................................		13,072,806
Total assets...		$390,134,309

Liabilities

Current liabilities....................................		$ 36,401,791
Deferred income.....................................		3,275,775
Stockholders' equity capital stock..............	$200,000,000	
(9,000,000 authorized, 8,775,000 issued)		
Earnings retained in business...................	150,456,743	
Total stockholders' equity............................		350,456,743
Total liabilities.....................................		$390,134,309

Statement of Consolidated Earnings for the Year 1955

Operating profit before depreciation, property losses, etc. (after eliminating inter-company profits)...........		$75,274,571
Deduct:		
Depreciation..............................	$18,023,508	
Property losses, net.......................	451,467	
Foreign exchange..........................	49,211	18,524,186
		56,750,385
Other income (interest, etc.).......................		1,368,981
		58,119,366
Provision of U.S. and foreign income taxes		24,580,000
Net earnings for the year 1955........................		33,539,366
Dividends declared $3.00 per share....................		26,324,991
Amount accruing to surplus or capital stock account...........		$ 7,214,375

[a] We give here a simplified version of the balance sheet that appears in the company's 1955 annual report, omitting subheadings that are not relevant to our inquiry. The published report, of course, can be readily obtained by anyone interested.

clear and complete picture of what United Fruit as an integrated operation has invested and what it earns.

THE UNITED FRUIT COMPANY AS AN INVESTMENT

OUR ANALYSIS STARTS with the consolidated balance sheet and income account for the year 1955. It will be noted from the simplified version given in Table 11 that the total assets of the company were over $390 million and its fixed assets, less accumulated depreciation, over $230 million. The original cost of the fixed assets it held at the end of 1955 is shown to have been $454 million, of which almost $334 million (including livestock) represented investment in the tropics, $99 million represented ships, and something under $21 million were for facilities located in North America, the United Kingdom, and Continental Europe. (If the 1955 asset account included the tropical investments that had been disposed of and written off prior to 1955, the total for this category would exceed $550 million.) Thus almost three-fourths of the company's fixed asset investments are committed to the tropical end of its operations.

The ownership of United Fruit is vested in 9 million shares of common stock without par value, of which 8,775,000 have been issued and 225,000 are held as treasury shares. The net worth of this holding at the end of 1955 was something over $350 million, of which $150 million represented surplus accumulated from past earnings that had not been paid out as dividends. Thus, the 1955 value of each outstanding share was carried on the books at about $40. Its market valuation, as shown by the range of prices for which the stock has traded on the New York Stock Exchange, has fluctuated between $42 and $74 between the beginning of 1946 and the end of 1955[2], with an average price of $54.50 per share for the 10-year period against an average book value of $34. Thus for the whole period, the market placed a value on United Fruit shares at 60 percent over their book value. The average annual earnings after taxes on each share of United Fruit stock during this period was $5.38. This indicates that investors generally were willing to pay 10 times the annual earnings rate for a share of United Fruit stock.

To provide perspective upon how U.S. investors rated United Fruit stock, it is necessary to compare this record with that of alternative investments. One of the most widely used yardsticks is provided by

[2] From Jan. 1956-Dec. 1957, the range was between $34 and $55 per share.

Standard and Poor's Index of 50 Industrial Stocks. On the market value to book value measurement, United Fruit stock ranked a fraction better than the average for the entire Standard and Poor's list (a 1.6 to 1 ratio for United Fruit against a 1.5 to 1 ratio on the Standard and Poor's index); but on the more important ratio of market price to annual earnings its 10 to 1 ratio was almost exactly the same as that of the 50 Standard and Poor's industrial stock average.

The ratio of market price to annual earnings, however, gives us only part of the relevant story. It leaves out completely the enormously important factor of growth. At the end of 1955, the price index for the 50 industrial stocks on the Standard and Poor's list was about three and one-third times its level at the end of 1946. The average annual earnings of these 50 companies had increased more than three and one-half times over the same period. But the average between high and low for United Fruit stock was $48 a share in 1946, and had risen to $55.5 a share for 1955, an increase of only 16 percent in value. Its earnings after taxes had actually declined from $39.6 million or $4.51 per share in 1946 to $33.5 million or $3.82 per share in 1955. Its peak earnings for the period of $7.53 per share, realized in 1950, had been only 70 percent higher than the 1946 earnings, and had fallen off drastically in subsequent years.

Clearly, the financial performance of the United Fruit Company has been substandard compared to the general growth record of United States corporations over the past 10 years. Its status has been essentially static in a dynamically expanding economy. It is not surprising then to find that the range of prices upon which United Fruit stock was traded on the New York Stock Exchange was from $33⅝ to $47⅝ per share for the year 1957, or appreciably lower than the average for 1946. Over the period of 11 years, its shares have yielded no capital gains to those holding them for the entire term. What is surprising is that despite the evidence of this comparative record, and the fact that the stock market consistently has placed a lower value on United Fruit stock than on the equities of growth corporations, the impression that this company is enormously profitable still has currency in Latin America and among many North Americans who do not follow the market returns.

UNITED FRUIT COMPANY EARNINGS

EVEN WHEN YARDSTICKS ignore the growth factor entirely, the United Fruit Company's earnings record is far from spectacular. From the 1955 income account given above, it will be seen that the company's earnings after taxes, *on its total operations including income from its funds invested outside of its own business,* were $33.5 million, a return of something under 10 percent on the stockholders' equity in the business. The dividend disbursement of $26.3 million represented a return of about 7.5 percent, with the $7 million difference actually committed to new capital investments authorized during the year.

We can compare the 9.8 percent return after taxes on net worth earned by the United Fruit Company in 1955, with a broad computation of the earnings records of 3,485 leading corporations compiled and published by the First National City Bank of New York.[3] This shows, in Table 12, the picture of net income after taxes related to net assets[4] or stockholders' equity for a thoroughly representative sample of the larger U.S. corporations.

Table 12 **Income after Taxes Related to Net Assets 1955**

No. of companies	Industrial groups	Return after taxes as % of net assets
1,843	Total manufacturing...................	14.9
63	Total mining and quarrying...............	13.0
204	Total trade	10.9
224	Total transportation...................	6.0
268	Total public utilities..................	9.7
116	Total amusements, services, etc............	12.3
767	Total finance.......................	7.6
3,485	Grand total........................	11.9
	United Fruit Company (consolidated)......	9.8

It will be seen from Table 12 that the less than 10 percent return realized on the United Fruit Company's net assets in 1955 was considerably lower than the almost 12 percent average for all of the companies in the leading corporation sample, and far below the almost 15 percent average of the 1,843 manufacturing corporations.

[3] The First National City Bank's *Monthly News Letter* of April, 1957.
[4] Defined as the "excess of total balance sheet net assets over liabilities," which is the base used in our United Fruit Company accounting, under the label of "stockholders' equity."

Chart XII
United Fruit as an Investment

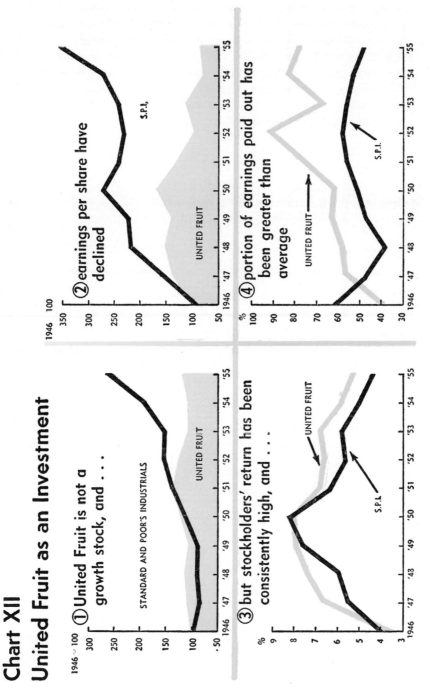

① United Fruit is not a growth stock, and . . .

1946 ~ 100

300 · 250 · 200 · 150 · 100 · 50

STANDARD AND POOR'S INDUSTRIALS

UNITED FRUIT

1946 '47 '48 '49 '50 '51 '52 '53 '54 '55

② earnings per share have declined

1946 100

350 · 300 · 250 · 200 · 150 · 100 · 50

S.P.I.

UNITED FRUIT

1946 '47 '48 '49 '50 '51 '52 '53 '54 '55

③ but stockholders' return has been consistently high, and . . .

%

9 · 8 · 7 · 6 · 5 · 4 · 3

UNITED FRUIT

S.P.I.

1946 '47 '48 '49 '50 '51 '52 '53 '54 '55

④ portion of earnings paid out has been greater than average

%

100 · 90 · 80 · 70 · 60 · 50 · 40 · 30

UNITED FRUIT

S.P.I.

1946 '47 '48 '49 '50 '51 '52 '53 '54 '55

111

In fact, if one goes back to the beginning of the United Fruit Company in 1899, one finds that its average annual net earnings on net assets for the entire period have amounted to just under 13 percent. This is 2 percent lower than the *1955 earnings* shown by manufacturing corporations in the above tabulation. We do not have a comparable general series that runs back that far, but we can compare the United Fruit position with the National City Bank series for leading corporations that has been carried back to 1928.

Table 13	Income after Taxes Related to Net Assets 1928-55	
		Return after taxes as % of net assets
Total manufacturing[a]		10.3
Total trade[a]		11.4
Grand total[a]		8.2
United Fruit Company (consolidated)		11.1

[a] First National City Bank series for leading U.S. corporations.

This record covering 28 years of operations shows that United Fruit's comparative earnings record over the longer-term period is somewhat better than it was in 1955, but it clearly establishes that record as close to the average for larger U.S. corporations engaged in the production and/or sale of commodities. Its long-term earnings record shows a return after taxes about three percentage points higher than the average for the total list including transport, public utility, and financial companies; less than 1 point higher than the average for manufacturing companies; and slightly lower than the average for companies engaged primarily in trade. In short, the long-term earnings record of the United Fruit Company, measured against net assets, is neither outstandingly better nor worse than the average for representative U.S. corporations, most of which are engaged wholly or largely in domestic operations far less hazardous than any enterprise concerned with foreign-based agricultural operations. United's profit margin clearly is not one that has afforded a premium to compensate for the fact that its production is of an unusually risky type and dependent upon international trade outlets.[5]

Upon the basis of the earnings record, if that were to be taken as the sole criterion, there would be little to support the U.S. government contention in the antitrust suit now in progress that the United Fruit Company has a monopoly on the banana trade. Its earnings record bears no relationship to the commonly held conception that a monopoly position is one that inevitably results in producing exorbitant profits to those exercising such control. There is equally scant ground for the frequent charges made abroad that United's profits have been of a dimension that represents "exploitation"—in the derogatory sense of that word—of the foreign countries in which it operates, to the point of enriching its stockholders beyond what they might have expected to receive from investment in a purely domestic enterprise.

Preconceptions that run along either of these lines are simply not supported by the earnings record. Investment in United Fruit Company stock at prevailing market prices has been moderately attractive, and no better, when measured by the yardstick of assets-earnings ratios in the U.S. market for corporate securities. It has been woefully substandard when the factor of capital appreciation is added. If United Fruit's earnings record were judged by the returns generally regarded as attractive to local investors in Latin American business enterprises, the record would mark the company as a singularly unrewarding venture. This may be one of the controlling reasons why almost no Latin Americans have availed themselves of the open opportunity to acquire a substantial ownership of the company through purchase of its securities. There has been ample opportunity for such acquisition since there has been a continuous turnover of United Fruit shares through trading on the New York Stock Exchange. It may explain also why more rival firms have not been established through the investment of U.S. capital to challenge United Fruit's position in this field.

Finally, the financial records of the company provide a decisive

---

[5] It is not practicable to compare the growth in the value of United Fruit's net worth with that of the companies listed in the First National City Bank's tabulation, since the latter represents an expanding rather than a constant company coverage over the years. But between 1946 and 1955, the book value per share of United Fruit's stock increased by only 66 percent, while the average value per share of Standard and Poor's 50 industrial corporations increased by 123 percent. There is evidence that the growth in stock values of the 1,200 to 1,800 leading manufacturing corporations covered by the First National City Bank would outstrip that of United Fruit by a comparable margin.

answer to any speculation as to whether or not its books have been kept in a fashion that tends to understate the profits of its banana business through apportioning more than their due share to shipping or other phases of its complex operational structure.

Table 15 shows the proportions of revenues and profits before taxes of the major segments of the company's consolidated business over the 16-year period, 1940-1955, as shown by its accounts:

Table 14 | **Breakdown of Gross Revenues and Earnings Before Taxes (Average for period 1940-55 inclusive)**

	Bananas	Sugar	Steamship traffic, etc.	Other	Total
Gross revenue............	60.3%	17.4%	12.7%	9.6%	100%
Earnings before taxes......	82.1%	7.3%	5.3%	5.3%	100%

Over this 16-year period, it is shown that the company's receipts from its banana sales provided only 60 percent of its gross revenues while accounting for 82 percent of its profits before taxes. Very clearly, it has been the banana phase of its business that has provided the preponderant share of the company earnings. If the company's system of accountancy had been designed to hold down the dimension of its banana earnings by overloading the charges against bananas for shipping or other services rendered, the ratio of earnings to gross revenue on the other phases of the consolidated operations would be higher than shown for bananas. In fact, they are drastically lower in every case. In Chapters III and IV our estimates of the profits on *banana operations* were based on the proportion of total capital that could fairly be attributed to that phase of the company's overall business.

WHO OWNS THE UNITED FRUIT COMPANY

To MANY PEOPLE in the countries in which the United Fruit Company's production operations are located, the company appears to be a corporate entity of truly colossal size, unlimited resources, and virtually untrammeled power. Much of the literature that has been written about it in Latin America reflects this concept of a business giant, serving the interests of a few North Americans

114

of enormous wealth, and fully capable of manipulating the foreign policy of the United States in the furtherance of its interests.

From the perspective of North American eyes, its stature hardly lives up to this billing. Its $390 million of total assets give it a ranking among the more important U.S. corporations, but there were some 34 U.S. companies (excluding banks and insurance companies), each of which had assets in excess of $1 billion at the end of 1955. The first 10 of these had assets ranging from six to 37 times as large as those of United Fruit. United Fruit's 1955 gross sales of approximately $288 million (excluding steamship traffic) were exceeded by about 120 industrial corporations and by 24 merchandising firms. The sales of Macy's Department Store and those of Gimbel's were both larger than United Fruit's. The total sales of at least five of the chain food-distributing companies that handle a large proportion of North American banana distribution at retail level ranged from 140 percent to more than 1,400 percent of the gross revenue of United Fruit, including its shipping receipts. In the U.S. business scene, the United Fruit Company is just one among about 500 of the larger corporations engaged in production enterprise, with a recent earnings record considerably below the average for this group.

The 8,775,000 outstanding United Fruit shares were owned, as of the middle of 1955, by 72,860 shareholder accounts. A considerable number of these accounts—particularly the larger ones—were in trust funds of various types, so that the number of individuals dependent upon United Fruit dividends for part of their income would be considerably larger. The 141 largest accounts represented holdings of 5,000 or more shares. The combined holdings of this group amounted to 2,424,141 shares, a trifle over one-fourth of the total ownership interest, with an average of 17,190 shares in each of these larger holdings. Since a $3 dividend was paid on each share in 1954, 1955, and 1956, the annual income realized on each of these 141 largest shareholder accounts averaged $51,570. But at the opposite end of the scale, there were 72,092 United Fruit stockholders owning less than 1,000 shares each. The total holdings of this group comprised 59 percent of the outstanding shares, but the average holding of each was only 71 shares, which yielded an annual income of $213 at the prevailing dividend rate in 1954 through 1956. Between these two extremes, there were 627 accounts with stockholdings amounting to between 1,000 and 4,999 shares. The average ownership bloc held by each member of this group was 1,933 shares and the annual dividend checks of each averaged $5,799 from 1954 through 1956.

The actual pattern of United Fruit's ownership distribution has little

Chart XIII
Who Owns United Fruit?

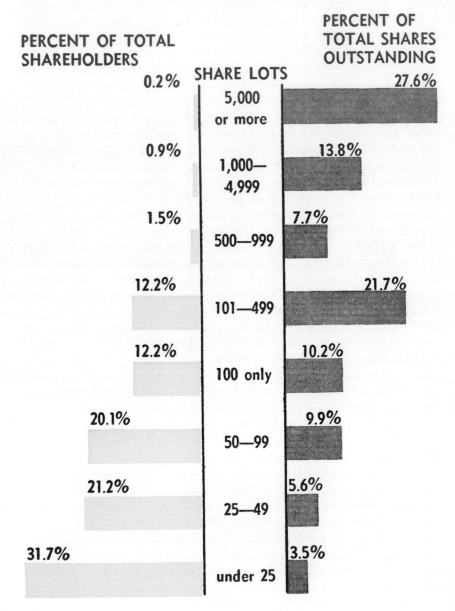

PERCENT OF TOTAL SHAREHOLDERS	SHARE LOTS	PERCENT OF TOTAL SHARES OUTSTANDING
0.2%	5,000 or more	27.6%
0.9%	1,000—4,999	13.8%
1.5%	500—999	7.7%
12.2%	101—499	21.7%
12.2%	100 only	10.2%
20.1%	50—99	9.9%
21.2%	25—49	5.6%
31.7%	under 25	3.5%

relationship to the preconceptions that are very widely held. Of the 500 largest industrial corporations in the United States, only 29 had more individual stockholder accounts than United Fruit, and the great majority of these had assets many times as large. It undoubtedly will come as a surprise to many Latin Americans that the number of North American investors who have a stake in United Fruit prosperity so closely approximates the 77,810 Latin American employees who in 1955 were dependent upon the company for wages and salaries. It may be even more of a surprise to learn that the dividend return of its average shareholder ($360 in 1955 on 120 shares) has been running at a level well below 40 percent of the average annual wage paid to each of its tropical employees ($942 in 1955). Finally, even the dividend returns of a trifle over $50,000 per year that represents the average taking of the 141 largest shareholder accounts are not of a dimension that would support many racing stables, steam yachts, or estates on the Riviera—even if they all represented returns to individuals, which they do not.

However it is viewed through North American eyes, the United Fruit Company's stature inevitably assumes gigantic dimension to the people of the countries in which its main production operations are conducted. For example, in Costa Rica, Panama, and Honduras central government revenues for 1955 totaled about $47 million, $44 million, and $30 million, respectively. In such countries, there is bound to be a perspective different from our own upon a company that showed a consolidated statement listing $330 million of gross revenue, $58 million of earnings before taxes, $33 million of profits after taxes, and $26 million in dividend payments for that year. It is understandable that they should tend to regard a company whose total operations dwarf their own national budgets as a colossus of almost unlimited power and resources. The evidence given above shows that this company's stature, in the North American scene, is of far more modest dimension. Both sides of the picture must be held in focus if the performance of United Fruit Company is to be appraised in balanced perspective.

UNITED FRUIT CONTRIBUTIONS To HOST COUNTRY ECONOMICS

A DETAILED ACCOUNTING for a year's operations of all of the United Fruit Company subsidiaries in the six countries is given in Tables 15 and 16. For this purpose, we have taken an average of the separate accounts shown on the company books for

117

1954 and 1955. This procedure was adopted because a reading of the 1955 account alone would be less than thoroughly representative, since deferred dividends from 1954 were remitted along with those for 1955, and there were also some advances on taxes that were paid in the latter year.

From the left-hand column of Table 15 one can read the record of subsidiary expenditures. These total $139 million, the sum that was left in the producing countries by the company's operations there. About $75 million out of this total—made up of wage payments, the value of company-produced meat for its workers, and taxes, including duties and consular fees paid to governments—represents direct payments of the sort generally credited as contributions to national income accounts. Something over $27.6 million covers payments by the subsidiaries to other local producers, including payments for bananas purchased for export. This is not income produced by the Fruit Company's subsidiaries, but it is local business generated by their operations and paid for out of their sales receipts. Another $35.6 million represents goods and services purchased abroad. All but a small fraction of this is for equipment, construction materials, chemicals, fertilizers, and the like, brought in and added to the production potential of the six countries. Something under 10 percent represents imported merchandise made available to company employees through commissary sales. All of this foreign expenditure is paid for out of the subsidiaries' total receipts. The final entry of $801,000 is largely for inventory increases—that is, goods purchased but not used in the year's current operations.

From the right-hand column of the table, one can see how the subsidiaries derived the funds to pay for these expenditures. The annual receipts from exports, preponderantly bananas, amounted to $122.5 million. Receipts from domestic sales of commissaries, for radio, railroad haulage, etc., totaled over $27 million, with another $635,000 earned in fees from abaca operations conducted for the account of the U.S. government. In addition, the subsidiaries' capital accounts were increased by about $6.6 million, representing additional investment commitments of the parent company in this area. All of this totals up to just under $157 million.

Dividends of $17.85 million were paid by these subsidiaries to the United Fruit Company. This represents the total amount that was withdrawn from the producing area out of the year's total transactions, upon an accounting that treats the investment of new funds as subsidiary income.

118

Table 15 | United Fruit Company Subsidiaries Combined Operations in Six Countries 1954-55 Annual Average (In thousand dollars)

Expenditures	1954-55 average
Value added by United Fruit	74,988
Salaries and wages	56,001
Cost of livestock butchered	960
Taxes and export duties	2,838
Import duties and consular fees	3,452
Income tax paid locally	11,737
Goods and services purchased locally	27,645
Bananas (purchase cost paid planters)	10,035
Cost of merchandise purchased locally	9,875
Cost of materials purchased locally	5,105
Transportation paid others	2,630
Goods and services purchased abroad	35,584
Cost of merchandise imported	3,160
Cost of materials and miscel. imported	32,424
Changes in inventories, etc.	801
Total	139,018

Sources of funds	1954-55 average
Export	122,514
Bananas	117,193
Cocoa, palm oil, and miscel. products	5,321
Domestic receipts	27,136
Merchandise (commissary)	15,608
Radio, traffic, etc.	5,405
Other	6,123
Fees for managing abaca operations, interest, etc.	635
Net increase in capital investment	6,583
	156,868
Less dividends	−17,850
Total	139,018

119

Table 16	United Fruit Company Subsidiaries Combined Operations in Six Countries 1954-55 Annual Average (In thousand dollars)			
	Expenditures	Sources of funds		Balance
Current account.......	122,176	Total receipts.	150,285	+28,109
Capital account.......	16,842	Net increase in capital invest-ment.........	6,583	−10,259
Total...............	139,018		+156,868	+17,850
Less dividends remitted				−17,850

Table 16 sets forth the same account in a slightly different form. The same totals are broken down to show how the annual transactions divided between current and capital income and expenditures. Current receipts were $150.3 million and current expenditures $122.2 million. The subsidiaries therefore showed an operating profit of $28.1 million. During the year, however, almost $17 million was spent upon the never-ending task of maintaining and adding to the production potential through land development and reclamation projects and in equipment, utility, and building investments. Of this capital commitment, $10.26 million was provided by reinvesting the difference between the current-account earnings and the dividends paid out; $6.6 million represented a new capital commitment.

A few general observations are in order. The dividend payments of $17.85 million withdrawn from the local economies can be compared with the $139 million that the United Fruit operations left behind in the producing countries. The dividends paid amounted to less than 12 percent of the subsidiaries' current account receipts, and to only about 11 percent of the $162 million of the company's investment in the area, appraised at depreciated book values. They were actually a shade less than the taxes and duties paid locally by the company to governments in the six republics and totaled less than a third of direct payroll disbursements there.

It would be difficult to contend that these returns are immoderate by any standards. Leaving out the commitment of new investment funds entirely, the 1954-55 record shows that about 92 percent ($139 million out of $150 million) of the subsidiaries' total sales receipts went into the local economies. The company's return in previous years had been only moderately larger. Average dividends withdrawn from the combined six-country operations over the five-year period, 1951-55, averaged $22 million per year.

Comparison With Other U.S. Direct Investments in Latin America

A RECENT STUDY by the U.S. Department of Commerce[6] provides data that allow us to make some comparisons between the impact of the United Fruit Company's operations upon Latin American economies and that of other enterprises in which U.S. investment has played an important role. This Department of Commerce survey was prepared upon the basis of specific questionnaires that were filled out by some 300 parent companies operating about 1,000 subsidiaries and branches in Latin American countries. Its coverage is estimated at about 85 percent of all U.S. direct private investment with interests in the area in 1955.

From Table 17 it will be seen that the performance of the United Fruit Company compares very favorably with other U.S. enterprises with direct investment in Latin America in terms of its impact upon local economies. The book value of its subsidiaries operating in the six countries of our study amounted to about 3 percent of the total for all the others covered. Its share of total sales was of the same relative magnitude and that of its export sales much larger. Its contributions to the local economies in the form of total payments were about average, with payroll payments high and tax payments somewhat low, due importantly to the relatively large weight of petroleum enterprises in the overall sample.

When the comparison is made with other agricultural enterprises in Latin America in which U.S. capital has a major interest United Fruit Company performance is outstanding. While the book value of its assets represented only 36 percent of that of other U.S. investments in this category, its total sales amounted to 54 percent, its exports to 55 percent, and its total local payments to 41 percent. Its wage payments were 65 percent of those made by all others in the agricultural group, and its taxes paid to central and local governments combined were 69 percent of the total, or almost twice its relative share based upon volume of funds invested.

Although the figures are not included in the above tabulation, the Department of Commerce estimates that the foreign exchange contribution on the favorable side of Latin American balance of payments accounts totaled about $1 billion for the entire group sampled in all industrial categories. The 1955 contribution of the United Fruit Company on this score amounted to about $80 million, or 8 percent

---

[6] *Survey of Current Business,* January 1957.

Table 17 | Comparative Record for 1955 United Fruit Company and other U.S. Direct Private Investments in Six Latin American Countries
(In millions of U.S. dollars)

	Book value of assets	Sales		Local payments by U.S. companies operating in Latin America					
		Total	Export	Total	Wages and salaries paid locally	Materials, supplies, equipment purchased in Latin America	Interest, royalties, dividends paid locally	Total taxes paid locally	Other and unspecified
All industries[a]	5,765	4,796	2,090	4,189	930	1,788	65	1,043	363
Agricultural enterprises[a]	455	277	221	265	88	118	2	29	27
United Fruit (six-country operation)	162	150	121	109	57	28	0	20	4
United Fruit as percent of all other industries	3	3	6	3	6	2	0	2	1
United Fruit as percent of other agricultural enterprises	36	54	55	41	65	24	0	69	15

[a] United Fruit Company omitted.
NOTE: All dollar figures rounded to nearest million; percentages rounded to nearest percentage point.

of the total. The normal annual transmittal of earnings by United Fruit subsidiaries appears to be quite closely in line with that of the average for all U.S. investments in Latin America when related to comparative capital assets. But when measured as a percentage of total exports, the $80 million of foreign exchange contributed by United Fruit's 1955 operations amounted to almost 70 percent of its total exports from the area, compared with a 50 percent ratio for U.S. Latin American investments as a whole.

United Fruit Contributions Compared With Local Agricultural Enterprise

To Latin Americans it may seem more relevant to compare their net gains from United Fruit Company operations with those derived from agricultural projects carried out through purely domestic enterprise and investment. This we shall attempt to do in Chapter VI, upon a country-by-country basis, for each of the six countries in which we made firsthand studies. In our judgment, this procedure is far more realistic than any generalized account of United Fruit impact upon the area as a whole since there is so wide a diversity in the size and pattern of the several economies and of the relative importance of the United Fruit Company operations among them. Furthermore, the general economic statistics for the six countries are far from uniform in coverage and probable degree of reliability. Nevertheless, a few overall comparisons on the combined six-country picture may be offered with some confidence that the general magnitudes at least are of the right order.

For the year 1955, and crediting to the United Fruit operations only the value that actually accrued to the national economies in question, it may be stated that:

United Fruit utilized about one-fourth of 1 percent of all improved agricultural lands including pasturage (2 percent of all croplands) and accounted for about 6 percent of the area's combined agricultural production. United Fruit's output per acre was from five to 16 times the national averages for the several countries.

● It employed about 1.2 percent of total agricultural employees. Its production per worker varied from three to 10 times the national averages in the several countries, and was about five times that of the area as a whole. In all cases, its wage rates were substantially higher than the reported averages for agricultural employees.

● United Fruit accounted for about 12 percent of the combined foreign exchange revenues of the six countries from exports of all types, varying from just under 2.5 percent in the case of Colombia to about 72 percent in the case of Panama.

● The taxes paid by United Fruit in 1955 to central governments of the six republics amounted to only about one-fifth of 1 percent of total revenues in the case of Colombia, but ranged up to 19 percent in the case of Costa Rica. If we exclude Colombia—in which United Fruit operations were too small to be significant and where the total government revenues are more than three times as large as those of the other five republics combined—United Fruit's taxes accounted for almost 6.5 percent of total government revenues in the remainder. This tax contribution was about twice as large as the proportionate size of United Fruit's operations in their overall economies as measured by its "value-added" contributions to gross national product.

THE STABILITY OF THE MARKET

A VOLUMINOUS LITERATURE documents the thesis that nations heavily dependent upon the export of primary products, either agricultural or extractive, are at a serious disadvantage. The argument is that both the prices and volumes of primary products moving in world trade are much more volatile than those of manufactured goods. Accordingly, nations heavily dependent upon foreign exchange earnings derived from primary product exports are alleged to be at a comparative disadvantage.

This thesis has gained sufficiently wide currency to cast something of a cloud upon the whole process of producing primary food and fibers, or extractive minerals of any type for export. The more moderate reaction has taken the form of a widespread demand for the establishment of a variety of international stabilization programs to protect primary product exporters from the instabilities to which their position is held to be peculiarly vulnerable. The extreme position has tended to write off primary product production for export as a venture of dubious merit at best, with disadvantages of such obvious severity as to discount whatever advantages such trade may bring.

Any definitive analysis of the validity of this thesis would require far more detailed exposition than could be justified for inclusion here. There is considerable evidence that on the long-term record of downturns in foreign exchange earnings (prices x volumes traded) derived from primary product exports *as a whole* have not been more extreme or frequent than in foreign exchange earnings derived from the export of manufactures *as a whole*.[7] The case for the relative volatility of trade in primary products appears to have been based largely upon studies comparing *one segment* of primary products trade—such as foodstuffs alone, industrial raw materials alone, or even trade in individual primary commodities—with trade in *all* manufactures. This merely demonstrates the statistical fact that the more the items included in a given time series, the smoother the curve. When one compares the foreign exchange earnings from narrow categories of manufactured products—such as cotton textiles, or iron and steel mill products, or machinery and equipment—with those realized from crude foodstuffs, or agricultural fibers, or metallic minerals or petroleum, the frequency and severity of yearly declines are no less striking in the former than in the latter categories.

What does seem to be well established is that foreign trade tends to be more volatile than domestic trade, and that the returns from any single export item may be exceptionally erratic. It is a thoroughly sound principle, then, for any nation to make vigorous efforts to broaden both the base of its exports and of production for its domestic market to the extent that this is economically feasible. Since efficient production requires both modern equipment and technology, and since most economies in the early stages of industrialization have no choice but to procure the more elaborate equipment from abroad, foreign exchange earnings are a key element in the determination of the speed with which industrialization in the broadest sense can go forward.

Therefore, any activity that produces foreign exchange earnings for countries in the early stages of development should be valued and cultivated along with import-saving enterprises. Export activities that yield a high level of foreign exchange with a minimum of declines from year to year will, of course, be most valuable. But even widely fluctuating exchange earners may be better than none at all, particularly if the high returns realized in windfall years are channeled into the development of additional activities that will broaden the area's economic base.

---

[7] See "Folklore and Fact about Underdeveloped Areas," by Stacy May, *Foreign Affairs*, January 1955.

Table 18 | Prices of Bananas and Other Agricultural Products in U.S. Markets
(Index numbers of annual average prices, 1940=100)

Year	Bananas	Annual % chg.	All fruits (U.S.-prodcd.)	Annual % chg.	Peaches	Annual % chg.	Oranges	Annual % chg.	Milk	Annual % chg.	Coffee	Annual % chg.	Cocoa	Annual % chg.
1940	100		100		100		100		100		100		100	
1941	118	+18	116	+16	115	+15	132	+32	117	+17	158	+58	146	+46
1942	164	+39	157	+35	190	+65	208	+58	151	+29	186	+18	173	+18
1943	193	+18	256	+63	340	+79	222	+7	166	+10	186	0	173	0
1944	181	−6	288	+13	297	−13	226	+2	175	+5	186	0	173	0
1945	168	−7	281	−2	282	−5	247	+9	176	+1	189	+2	177	+2
1946	176	+5	296	+5	267	−5	131	−47	220	+25	260	+38	232	+31
1947	208	+18	230	−22	207	−22	110	−16	238	+8	366	+41	696	+200
1948	233	+12	205	−11	254	+23	147	+34	270	+13	372	+2	791	+14
1949	258	+11	242	+18	186	−27	187	+27	220	−19	442	+19	429	−46
1950	266	+3	240	−1	259	+39	166	−11	216	−2	705	+60	640	+49
1951	264	−1	223	−7	255	−2	126	−24	254	+18	754	+7	708	+11
1952	261	−1	236	+6	254	0	123	−2	270	+6	751	−1	707	−1
1953	270	+3	258	+9	241	−5	165	+34	241	−11	812	+8	738	+4
1954	265	−2	270	+5	253	+5	141	−15	223	−7	1,088	+34	1,147	+55
1955	271	+2	262	−3	276	+9	n.a.		n.a.		791	−27	746	−35
1956	259	−4	278	+6	266	−4	n.a.		n.a.		810	+2	541	−27
1957a	255	−2	n.a.		n.a.		n.a.		n.a.		831	+3	497	−8

a First half of 1957.

n.a.: Not available.

Sources: Bananas—United Fruit average return per 100 lbs. of stem-weight fruit for U.S.A. and Canada.
Fruits (U.S.-produced)—Prices received by U.S. farmers, *Statistical Abstract of the U.S.*
Peaches—Annual average return to growers per bushel marketed (Department of Agriculture).
Oranges—Annual average return to growers per box sold (Department of Agriculture).
Milk—Annual average return to farmers for 100 lbs. milk sold for all purposes (Department of Agriculture).
Coffee—Annual average spot price per lb. in New York (Bureau of Labor Statistics).
Cocoa—Annual average spot price per lb. in New York (Bureau of Labor Statistics).

How does the banana industry rate in terms of its consistency as a producer of foreign exchange revenue for countries of production? Unfortunately, a direct measurement of foreign exchange yields from this activity cannot be made over an extended period. As we already have noted, even the current reporting of export and import values for bananas is grossly inaccurate. An attempt to work out from official foreign trade figures a time series covering an extended period would result merely in a compounding of errors.

We do have, however, an accurate record of yearly stem imports to the North American market, and of the share of this handled by the United Fruit Company. Upon the not unreasonable assumption that the prices and stem weights of its competitors' imports maintained a reasonably constant relationship to those of United Fruit over the period, we are able to construct what we believe to be reliable indices of banana prices and total sales for this market from 1940 through 1955. We shall start by giving consideration to the price index:

Table 18 shows the behavior of banana prices from 1940 through 1955, compared with a general price index for fruits produced in the United States, and for five individual food items, three of domestic origin and two imported. In each case, an adjoining column shows the percent of price increase or decrease from the preceding year. The following comments may be useful in interpreting these indices:

● Banana prices, over the 15-year period covered by most of the series, have shown a general upward trend, with 1955 prices 171 percent higher than those prevailing in 1940. There were two periods of three years each in which there were sustained rises of considerable magnitude—from the early war years 1941-43 when shipping shortages sharply curtailed banana imports, and from 1947-49, when there was a sharp rise in all U.S. prices following the removal of wartime price controls. There were only two years in the series in which banana prices fell significantly, a 6 percent fall in 1944 followed by a further 7 percent fall in 1945. This clearly was a readjustment reflecting the re-established trend toward normal volume of banana shipments as the effects of the submarine blockade were overcome. Even with the reduced prices, the total value of banana imports increased sharply in these two years.

● It is evident that banana prices in this market have conformed closely to the general price trend of the combined index for fruits produced domestically in the United States. The trend in banana

Chart XIV
U. S. Banana Prices Conform Closely to Prices of U. S.-Grown Fruit, rather than Following Prices of Coffee and Cocoa Imports

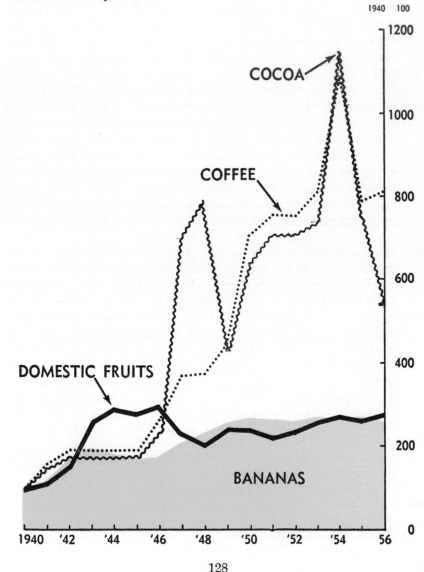

1940 100

COCOA

COFFEE

DOMESTIC FRUITS

BANANAS

1940   '42   '44   '46   '48   '50   '52   '54   56

1200
1000
800
600
400
200
0

prices has been somewhat steadier than the general index, but except for the late war years the conformity of the two series suggests that banana prices here are importantly affected by the competition of other fruits that are offered to the American public.

● Banana prices have followed the general long-term price trend of peaches, though the banana trend has been somewhat more regular. It has departed widely from the price trend for oranges, but the latter has been importantly affected by a revolution in marketing procedure. To an ever-increasing extent in recent years, oranges have been marketed in the form of frozen and refrigerated orange juice rather than as fresh fruit. Accordingly, the average quality of oranges sold by growers has been consistently downgraded, so that the product marketed by growers has undergone a drastic change. If banana prices are compared with farm prices paid in the United States for milk, a food product not directly competitive but one that presents somewhat similar handling problems, there is again a considerable similarity in the general trend, at least through 1952.

● When the comparison is shifted to two other major import food crops—coffee and cocoa—the picture is quite different. Prices for both of these commodities skyrocketed on an almost unbroken upward trend through 1954, by which year their indices had risen to a level more than four times that attained by banana prices. In 1955, there was a major break in the annual averages of both coffee and cocoa prices, of a dimension much larger than any shown in the banana price series. The price slump has continued in cocoa, and by the first half of 1957 cocoa prices were off almost 60 percent from their 1954 level. Coffee prices meanwhile had firmed slightly after the 1955 break, but were still almost 25 percent below the 1954 average. The index of banana prices at importer level rose by 2 percent in 1955 over 1954 levels, and then declined by a moderate 4 percent for 1956 and by an additional 2 percent for the first half of 1957.

Although the United Fruit Company is presently being accused of having maintained a monopoly control over banana prices at importer level in this market, it would be hard to support this upon the evidence of these statistics. If banana prices are compared with coffee and cocoa prices, it would be far easier to establish a prima facie case for inferring the incidence of artificial manipulation of prices with respect to the last two than it would be for bananas. Again, the inference of price manipulation by the United Fruit Company would raise puzzling questions as to the rationale of such control, since the earnings record of the company cited earlier in this chapter bears not the slightest relationship to what are generally conceived to be monopoly profits.

The very strong inference from the indices presented is that banana prices are importantly determined by the competition of domestically produced fruits, and that there is an effective pressure that prevents banana prices from diverging markedly from the general fruit price trends for sustained periods. One would not expect to find such a degree of concurrence in the case of a commodity for which prices were "administered." With respect to coffee and cocoa, no such competition from domestic crops has existed, but the large returns accruing to producers from soaring prices is offset by evidence of greater instability.

There is another line of evidence that strongly challenges the thesis that banana prices have been arbitrarily controlled. We have tabulated the average prices by months for which United Fruit has sold its bananas in the North American market for each year from 1940 through 1955. The average deviation between the high and low monthly prices for the period was 20 percent per year. In 1953, the high monthly average was only 6 percent greater than that of the low month. In 1954, there was a 37 percent divergence; in 1955, a 29 percent spread. Earlier years show both lower and considerably higher monthly deviations than those cited. There does not appear to have been any consistent seasonal movement in banana prices over the years. We have been unable to visualize any rational basis upon which an administered price policy might operate that would have produced the price pattern that has obtained for bananas in the North American market. In our judgment, only supply and demand, the competition of other distributors of bananas and of other fruits, and the general price trends in the American market could account reasonably for what has happened to banana prices.

From the standpoint of countries which produce bananas, the price trends for their product in the North American market has been highly advantageous. Not only has it shown an upward trend of extraordinary year-to-year consistency, but the 171 percent rise between 1940 and 1955 has been of a dimension that has been favorable to Latin American producers in that it has improved their "terms of trade." The index of prices of all U.S. exports over the same period rose by 100 percent, and that for U.S. exports of all finished manufactures by only 86 percent. Thus, Latin American banana producers could buy over 35 percent more of general U.S. exports and over 45 percent

Table 19 | Import Indexes [a] for Banana and Other Crude Foodstuffs (1940=100)

| | Banana sales to U.S. and Canada | | | | Value of U.S. imports | | | | | |
	(1) By United Fruit	Annual % chg.	(2) Estimated total [b]	Annual % chg.	(3) Crude foodstuffs	Annual % chg.	(4) Coffee	Annual % chg.	(5) Crude foodstuffs ex. coffee	Annual % chg.
1940	100		100		100		100		100	
1941	110	+10	115	+15	132	+32	139	+39	126	+26
1942	76	−31	89	−23	122	−8	161	+16	91	−28
1943	54	−29	82	−8	205	+68	215	+34	197	+116
1944	79	+46	109	+33	295	+44	257	+20	326	+65
1945	103	+30	133	+22	243	−18	272	+6	220	−33
1946	147	+43	211	+63	286	+18	372	+45	216	−2
1947	208	+41	287	+36	357	+25	473	+27	263	+22
1948	268	+29	305	+6	446	+25	550	+16	363	+38
1949	269	—	311	+2	468	+5	626	+14	340	−6
1950	296	+10	326	+5	614	+31	860	+37	416	+22
1951	287	−3	316	−3	728	+19	1,073	+25	452	+9
1952	272	−5	310	−2	726	−1	1,083	+1	438	−3
1953	291	+7	315	+2	767	+6	1,157	+7	453	+3
1954	274	−6	302	−4	771	+1	1,170	+1	452	−1
1955	268	−2	300	−1	701	−9	1,068	−9	406	−10

[a] Columns 1 and 2 cover banana sales at importer level for both Canada and the United States. All but a small fraction of Canadian sales are transshipped from the United States. Columns 3, 4, and 5 represent U.S. imports only.

[b] Figured upon proportion of United Fruit *stem* imports to total *stem* imports. Since we do not have accurate weight or price figures for fruit handled by United Fruit's competitors, the total index has been constructed upon the assumption that the relationship between weights and prices of United Fruit's imported stems and those of its competitors has remained constant for the period covered.

131

Chart XV
United Fruit Bananas Are a Steady but Slowly Expanding Source of Income to Producing Countries

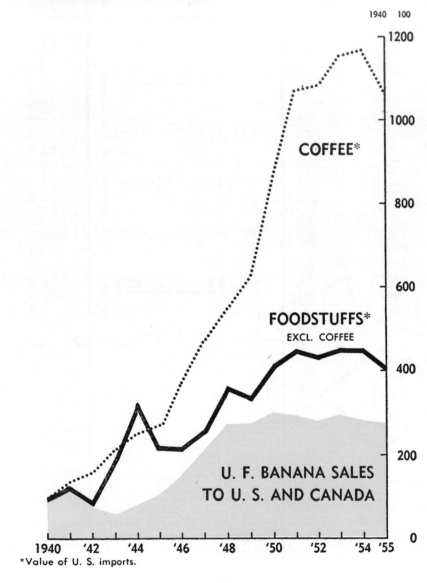

1940 100

COFFEE*

FOODSTUFFS*
EXCL. COFFEE

U. F. BANANA SALES
TO U. S. AND CANADA

1940 '42 '44 '46 '48 '50 '52 '54 '55

*Value of U. S. imports.

more of U.S. manufactured goods in 1955 than in 1940 from their exports to us of a given quantity of bananas.

Of far more basic importance to producing areas, however, is the combined effect of prices and volumes shipped. A reasonable measure of the trend in revenue obtained by producing countries from their banana exports and how it compares with that from other traded food crops can be inferred from the following indices of import values for bananas, coffee, and for all crude foodstuffs with coffee both included and excluded. In the case of bananas, we have included imports for both U.S. and Canadian consumption since, as has previously been noted, all but a very small fraction of the latter are transshipped from the United States.

Column 1 in Table 19 may be read as an approximate index of the trend of returns realized by producing countries from United Fruit banana sales in the North American market. The indicated increase of 168 percent from 1940 to 1955 undoubtedly understates the increased realization of producing countries, since the rate of income taxes paid to those countries has increased markedly in recent years. This volume-times-price index moves in a pattern very similar to the price index alone, except for the fact that on this index the drastically lowered volumes during 1942 and 1943 caused by the non-availability of shipping, and the rapidly increasing volumes from 1944 through 1948 intensify the yearly changes during those years.

One thing that stands out from the record is that the weight volume of United Fruit banana imports to North America was virtually the same in 1955 as in 1940. A 15 percent increase in the average weight of each stem imported was almost completely offset by a decline in the number of stems imported by the company. From the perspective of the producing countries this may offer a legitimate cause for complaint, on the ground that the company representing their largest distributive channel has not been able to add the revenue increases that would have accrued to them from enlarged volume to those that it has provided through higher prices. Anyone taking this position, however, is wielding a two-edged sword. Its backswing is lethally destructive to the argument that the United Fruit Company's share of the North American market consistently has been too big, and that the interests of both producers and consumers would be furthered by its relative curtailment.

Column 2 gives the realization in the North American market from total banana sales, by United Fruit and its competitors combined, from 1940 through 1955. On this index, the effect of price increases

133

is enhanced by a moderate 10 percent volume increase as well. While the weight volume of United Fruit's imports to this area in 1955 was almost the same as it had been in 1940, its competitors' 1955 imports are estimated to have increased by almost 30 percent over this time.

This, of course, is further evidence that the weight of the United Fruit Company's position in the North American market has been waning rather than waxing, a situation that is hardly compatible with a status of monopoly control. More important perhaps from the producing countries' viewpoint is the recorded trend of how the market as a whole has served them over an extended period. This index, reflecting the combined influence of price and volume, indicates that their dollar earnings from banana shipments tripled over a period of 15 years. With the shipping-short war years of 1942 and 1943 excepted, there were no instances in which overall annual foreign exchange earnings from this trade fell off sufficiently to present balance-of-payment problems of any moment.

There is one negative factor in the showing that should not be ignored—the failure of the trade to expand since 1948. It would be plausible to impute at least part of the responsibility for this leveling off to lack of aggressive merchandising on the part of banana importers were it not for the fact that the American consumption of all other fresh fruits combined shows an absolute decline in the same period. Ever since World War II, the per capita consumption of fresh fruits generally has fallen off in the United States while overall per capita fruit consumption has advanced. All of the gain, and more, has been accounted for in the increased consumption of processed fruits—frozen, canned, or otherwise preserved. Since, as yet, there has been no notable success in finding a way to process bananas in a form to provide volume outlets, bananas have not benefited importantly from the gain in processed fruit consumption. But it is rather remarkable that the market for this imported fresh fruit should have held up better than that for competing fresh fruits of domestic origin.

There appears to be an unmistakably growing preference in the North American market for foods that are the least demanding in carriage, storage-space requirements, and preparation. In the light of this there is a strong implication that banana consumption in this market is not likely, at best, to expand much faster than population growth, except through the development of broader uses in processed form for baby foods, ice cream, or confectionery and cereal fabrications, or in combinations for the housewife of the outlandishly wonderful, ready-mix variety. Fresh bananas, of course, are not difficult to eat, but they are a bulky, heavy item for the housewife to carry; they take considerable space; and have a limited holding period in the vanishing American pantry or on the increasingly typical kitchenette shelf. As everyone knows from Chiquita Banana's admonitions, they are a tropical fruit not well adapted to storage in home refrigerators.

Columns 3, 4, and 5 provide yardsticks for comparison of bananas and imported crude foodstuffs in general. It is obvious that foreign exchange earnings from the banana trade have expanded far less rapidly than from crude foodstuff exports as a whole to this market. Coffee clearly has dominated the general index, with price increases on this commodity far outweighing the increases in volume traded. When the banana index is compared with that of crude foodstuff imports other than coffee (Column 5) the showing is better but is still under average by about 25 percent in terms of overall growth. When judged on the stability factor, the showing of the banana trade is definitely superior.

The horizon of opportunity for countries producing bananas is by no means limited to the North American market. Europe, in the years immediately preceding World War II, consumed a relatively low percentage of world banana shipments. From 1941 through 1945, Western Europe imported scarcely any bananas. Then, with the vigorous resumption of postwar economies, the flow of bananas to that area was resumed. By 1950-51, the volume had regained its prewar levels, and the upward trend continued through 1956. In the latter year, Western Europe's banana imports were well above 50 percent higher by stem count than the five-year average of 1935-39. Since the per capita banana consumption in Europe is still well under that of the United States, there would seem to be considerable room for further expansion of the volume that Europe can absorb.

We have not been able to obtain satisfactorily complete price data on European banana imports. From the record of Latin American bananas exported to Europe, however, it is evident that the price trends at importer sales levels have differed widely between Europe and North America. As we have explained previously, European prices per pound of stem weight have been consistently higher than American prices on the same basis. In 1940, European import prices per pound averaged 55 percent higher. When volume trade was resumed in 1946 after the wartime stoppage, European banana prices averaged 130 percent higher. Since then, there has been a gradual closing of the gap as North American prices have risen and European prices have fallen off 30 percent. By 1955 and 1956, Latin American bananas shipped to Europe were sold by importers at a price only about 10 percent more per pound in that market than they were bringing in North America. A large fraction of the price differential between the two markets in these two years represents the higher freight costs of shipping Latin American fruit to Europe.

Thus, for the past several years, the profit margin on bananas exported from Latin America to Europe has been decreasing. This factor may blunt somewhat the appeal of the greater growth capacity of the European market. There is a distinct possibility also that, under the proposed tariff standardization program of the European Common Market, bananas from overseas European dependencies may be given a general advantage over those coming from Latin American republics. If so, the latter may find it more difficult to export their product to some European countries in which they now find outlets.

The role of the United Fruit Company as a supplier of the European market has shown a steady decline. Before World War II, United's proportionate share of the European market was quite comparable to its share of the North American market. Since the end of the War, the company has never supplied more than 12 percent of European banana imports, and in most years its stem shipments to Europe have been well under 10 percent of the total. Its current position in that market is obviously not of a dimension that would allow it to exercise any important influence upon price or volume trends; yet the record of recent years shows that prices and even volumes in the two markets are drawing closer together in a way that suggests a growing competition between them for the available supplies of acceptable fruit.

In Summary

OUR CONCLUSIONS on the economic record of the United Fruit Company can be summarized in the following terms:

United Fruit is a large but far from a giant corporation by U.S. standards. Over the years, its business has been only moderately profitable as measured by return on value of funds invested when compared with other large U.S. corporations doing primarily a domestic business.

The earnings record of the United Fruit Company has been substandard when measured by the criterion of growth. Holders of United Fruit stock have realized no capital gains, on the average, from sales on the New York Stock Exchange over the past 11 years.

The ownership of the United Fruit Company is very broadly dispersed, even when judged by U.S. standards. The company has almost as many stockholders as it has tropical employees and the annual dividend return of its average shareholder is less than 40 percent of the wage earned by its average tropical employee.

On the basis of the record of United Fruit's 1955 operations in the six countries in which all but a small fraction of its bananas are produced, the company's direct contributions to the national economies are surprisingly large. They have amounted to about 95 percent of its total revenues from export and domestic sales in the area. On the very important item of net foreign exchange contributions, the local economies retain about 70 percent of the value of the total export sales of the company.

When United Fruit's contributions are compared to other direct U.S. private investments in Latin America its comparative record is outstandingly favorable among total investments in the agricultural category upon virtually every count. When compared with U.S. direct private investments in Latin America in all fields, its comparative contributions are far above average in employment and wage payments, for export trade generated, and for foreign exchange returns accruing to local economies; its total contributions to local economies are about average; its tax payments somewhat below average, which reflects the fact that its total earnings have been relatively modest.

Compared to locally owned agricultural enterprises of all types, the efficiency of United Fruit operations and the returns that accrue to local economies from them are uniquely high. By a wide margin, no purely local agricultural ventures contribute as much per acre or per man employed as producing countries derive from United Fruit operations.

Finally, on the controversial issue of whether or not the returns from primary product exports are so comparatively volatile as to prejudice their value to countries importantly committed to such activity, the record of banana exports has been consistently excellent. The value of banana imports into North America tripled between 1940 and 1948 (and have since held about level), with price increases accounting for all but about 10 percent of the gain. The only serious setbacks in the period occurred in 1942 and 1943, and were directly chargeable to the submarine blockade. The price index for European banana imports has been far more irregular, but the effect of this on banana export earnings has been more than offset by the far greater and remarkably steady increase of the volume of European banana imports in the postwar period. In recent years, prices in the two markets have been drawing closer together and currently the price per pound of Latin American bananas shipped to Europe exceeds the price of their North American shipments by little more than enough to cover the freight differential. Similarly, the volume of per capita banana consumption in Europe is gradually drawing nearer to the North American level, though the latter is still appreciably higher.

The weight volume of United Fruit banana imports to both North America and Europe was about the same in 1955 as in 1940. Other importers accounted for the small increase in the former market's volume and the much larger increase in the latter. United Fruit now accounts for so small a fraction of the European trade that there could be no reasonable ground for assigning to it a capacity to influence price trends or marketing policies in that area. In the North American market, where it is still the principal importer though to a less degree than formerly, the preponderant evidence indicates that banana prices are importantly determined by the general price level for domestically produced fruits with which bananas must compete for the consumer's dollar. There appears to be as little ground for crediting United Fruit with having maintained a price structure that has been genuinely advantageous to the interests of producing countries as there would be to chide it for the failure of the North American market to absorb ever-increasing quantities of banana imports. In both instances, what has taken place appears to have been largely caused by factors beyond the capacity of the United Fruit Company to control.

There is a final comment that seems worth recording before we proceed to an examination of the economic impact of the United Fruit Company's operations on a country-to-country basis. The picture that has been drawn of the banana market, as one that has offered a regularly increasing return to producing countries with remarkably few and exceptionally mild annual recessions, is accurate when applied to producing areas as a whole. The record for individual countries, or even for specific areas within a given country, has been far less stable.

Within the Western Hemisphere, banana production in Cuba, Jamaica, Mexico, British Honduras, Nicaragua, Dutch Guiana, and the Windward Islands has blossomed and withered within the past few decades. In Costa Rica and Panama it first flourished on the Atlantic Coast, then died out there and was reconstituted on the Pacific side of both countries, followed by recent signs of rehabilitation on the original sites. In Ecuador, banana culture has flowered in the classically exuberant pattern that has characterized its early stages in other areas, and is now undergoing the historic travail that has beset this venture in country after country in the past.

Unless and until more efficient control measures are devised to check known banana diseases, and in all likelihood new blights that are as yet unknown, it is likely that the locus of large-scale banana cultivation will keep changing, sometimes from plot to adjacent plot, and sometimes in leaps spanning hundreds of miles. So long as the recurring floods and blowdowns continue to decimate annual banana cultivations in a given country, it seems inevitable that large markets like North America and Europe will need multiple sources of supply, rather than one or two, in order to assure the continuity of their import volumes.

Because of the inherently perishable nature of this tropical commodity and the huge distances that it must travel in order to keep every corner of its far-flung markets supplied without shortage or glut, there is no prospect that the future will tolerate any relaxation in the precise time and flow schedules that banana distribution has been forced to meet in the past.

All of these considerations—disease incidence, natural disasters, and the exceptionally demanding logistics of banana distribution—promise to keep the pattern of enterprise in this field one in which large-scale, vertically integrated operators predominate. Without them, it is difficult to visualize how world trade in bananas can be maintained on a scale that is uniquely large for a commodity of this general type.

For over half a century, the United Fruit Company has been the outstanding pioneer in this field. To a unique degree the world banana trade is its creation. It has initiated most of the procedures, from cultivation through distribution, that have built the trade to its present dimension. Whether its relative position in the industry is maintained or continues to decline, the general organizational patterns it has established seem likely to persist.

This does not mean that there will not be a continuing evolution in the detail of procedure, or even in the basic organizational pattern of some important segments of banana enterprise as a whole. The direction of a number of the more important changes that appear to be in the making will appear as we turn now from the general to the particular. In Chapter VI we shall weigh and appraise the impact of the United Fruit Company's operations upon the several economies of the six countries that produce most of the bananas that enter into world trade and examine some of the problems and trends that are indicated by this record.

139

VI.

Contribution to the Several Local Economies

Two CONDITIONS, we believe, must be satisfied before investment funds will move from one nation into another: First, the return to the investor supplying the funds must be satisfactory in that it compares favorably with alternative uses of funds in his own nation. Second, the net return to the host nation, after deducting all outpayments, must make a contribution to the local economy that would not otherwise be realized and that compares favorably with the contribution of locally financed activities. If these conditions are met, both sides have an interest in encouraging private investment.

In the previous chapter we looked at United Fruit's operations from the standpoint of an investor in the company's stock. We saw that it has yielded a steady, though far from spectacular, return to the shareholder. The main purpose of this chapter is to measure the economic impact of United's operations in the six countries that produced about 92 percent of North American banana imports in 1955—Costa Rica, Honduras, Panama, Guatemala, Ecuador, and Colombia. In the process, we shall try to show how the company's production operations differ from nation to nation, thus amplifying the general discussion presented in Chapter IV.

How should one go about measuring the economic impact of the United Fruit Company on these nations? There are various procedures that have been used in measuring a company's contribution to the economy in which it operates. One widely used procedure is to measure what is termed the "value added" by a company's operations. The cost of purchased materials, services, parts, and fuels that a company purchases from other business concerns is deducted from the market value of what it sells and the remainder is the "value added" by the company's operations to the gross national product of the country in which it operates. Depreciation and indirect taxes are deducted to compute the value added to national income by the company's operations.

Such calculations would in some respects understate and in others overstate the United Fruit Company's contributions to the nations in which it operates. Since its banana plantations have literally been hacked out of the jungle, all of its expenditures within a nation where it operates represent an addition to the economy of that nation. Its purchases of materials and supplies within the nation add to production and employment. Moreover, the major portion of its imports increase the supply of consumer goods or the stock of capital available in the country. It pays taxes to central and local governments. Moreover, it reinvests part of its net earnings after taxes and frequently brings in capital to support new investment. On the other hand, the portion of earnings remitted to the United States by the wholly owned subsidiaries of United Fruit cannot appropriately be regarded as a contribution to the economies in which it is earned—it should be deducted from the accounts in measuring United's contribution to host nations.

United Fruit's Net Contribution

From the company's accounts we have assembled a set of statistics which measure the "net contribution" of United Fruit operations to each nation for the years 1951-55. Stated briefly, this method takes the company's total expenditures[1] upon both current and capital account within each country in a given period and adds the value of imports. The resulting figure shows the amount that remains in the country as a result of the company's operations. The funds to pay for these contributions come from the total receipts of the company's subsidiaries within a given country—from its exports, fees derived from abroad for services, and local sales—plus net additions to their capital accounts representing new company investment commitments. When dividend transmittals are subtracted from this total, the remainder represents the sum of payments within the country plus the value of imports added to the country's stock of capital or consumers' goods.

Wherever available statistics permit, we shall compare the United Fruit contribution with that of other economic activities in the six countries in terms of the return to the nation per acre for farm products, per man employed, and per dollar of investment. We shall look also at the contribution to foreign exchange availability and to government revenues. Our objective is to measure as accurately as pos-

---

[1] Measured on an accrual basis as is usual in accounting statements. Thus, the figures will differ from those on a cash expenditure basis to the extent that cash payments are made before or after obligations are incurred.

141

sible what the company's operations leave in each nation both in absolute terms and in comparison with other agricultural and industrial operations. In doing this we shall see whether United Fruit is making the sort of economic contribution that should encourage continued hospitality on the part of host countries. In later chapters we propose to consider the social and political impact of the company's operations on the six nations.

As was pointed out earlier, the economic impact of United's operations differs markedly among nations. Accordingly, we propose to consider first the three countries in each of which the impact is clearly of major importance to the local economy in that the company accounted for more than a third of export receipts in 1955. These nations are: Costa Rica, Honduras, and Panama. Then we shall turn to Guatemala, Ecuador, and Colombia where the United Fruit Company's contribution to exports was considerably smaller.

COSTA RICA

DURING 1955, United Fruit shipped 6,910,000 stems from Costa Rica, or one-fifth of the company's total shipments. Over nine-tenths of the company's total Costa Rican shipments came from its Golfito Division, located near the southern boundary on the Pacific Coast. The remaining production came from the Quepos Division further north on the Pacific side which was going out of banana production during 1955.

General Description

The Golfito Division was set up between 1937 and 1939. The company built a pier and established a port. Then a railroad was driven back into the virgin jungle behind a low range of coastal hills and the banana plantations were set up. In 1955, the company had 25,000 acres in bananas at Golfito. In addition, United Fruit was purchasing bananas under contracts with local producers operating 4,600 acres. (In connection with such purchases, United installs, maintains, and operates the sigatoka control system, provides irrigation, and furnishes transportation to the port.)

If any division of United could be said to be an average division in 1955, Golfito was it. Production per acre (210 stems in 1955) and cost per stem were close to the divisions average. In housing, transportation and most physical aspects Golfito is also close to average.

142

Golfito does, however, have certain special problems. It is particularly susceptible to flood damage. In 1954, floods wiped out a major portion of the division. In the Palmar region, 11,000 acres were hit by floods two years running. In addition, Golfito has certain special labor relations problems, a point we shall return to in Chapter VIII.

United's Costa Rican operations also encompass production of cacao, African palm oil, and abaca. At Quepos, 10,000 acres are planted in African palm and 5,000 in cacao. Near Limón on the Atlantic side the company has almost 19,000 acres in cacao as well as 5,000 acres in abaca (under a contract with the U.S. government). Almost as much land is planted in these other crops as in bananas.

Before turning to an examination of United's contribution to the Costa Rican economy, it might be well to set forth the facts relating to present and past land use. Experience in Costa Rica points up the problem of what to do about abandoned banana lands in perhaps its sharpest perspective. In 1955, the company owned almost 500,000 acres of land, or almost 4 percent of the national total. Slightly under a fifth of company land was planted in crops or was in pasture, but including the land in use for roads, structures, drainage, etc., perhaps a fourth of landholdings were in use.

Part of the idle landholding is being held in reserve. If flood fallowing proves economical, it would be possible to set up a division in the Limón area. It might also be possible to establish a division on a tract of swamp land held in the Quepos area through the use of pump drainage and silting. Virtually none of these lands could be used for commercial production if they were released, so the fact that United Fruit is keeping them in reserve imposes no limitation on Costa Rican agricultural development.

The company has turned over large tracts of land to the government. Company policy is to offer land which it has purchased but cannot use to the government as a part of the consideration involved in working out a new contract with the government. Thus, the company has expressed a willingness to sell excess land to individuals or to turn it over to the government under reasonable terms.

Land Problems at Quepos and Limón

The history of the Quepos Division points up the problem of making more effective use of land that is forced out of banana production by the advance of Panama disease. Quepos was developed in the mid-1930's as a major division. World War II slowed the growth of the Quepos Division, but production rose rapidly after the war. In

1947-48, banana production topped 2 million stems a year and 25,000 acres were planted in bananas. However, Panama disease spread so rapidly that banana production ceased in mid-1956. The 10,000 acres in African palm and 5,000 acres in cacao at Quepos furnish employment for 700-800 persons as compared with a peak employment of 5,600 in 1947. The company provided financial aid to farmers who wanted to go into rice production. And it set up a program to transfer employees to other divisions (most employees elected to take their severance pay instead).

The government discussed the possibility of taking over parts of the property, and the company would have been willing to work out a reasonable arrangement. However, the government lacked the funds to take over and develop the land for other uses. Consequently, most of the land has gone into subsistence farming.

Land that has gone out of banana production is first-class land for most crops that thrive in the tropics. Moreover, it is land that has been cleared, drained, irrigated, and provided with transportation and other facilities. In a nation that needs to expand agricultural output both to provide food for a growing population and to increase export earnings, it would seem self-evident that every effort should be made to shift abandoned banana land into commercial production of other crops.

The economic waste involved in the failure to make most effective use of land at Quepos is actually the second such experience in Costa Rica. Near Limón, United Fruit once had a large division that went out of banana production in 1942. Acreage planted to bananas there had reached a peak of 34,600 in 1908 and as late as 1931 exceeded 8,500 acres. However, the inroads of Panama disease forced abandonment of banana production. In addition to United Fruit's 10,000 acres in cacao and 5,000 acres in abaca in the Limón area, local farmers are growing cacao, some of it on land formerly in bananas. Most of the remaining acreage is in local food crops.

Nevertheless, the Costa Rican economy has suffered in the process. Despite continued efforts by United Fruit to improve cacao yields, cacao has not as yet made a significant contribution to the nation's total production or exchange earnings. Results during 1955 showed that the contribution to the local economy from cacao was far below that from bananas on a per-acre or per-employee basis. Thus, output per acre of banana production was more than five times that per acre in cacao. This, together with the low level of earnings by United Fruit on cacao operations (and, hence low tax payments), explains

ECONOMIC CONTRIBUTIONS TO HOST COUNTRIES

There are marked differences in the levels of economic accomplishments, as there are in cultural patterns and social development, in Colombia, Costa Rica, Ecuador, Guatemala, Honduras, and Panama. And within each country there are sharp contrasts from area to area. Each contains vast undeveloped areas, isolated and primitive farms, and bustling cities which are becoming increasingly modernized.

Although mechanization is moving forward, there is still a great deal of dependence upon primitive tools and animal power.

AN INDEPENDENT FARMER and his family in Costa Rica is one of many who profit from United's policies designed to encourage production of bananas and other crops by local growers.

By developing land that otherwise may have remained unused for decades, United Fruit has stimulated new settlements around its plantations and productive activities by local entrepreneurs who can take advantage not only of the company's transportation, communication, and purchasing facilities, but also its research and advisory services.

RAILROADS which United has built for its own use benefit the countries as a whole. These Panamanians, bound for a holiday outing, board a United Fruit train.

LAND DONATED by United Fruit is used for this governmental agrarian project in western Guatemala. Since 1935, the company has reduced its total acreage of land by about one-third, and a great portion of such land has been deeded to central or local governments.

By constant improvement of fa-cilities vital to its own integrated operations, United has helped to reduce barriers to communica-tions in host countries.

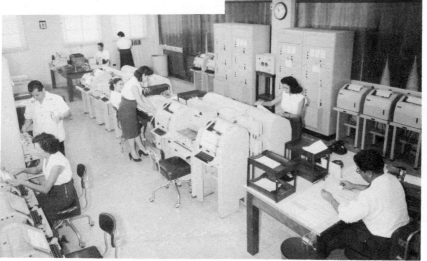

AS EARLY AS 1903, United began working on radio and telegraph services; in 1904, it was first to put commercial radio on shipboard; by 1910, uninterrupted radio communication between the United States and Central America was estab-lished. The Tropical Radio Telegraph Company, incorporated as a subsidiary of United Fruit, now operates as a regular public utility.

ANY IMPROVEMENT IN PORT FA-CILITIES by United is also shared by the public in its host country. And there have been vast improvements during the past half century, as indicated by the 1924 scene below and the present-day port in Latin America.

One of United Fruit's most important economic contributions to host countries has been the introduction of needed new skills. Many thousands of nationals of the six countries during the span of United's existence have had on-the-job training in the varied skills needed in large-scale development and operation of farms, in communications and transportation facilities, in processing plants, in depots and machine shops, and, importantly, in laboratories and business offices.

MODERN managerial methods and business machines are put into practice in such offices as this accounting section.

SKILLS in hydraulic engineering are acquired in the process of clearing land and constructing the many facilities necessary for United's integrated operations. The intimate knowledge of tractors, cranes, and other mechanical processes learned at United installations is adding to the trained labor pool in each host country.

Continuous research and advance planning is particularly important in the cultivation of a fruit so susceptible as bananas to the hazards of weather, disease, and spoilage. In addition to providing research data to local farmers from whom it buys, United also supplies findings to competitors, educational institutions, and government officials.

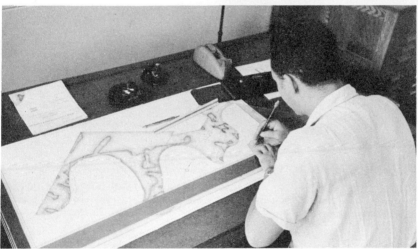

COMPANY SPECIALISTS map every farm development to show areas best suited to banana production. United Fruit research teams visit their own and other farms whenever blight, insects, or other factors impair production of fruit. Samples of earth disclose adaptability for growing bananas; chemist takes field tests of seed-sterilizing solution.

The Pan American Agricultural School in Honduras was founded and is financed by United Fruit. However, none of the graduates of the three-year course in all aspects of agriculture and farm management is allowed to enter United's employ. The school is dedicated to the formation of a growing corps of trained and experienced farmers who will be able to disseminate their knowledge and techniques to their fellow Latin Americans. Many graduates become teachers, agricultural extension agents, and farm managers.

YOUNG LATIN AMERICAN learns the correct time to harvest papayas at the Pan American Agricultural School.

A GOVERNMENT EMPLOYEE, graduate of the Pan American School, surveys land for a local farmer.

PROFESSOR of cattle raising at a government-sponsored school in Honduras is a graduate of the Pan American School. Here he explains tractor mechanics.

ANOTHER GRADUATE of the United-sponsored school of agriculture, now a government agent, talks with a farmer about insects found in a cotton crop.

DIVERSIFIED CROPS

United Fruit has almost as much land in other crops as in bananas. And it conducts research in each and offers advice to many producers in host countries. None of the other crops—which include African palm oil, abaca, and cacao—yields a profit to United comparable to its banana operations, but local economies are benefiting from United's introduction of some new crops and its improvements in planting stock and growing methods for others.

AFRICAN PALM OIL—a fairly new crop grown in Costa Rica and Honduras—now supplies an important portion of local demand for edible oils and soap, thus saving foreign exchange. Shown here are United Fruit seedlings, the fruit, mechanized harvesting, and the first step in processing.

ABACA—introduced by United Fruit Company during World War II when other sources of Manila hemp were closed—is grown under contract for the U. S. government. United's abaca operations in Panama, Costa Rica, Honduras, and Guatemala have shown that the Western Hemisphere can meet its requirements for rope fibers. Here stalks are loaded at railroad tracks alongside abaca field for trip to the factory where they are pressed, shredded, and dried for baling before shipping to the United States.

CACAO RESEARCH has resulted in measurable increases in United's yields per acre. Developing high-yield, disease-resistant strains of the cacao plant and improving agricultural practices are benefiting both the company and local producers. Cacao plants, started from cuttings at United's propagating beds, now grow many clones. After roasting, beans are sorted and graded before being bagged.

CATTLE RANCHES and dairy herds are maintained and other crops grown on United's plantations to assure adequate food supplies for its employees.

RESEARCH AND DEMONSTRATION on still other agricultural resources and practices is geared to a variety of needs felt in the host countries. These range all the way from reforestation and preservation of timber to spraying of crops by helicopter.

A measure of United's economic contributions in agriculture alone is indicated by figures on yields per acre and per worker and on wages. The yield per acre of land owned or contracted to United Fruit in the six countries was more than 20 times the average for all other improved agricultural land; and from the company's cropland it was three times the average from all other cropland in the host countries. Similarly, yield per worker employed in agriculture on United's operations was about five times as high as the average for the six countries. And wages paid were substantially higher than the average for agricultural employees.

why cacao has made a lesser contribution than bananas. Similarly, experience in abaca and in African palm oil shows lower returns both to the local economy and to the company than banana operations.

Problems of Developing Other Crops

As a broad generalization, United's experience with crops other than bananas—not only cacao, abaca, and African palm oil, but also rubber and timber (mainly teak)—has proved disappointing earnings-wise. Despite this experience, it may be that efforts to develop better methods of producing other crops could produce better results in the future.

Progress in increasing yield per acre in cacao production at Limón would appear to be most encouraging. The work in developing high-yield, disease-resistant strains of the cacao tree and in improving agricultural practices may benefit both the company and local producers if the cacao situation should favor production in the Western Hemisphere as related to Africa in the years ahead. African palm oil production in Costa Rica and other nations has developed to the point where it supplies an important portion of local demand for edible oils. In this manner, a saving in foreign exchange is effected. As local demands grow, it may be possible to expand acreage in palm oil.

The problem of utilizing most economically lands no longer suitable for bananas is not unique to Costa Rica. For example, in Honduras an entire banana division at Trujillo in the late 1930's was lost to Panama disease—the area was given to the government and has since largely reverted to jungle; disease led to cessation of United's banana production in Nicaragua in 1942 and to the virtual elimination of production on the east coast of Guatemala by 1955. As was pointed out earlier, the ravages of Panama disease in all producing areas have spread over 900,000 acres in the past half century, or six to seven times as much land as United Fruit now has planted in bananas.

In most cases, as in Limón and Quepos, the opportunities offered by the termination of banana production have not been fully realized. Abandoned banana land, with its improvements and supporting facilities, represents an investment by United Fruit in today's prices of some $2,000 per acre. Production of other crops would not entail as heavy an investment. Even so, the investment needed to set up farmers in production of other crops on retired banana lands is obviously far less than that required to develop virgin jungle lands. Thus, the cessation of banana production offers a great opportunity to establish commercial production of other crops. They may not yield as great a return to the nation as bananas, but they will yield far more than if the land goes back into jungle or is used for subsistence crops.

In general, the company's efforts to develop other crops represent the sort of technical assistance that U.S. companies can offer to other nations. Thus, it would seem that such efforts should be continued, and that they might offer one solution to the problem of making efficient use of abandoned banana land.

A National Responsibility

The chief responsibility, however, for making the most economical use of abandoned banana acreage must rest with the national governments. It is clearly their responsibility to provide the education necessary to teach people to operate successful commercial farms and to provide such credit facilities and technical assistance as may prove necessary to enable them to take over lands released from banana production.

At the same time, the United Fruit Company, or any similar company, would seem to be under obligation to cooperate fully with national governments in working out feasible arrangements to shift land no longer suitable for bananas to the most productive uses. This responsibility includes such measures as: providing as much advance notice as possible of acreage that could be used by local farmers; disposing of such surplus lands at reasonable prices; furnishing transportation and other services at reasonable prices to local farmers; and, in general, facilitating local efforts to make good use of the land.

At least in the period covered by this study, the general policy of the United Fruit Company has been fully in line with these specifications. There has been an understandable tendency to use surplus land as a bargaining point in negotiating contracts with local governments, a process which in some cases may have delayed the transfer of retired banana lands to local users. In addition, the transfer of land that forms part of a banana division still in operation poses special problems. For efficient operation of banana farms it is necessary to control a complex system of rail and road transport, irrigation, and drainage facilities. Thus, there may well have been a general reluctance on the part of managerial personnel in the field to expedite the process of turning land over until large tracts went out of bananas.

Consequently, it may be that United Fruit's land policies should be set forth more explicitly for the guidance of field personnel. Field managers might be specifically directed to facilitate the transfer of Panama disease-infested lands to local production. In their capacity as good agriculturalists with intimate knowledge of the local situation they might do much to stimulate local production.

As a practical matter, however, the national government must take the initiative in this matter. Up to the present, the major problem has been a lack of funds to provide agricultural credit and the educational services that are provided by a trained agricultural extension service. Thus, the failure of the Costa Rican government to take advantage of opportunity presented at Quepos was due to a lack of money and trained personnel.

This would seem to be a fruitful field for the International Bank for Reconstruction and Development and the Export-Import Bank to investigate. Loans to support supervised agricultural credit programs in areas where further abandonments of banana land can be expected would appear to constitute sound and desirable undertakings for these institutions. In addition, programs to resettle persons from Europe might well be geared to utilize such retired banana lands.

Sources of Funds

Now that we have considered the problem of using to best advantage land forced out of bananas by disease, let us turn to the contribution made to Costa Rica from United Fruit operations on land it is using. United Fruit owns or controls some 5 percent of Costa Rica's agricultural land and about 10 percent of acreage under crops. In the five years 1951-55, the average annual contribution from all United Fruit operations worked out to $34,414,500. That amount was equal to about 20 percent of the value of the country's total agricultural production.

To see how the measurement of the United Fruit contribution is derived, consider the accounts for the year 1955.[2] The company's exports were valued at $35.9 million in that year. Bananas made up 92 percent of the total, while cacao accounted for most of the remainder. The company also took in $7.7 million from sales of merchandise in Costa Rica and receipts from Tropical Radio and other local operations. Thus, total receipts from current operations amounted to $43.6 million.

In addition to these funds generated from current operations, capital funds were increased by $13.2 million (of which over $3 million repre-

---

[2] In the case of Costa Rica as well as each of the other nations studied, these statistics are based upon, and are consistent with, United Fruit's accounting records. These records are, of course, reviewed by independent accounting firms and by the U.S. Treasury Department.

147

sented advance payments on income taxes). Thus, the total funds available to United's operating company, the Compania Bananera de Costa Rica, amounted to $56.8 million. Dividends of $14.8 million were remitted to the United States. Thus, the amount remaining in Costa Rica was $42.0 million.

In other words, the amount remaining in Costa Rica equaled to 96 percent of United's receipts from sales of all products and services in 1955. The year 1955 happened to be unusual in two ways. In the first place, income tax liabilities were doubled as a result of a new contract which raised the tax rate from 15 percent of net earnings to 30 percent. A second factor is that dividend payments were unusually large in 1955—no dividends were paid in 1954 and dividend outpayments in 1955 represented two years' return from the standpoint of the U.S. company. Tax considerations in the United States led to the decision to defer dividends from 1954 to 1955.

Uses of Funds

The $42 million remaining in Costa Rica during 1955 was used in these ways:

Wages and salaries ....$15.3 million or 36%
Taxes .... 8.8 million or 21%
Purchases of goods and services .... 4.5 million or 11%
Imports of capital goods, materials, and of
    goods sold in commissaries .... 9.9 million or 24%
Other (largely additions to inventories) ... 3.5 million or 8%

The $15.3 million for wages and salaries covers the costs of fringe benefits. For example, the company operated three major hospitals, 39 dispensaries, and 62 schools. Average annual earnings of the 15,500 persons employed amounted to almost $1,000 per employee, well above the average for the nation as a whole.

United's tax payments in 1955 accounted for over 18 percent of the central government's revenues. That was about double the share in 1954. The increase was caused partly by the new contract which increased the company's income tax liability and in part by the fact that the company made substantial advance tax payments in 1955. However, if an adjustment were made for the advance payments, the company's contribution to government revenues would work out to about 15 percent. The United Fruit Company's operations accounted for 8 percent of Costa Rica's national income in 1955 (national in-

Chart XVI
Sources and Uses of the
United Fruit Company Contribution
to the Costa Rica Economy in 1955

The United Fruit Company
in Costa Rica had receipts
from all sources totaling

(in millions of dollars)

$56.8

SOURCES OF INCOME

$32.9 came from
banana exports

$7.7 from
domestic sales*

$3.0 from
other exports

and $13.2
new capital
was invested
by UFCO

*Includes General Services Administration fee.

USES

Of the $56.8 .... $14.8 was paid out in
dividends*

$42.0 remained in
Costa Rica .... and was used in this manner:

$3.5 — inventories and misc.

9.9 imported goods
and equipment

4.5 local purchases

8.8 taxes and duties

15.3 wages and salaries

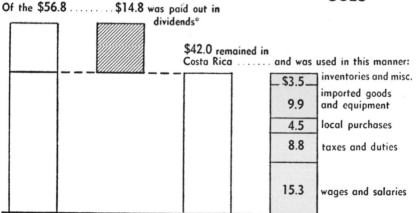

* No dividends remitted in 1954; 1955 dividends covered both
1954 and 1955 operations.

come was estimated at $300 million while value added by United's operations was $24.1 million).

Other Comparisons

We have seen that the United Fruit Company owns or controls about 5 percent of Costa Rica's agricultural land and about 10 percent of land planted to crops (the last census covered only about one-third of the nation's land area, so exact figures are not available). In 1955, the company owned or had under contract about 65 percent of acreage planted in bananas. The amount left in the nation by United's operations amounted to between a fifth to a fourth of the nation's total farm output in the 1951-55 period, and to one-fourth to one-third of total crop output. The company accounted for 90 percent of banana production and over 98 percent of export receipts from bananas.

Thus, the contribution to Costa Rica's economy from each acre of banana land owned and controlled by United Fruit was more than five times as great as the average for all cropland, almost five times the return on acreage devoted to banana production for domestic consumption, five and one-half times the return per acre on cacao, and three times the return from coffee.

United Fruit employs about 5 percent of the total labor force and almost 10 percent of those working on farms. The contribution to the economy per person employed by United is two to two and one-half times as great as the average output per worker in agriculture generally.

United's exports at $35.9 million accounted for 44 percent of the nation's total foreign exchange receipts in 1955. Coffee exports were somewhat larger; they amounted to $37.4 million or 46 percent of the total. In neither case, does the gross export figure give an accurate reading of the net foreign exchange returns to national balance-of-payment accounts. For United Fruit operations, such contribution amounted in 1955 to $24.4 million.[3] This would work out to an average of about $381 per acre of *net* foreign exchange earnings for each of United Fruit's 64,000 acres planted to its export crops.

This may be compared to the foreign exchange return that Costa Rica derived from coffee, a crop that is grown preponderantly by local producers so that no considerable deduction for dividend transmittals abroad is involved. Costa Rica's foreign exchange return in

[3] $49.1 million (exports of $35.9 million plus net capital commitments of $13.2 million) minus $24.7 million (imports of goods, materials, etc., of $9.9 million plus dividends remitted at $14.8 million) equal $24.4 million.

1955 from each of the estimated 119,000 acres[4] planted to coffee that was exported works out to about $315.

The net foreign exchange return per acre is clearly higher in the case of United Fruit's operations, even though this net is derived by deducting both dividend payments abroad and the cost of all imported goods and materials from export receipts. There undoubtedly were foreign purchases of equipment, fertilizers, chemicals, and the like by coffee growers. These should be deducted from coffee export receipts to make our accounts strictly comparable, but the requisite data for this are not available.

On every economic measurement, therefore, the company's contribution to the Costa Rican economy compares most favorably with the contribution of domestic activities. By the same token, United Fruit's operations make a substantial contribution to the nation's growth and prosperity.

HONDURAS

BANANAS HAVE BEEN GROWN in the fertile soil of the Ulua River valley of Honduras since the earliest days of the banana trade. In 1955, United Fruit had 34,100 acres planted in bananas, of which 13,000 were not yet mature. In addition, the company purchases fruit from independent farmers operating 6,400 acres. Plantations stretch for some 50 air miles along the winding banks of the Ulua River. The river carries unusually heavy amounts of silt from the continual erosion of the mountains through which it flows. As a result, the riverbed lies well above the surrounding lands.

The physical characteristics of the river affect the company's operations in several ways. In the first place, huge drainage canals had to be dug on either side of the valley to drain swampland and carry away flood water. The main canals are as wide as ship canals and approximately 20 miles long. Secondly, operations are especially vulnerable to floods so that a large network of dikes and water control facilities had to be built. Despite these precautions, the plantations were inundated in 1954, wiping out an entire crop and damaging facilities extensively. Operations are also subject to the hazards of blowdowns (in early 1957 high winds flattened the farms and 6 million stems were lost).

---

[4] The total acreage planted in coffee was reported as 137,000 acres for 1955, but 13 percent of the coffee produced appears to have been consumed in the local market rather than exported.

However, there are some favorable aspects. The heavy silt content of the river makes it possible literally to create new banana acreage. A complex system of flood gates and dikes diverts flood waters into cleared land. When the water is trapped the silt is deposited. This process is repeated for several years until five or six feet of new soil has been built up. Then bananas are planted. New banana acreage is also obtained by the process of pump drainage. Dikes are built by drag lines to surround swampland and then huge pumps are set to work to remove the ground water and thus make the land usable.

Flood Fallow

The amount of heavy engineering work involved in the company's Honduran operations is increased by the effort to develop flood fallowing. As was explained earlier, this process involves the erection of dikes around each farm so that water can be let in to flood the land for the period necessary to kill the fusarium that bears Panama disease. In 1956, plans called for 15,000 acres under flood fallow, supplemented by enough other land from siltation, pump drainage, and continued use of land not yet affected by Panama disease to keep 35,000 acres in banana production.

While the company holds 300,000 acres and leases 67,000 acres in Honduras, the amount of land that can be planted economically in Gros Michel bananas is being used up. Uses of the land owned or controlled by the company line up this way:

Thousand acres

Banana acreage owned by United Fruit	34.1
Banana acreage under contract	6.4
Pasture	31.0
Palm oil	4.0
Abaca	5.0
Timber	4.0
Forest to protect reservoir	5.0
Floodways and spillways	40.0
Leased to individuals for food crops	19.9
Held for future banana planting	12.0

The remaining 200,000 acres consists largely of land that cannot be used for banana production. Most of it is jungle, swamp, or hillside acreage.

In the 1950-55 period, the company disposed of 65,000 acres, most of which was donated to the Honduran government. Of this total,

20,000 acres was cleared, drained, and served by roads. Most of this area is now being used by squatters for subsistence farming. As was the case in Costa Rica, an opportunity to shift abandoned banana land to productive use by commercial farmers was allowed to go by the board.

Contract Farms

Before sigatoka hit in the mid-1930's, the company bought bananas from a large number of independent producers. Their farms were wiped out by disease. However, the company drained and planted 6,440 acres of land in the El Higuerito district and turned the farms over to 120 Honduran citizens, most of whom were former employees. United provides the disease control and technical assistance. The planters sell their bananas to the company under a long-term contract which provides for a deduction from the price of each stem to pay off the loan made to finance purchase of the farm.

The successful development of flood fallow would probably preclude a large-scale extension of the contract system. The heavy investment required and the large units involved (usually 1,000 acres), to say nothing of the fact that the land is out of production a considerable part of the time, combine to make operation by an individual farmer impracticable. However, the land created by silting or pump drainage could be used to set up contract farms.

Research Center

The company's tropical research activities are centered in Honduras, although smaller stations are in operation in Costa Rica and Colombia. Currently, United's budget for fundamental research on banana culture is well in excess of $1 million a year. Such a sum is not out of line with the amounts spent by other enterprises facing similar problems (the Hawaiian sugar and pineapple companies spend 1 percent to 1.5 percent of sales on fundamental research, or a somewhat higher proportion than United).

However, the United Fruit Company has been striving to build up its research activities in the past five years after a long period of inactivity in the field of basic research. It takes time to recruit and train a staff for the sort of specialized activities required. A brief review of the history of the company's research activities may help provide perspective on current problems.

Panama disease first became a serious problem as far back as 1915.

Initial research efforts began before World War I but were suspended during wartime. In 1922, two plant pathologists were added to the staff and a program of basic research that was notable for the times was set in motion. A number of fundamental studies of Panama disease were completed and published between 1922 and 1933.

In 1926, the Lancetilla experiment station was set up as the headquarters for agricultural and horticultural studies. While research activities have been shifted to La Lima, Lancetilla has been maintained as a unique horticultural center. Plantings there include virtually every variety of tree or shrub grown anywhere in the world's tropical areas. Propagations from Lancetilla have been used to start company operations in such fields as rubber, African palm oil, teak, abaca, and cacao. Planting stock of new and improved varieties of tropical fruit and ornamental trees and shrubs has been supplied to all who will make use of them as well as to the company's own divisions.

Fundamental research was a casualty of the great depression of the 1930's. The research staff was cut back drastically after 1929 and remaining efforts were concentrated on day-to-day operating problems. In 1935, United was faced by what might well be termed its most serious crisis. Sigatoka disease began to spread like wildfire throughout Central America and Colombia. (This wind-borne banana leafspot disease originated in the Sigatoka Valley of Fiji as early as 1913.) In a year, it had infected 80 percent of the Honduran crop and it spread rapidly to other areas.

By an heroic effort, the research workers discovered a practical control method within a period of months. Further experimentation showed that the most economical disease control method consisted of the periodic applications of Bordeaux mixture (described in Chapter IV) through central pumping installations, each serving up to 1,000 acres through a network of spray pipe. By 1939, virtually all producing acreage in Honduras, Guatemala, Costa Rica, and Panama had been equipped with spray installations—over 100,000 acres were covered with 5,200 miles of pipe.

In a very real sense, the banana industry in Central America and Panama was saved from extinction. Export production was decimated in Mexico, where effective disease control methods were not undertaken. And many independent producers were wiped out in other countries. Sigatoka control requires both a relatively high level of technical skill and a relatively high investment. In 1955, the United Fruit Company spent an average of 56.4¢ per stem (44 percent of total farm cost excluding depreciation) on spray. At the time, few independent producers were able to undertake control measures.

By the late 1930's research emphasis shifted to Panama disease and the first flood-fallow experiments were undertaken in 1939-40. Flood-fallow had been tried on other crops—notably on sugar cane to wipe out insect pests. Initial experiments on bananas were promising, and work was renewed after World War II. In recent years, the company has undertaken a massive investment in flood fallow while simultaneously supporting an expanded program of basic research on Panama disease. At the end of 1955, land surrounded by dikes and set up for flood fallow in all divisions represented an investment of about $2.25 million—or more than had been spent in research on the characteristics of the disease.

To date, results from flood fallow have been mixed. Some farms have become infested with Panama disease within a discouragingly short time after being subjected to flooding, while other areas seem to show a good resistance. Meantime, experimental work has continued along such lines as: draining the land and plowing under the soil and reflooding; and the use of fungicides to treat lands after flood fallowing. It should be pointed out that considerable travail always surrounds attempts to introduce new techniques on a mass scale. Thus, the difficulties surrounding flood fallow may well be worked out as more experience is accumulated.

Even if such favorable results are obtained, however, it would seem desirable to continue and intensify efforts at basic research. One estimate is that United Fruit spent $140 million in the 1946-56 period on Panama disease and sigatoka control. This should constitute a considerable incentive to support research designed to seek out more economical methods of dealing with the disease problem. Lines of approach that might prove promising (and some of which are now being pursued) include: those pertaining to basic plant physiology; the assimilative processes of the banana plant, its biochemistry, its ecology; the influence of interactions of plant nutrition and environment on plant growth and on fruit quality; cytogenetics, variety selection, and breeding; broad studies of fauna, particularly banana insects and other insects in the banana zones—their parasites and predators; micro- and macro-floral studies; the biology (contrasted to the chemistry) of the soil in "natural" and modified cultural states; and other fundamental and basic studies.

In general, it would seem that the company has not, until recently, devoted a sufficient effort to research directed at the basic characteristics of banana growing and banana diseases. This is, of course, a judgment that is based on a quick review of the evidence. Moreover, it should be tempered by the understanding that: 1) research efforts have been intensified in recent years; 2) the problems of putting out the "brush fires" of sigatoka and a host of less difficult diseases and insects have been dealt with in exemplary fashion; and 3) the general progress in raising productivity per acre and per employee through improved farming methods constitutes an outstanding achievement.

In addition, research has played an important role in the introduction of new crops or in improved procedures for handling existing crops. Production of African palm oil in Honduras and Costa Rica fills a substantial portion of local needs for margarine, shortening, and soap. The abaca operations in Costa Rica and Guatemala have shown that the Western Hemisphere can meet its requirements for rope fibers. And research has resulted in spectacular increases in yields in cacao production.

Standard Fruit and Steamship Company

An alternative approach to flood fallow is being tried by Standard Fruit and Steamship Company on its division near La Ceiba, some 75 miles east of the United Fruit plantations. Standard has about 19,000 acres planted in varieties which are resistant to Panama disease. Apparently the Giant Cavendish variety has proved most satisfactory, although a considerable acreage was also in Lacatan bananas. While the varieties are resistant to Panama disease, they are subject to sigatoka and have certain significant disadvantages. They are subject to chill damage if the temperature drops below 57° F. for several hours. The Gros Michel banana will not chill until the temperature drops below 54°. In Honduras, the temperature frequently gets down to 56° but seldom goes below 54°. Thus, Standard lost an important portion of a banana crop through chilling in early 1955. Its shipments from La Ceiba dropped from 4 million stems in 1954 to 3 million in 1955. The Giant Cavendish is also more difficult to handle because the stem is less compact.

Certain disadvantages of the Giant Cavendish banana from a marketing standpoint were set forth earlier. For all these reasons, United Fruit has persisted in attempts to perfect flood fallow and in research directed at finding other methods of controlling Panama disease. If this disease can be controlled, the basic pattern of banana production will be altered markedly. Production would be stabilized in given areas and it would no longer be necessary or economical to hold

Chart XVII
Sources and Uses of the United Fruit Company Contribution to the Honduras Economy in 1955
(in millions of dollars)

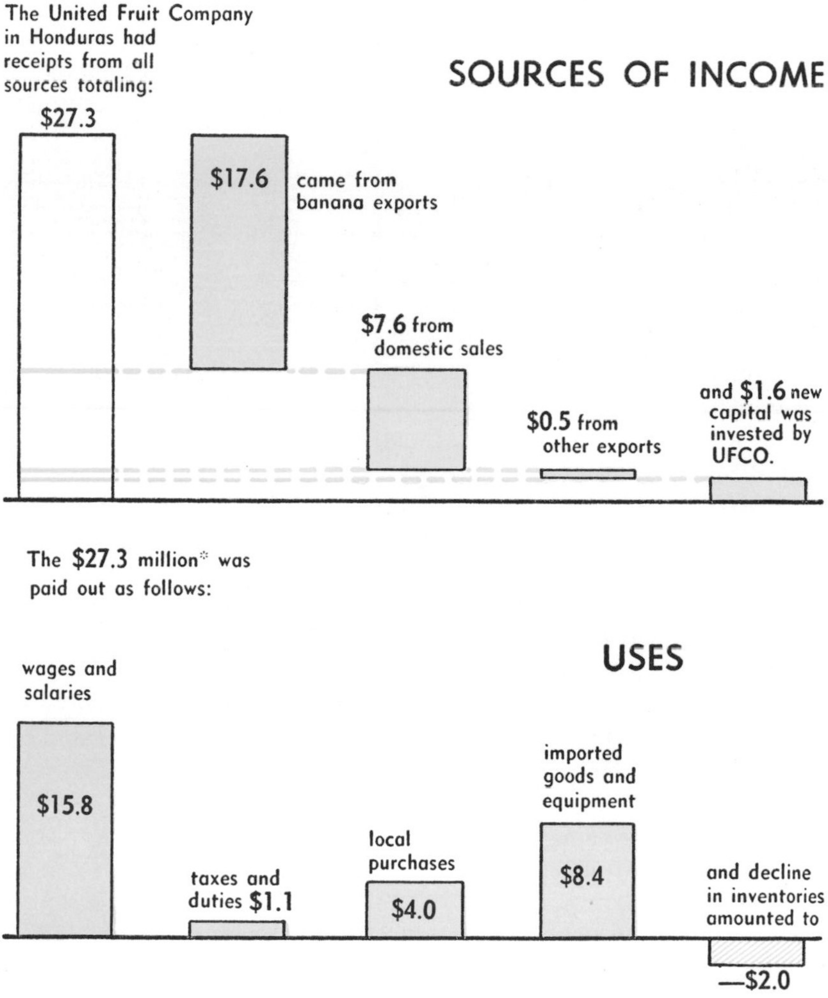

The United Fruit Company in Honduras had receipts from all sources totaling:

SOURCES OF INCOME

$27.3

$17.6 came from banana exports

$7.6 from domestic sales

$0.5 from other exports

and $1.6 new capital was invested by UFCO.

The $27.3 million* was paid out as follows:

USES

wages and salaries

$15.8

taxes and duties $1.1

local purchases $4.0

imported goods and equipment $8.4

and decline in inventories amounted to —$2.0

*No dividends were paid by U. F. subsidiaries in Honduras for either 1954 or 1955.

157

vast tracts of land to move to when planted current acreage became infested by Panama disease. Thus, many of the problems surrounding land acquisition and use would be solved.

As a matter of fact, a complete failure of the attempts to combat Panama disease might well lead to the adoption of variety bananas by United Fruit. The costs of opening up new banana lands under today's conditions might well force such a shift.

Impact on the Local Economy

The United Fruit Company is by far the largest enterprise operating in Honduras. In the 1951-55 period, its operations contributed an average of $35 million a year to the local economy. That was almost one-sixth of the nation's total production. (On a value-added basis, United's contribution works out to about one-tenth of national production.) To be as large relatively in the United States, General Motors would have to be more than four times its present size. The mere fact that United's operations are so big in relation to anything else in the nation raises a series of social and political questions which are discussed in later chapters. The objective here is to see how the company's contribution compares with other economic activities when measured on a common basis.

The 40,500 acres of bananas owned or under contract to the United Fruit Company amounted to 2 percent of land planted to crops in 1955. By contrast, United's contribution to the economy—the amount left in Honduras after all out-payments of dividends were deducted— came to $27.3 million in 1955. That was almost 20 percent of the estimated value of total agricultural production.[5] On an overall basis, then, United's contribution per acre was 10 times as great as the average return to the local economy from other farm activities.

The contribution per man employed by United Fruit was more than seven times the national average in other farming occupations. The company had 14,800 people on its payrolls or 2 percent of the estimated 740,000 people employed throughout the nation. Production per United Fruit employee worked out to $1,791 in 1955 as against an average of $245 for all farm workers.

While the statistics are subject to many qualifications, estimates

---

[5] This measurement (and similar ones later in this chapter) may overstate the relative contribution made by United Fruit. Estimates of the value of total farm output are probably based on prices at the farm, whereas the company's contribution is based on an adjusted export value computation.

show that United's operations account for about 8 percent of the invested capital in the nation and for about one-fourth of investment in agriculture. Therefore, output per unit of capital was only a little better than the national average, a fact that reflects the huge investment per acre involved in United's operations ($830 per acre for United compared with an average of $32 per acre in other farming). It is the huge investment made by the company that supports the high level of output per acre and per man employed.

In 1955, United's exports accounted for 35 percent of foreign exchange receipts. Tax payments were unusually low in 1955 because of the blow dealt to the company's production by a strike in 1954 and floods in 1955, but for the five years 1951-55, they amounted to almost 10 percent of central government revenues.

Every available statistical measurement shows that the United Fruit Company's operations made a substantial contribution to the Honduran economy in the five-year period covered by this study. In that period, the overall contribution averaged $35 million annually. In contrast, dividends paid out to investors in the United States averaged only $4.35 million, an 11 percent return on the book value of the United Fruit Company investment.

Stable Contribution

Experience in Honduras during the five years 1951-55 provides an excellent example of the stabilizing influence of the United Fruit Company operations. Although the company's banana exports in 1955 were only slightly more than half what they had been in normal years, primarily because of floods, United rather than the Honduran economy bore the brunt of this loss. Wage and salary payments actually increased as the company set about rehabilitating plantations. The overall contribution of the company's operations declined by one-fourth—but about half the decline was accounted for by a reduction in inventories and lower imports of fertilizers, chemicals, and other materials.

In all, a reduction in United's earnings from exports during 1955 of almost one-half from the previous good years was accompanied by a decrease in its direct payments to Honduras of only about one-eighth. In other words, U.S. investors and foreign suppliers absorbed three-fourths of the adjustment, whereas only about one-fourth had a direct impact on the local economy. This illustrates one of the major advantages of foreign investment to the host nation— risks of loss as well as actual losses are shared.

159

Chart XVIII
Sources and Uses of the United Fruit Company Contribution to the Panama Economy in 1955

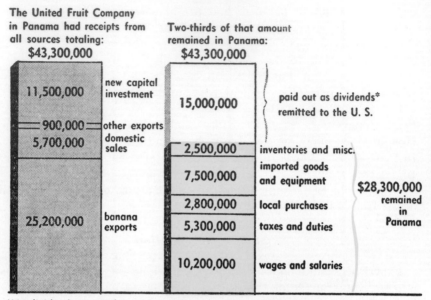

The United Fruit Company in Panama had receipts from all sources totaling: **$43,300,000**

Two-thirds of that amount remained in Panama: **$43,300,000**

11,500,000	new capital investment	15,000,000 → paid out as dividends* remitted to the U. S.
900,000	other exports	
5,700,000	domestic sales	2,500,000 — inventories and misc.
		7,500,000 — imported goods and equipment
		2,800,000 — local purchases
25,200,000	banana exports	5,300,000 — taxes and duties
		10,200,000 — wages and salaries

$28,300,000 remained in Panama

*No dividends remitted in 1954; 1955 dividends covered both 1954 and 1955 operations.

PANAMA

UNITED FRUIT OPERATES two divisions in Panama, one at Almirante on the Atlantic side and the other at Armuelles on the Pacific. In 1955, Armuelles was the company's top division—it shipped 6.6 million stems from 22,000 acres and had the lowest-cost and the best-quality bananas. It was in every way a prosperous and active division with good housing, and all buildings and grounds kept up in fine fashion. Armuelles is located in Chiriqui province, the most advanced agricultural area of the nation and one that has a thriving cattle industry.

The Bocas Division at Almirante presents a dramatic contrast. It is being rehabilitated after having been completely out of banana production from 1936 to 1953. Bocas was one of the large fruit producers early in the century, but Panama disease struck in 1911 and completely wiped out production by 1936. Some abandoned banana land was planted in cacao. In 1950, the company decided to re-establish banana production in the Bocas Division by use of flood fallow. Since rain is virtually continuous in that area, the building of dikes for flood fallow involves most difficult engineering operations in moving mud and muck under extremely unfavorable conditions. In 1955, 12,000 acres had been planted and shipments reached 1.7 million stems. The goal is 17,000 acres and 5 million stems a year. The hope was that flood-fallowed lands would produce in volume for an average of at least five years before flooding would have to be repeated. However, many farms have become infested with Panama disease in two years or less. So the future of Bocas hangs on the company's ability to combat Panama disease successfully.

Contribution to the Economy

United Fruit's overall contribution to the Panamanian economy totaled $28.3 million in 1955 and averaged $21.5 million in the 1951-55 period. The company's earnings from Armuelles were unusually high in 1955. However, the major portion of these earnings were, in effect, reinvested in the rehabilitation of Bocas. From the standpoint of the Panamanian economy, United Fruit's operations yielded more in 1955 than the company earned from exports. Thus, banana exports were valued at $25.2 million and cacao brought in another $900,000, while the company's contribution was $28.3 million.

Comparisons With Other Activities

United Fruit owns or controls a bit more than 2 percent of the nation's total agricultural land and its plantations account for 4.5 percent of all crop lands. About 4 percent of the labor force is employed by the United Fruit Company.

Unfortunately, the statistics necessary to compare the amount left in Panama by the company's operations with alternative activities are not available. A very rough estimate would place United's total contribution at about 5 percent of total economic activity in the nation. Its exports accounted for 72 percent of total export receipts in 1955, and tax payments equalled 12 percent of the central government's tax receipts. The company's income tax payment—$4.6 million in 1955—compares with the U.S. government payment of $2 million on the account of the Panama Canal. In overall terms, United's contribution to the Panamanian economy is probably 75 to 80 percent of that provided by net transactions with the Canal Zone. The company's contribution per acre planted to crops works out to $1,000 for 1955. No comparable statistics are available for local crops. However, the value of output of rice, coffee, and sugar crops in 1954 is estimated at $15 million, while cattle slaughter was valued at $6,850,000. In addition, production of local food crops might be estimated roughly at around $20 million. These very rough calculations would point to total agricultural production (excluding United's output) of around $50 million, yielding an output per acre of cropland of $80 per annum. That is less than 10 percent of the per-acre contribution of the company's operations. Using the same rough estimates, output per worker in local farming activities would come to about 20 percent of the contribution per worker on United Fruit farms.

United Fruit's Contribution to Development

Continued growth of the company's operations could make a most significant contribution to the development of the Panamanian economy. In economic terms, Panama's problem is to develop new activities in the agricultural, manufacturing, and distributive fields to provide an expanding standard of living for a growing population. Earnings accruing to the Panamanian economy from banana production can provide an important source of the foreign exchange needed to support general economic development.

GUATEMALA

THE UNITED FRUIT COMPANY enjoys the unenviable position of being by far the largest private economic entity and of contributing a major portion of foreign exchange earnings in Honduras, Costa Rica, and Panama. In Guatemala, United Fruit is also the largest private enterprise. However, its impact on foreign exchange earnings and on the economy generally is relatively smaller than in the three countries already discussed.

As in Costa Rica and Panama, United Fruit operates plantations on both coasts of Guatemala. The major operation is in the Tiquisate Division on the Pacific side where the company has 18,000 acres in bananas. In addition, the company has contracts with local producers operating 10,000 acres.

Tiquisate has several notable characteristics. It is one of the plantations where overhead irrigation is used—revolving nozzles on steel towers spray a circle covering an area of 3.3 acres. The newer plantings, however, are equipped with "under-tree" irrigation—small sprinklers placed in concrete sockets arranged to provide an even distribution of water among the group of plants served by each hose.

A second noticeable characteristic of Tiquisate, and one particularly evident from the air, is that it is pock-marked by areas that have gone out of production because of Panama disease. Unlike most other divisions, where banana plants form a smooth and level lawn when viewed from an airplane, Tiquisate is marked by patches where bananas can no longer be grown. Each of these patches is planted to corn or beans—virtually all improved land is in use. The company rents land that has gone out of bananas to its workers or to others for $1.00 per year (which is seldom, if ever, collected).

To turn to more technical considerations, banana production on the Pacific side is subject to two main hazards: First, the advance of Panama disease, while slower than in many other areas, is inexorable. In general, a farm will last about 10 years before Panama disease forces its abandonment. Flood fallow is not practical because the porous subsoil would not permit flooding for an extended period. However, the company holds enough potential banana land to maintain production by new plantings for 30 to 40 years at the current rate of advance of Panama disease.

A second hazard is that of blowdowns. In the past 10 years, the company has lost about half its potential production to the winds that sweep in from the Pacific, usually in the month of May. Even 15 minutes of moderately heavy winds suffice to blow the entire 18,000 acres flat. It is thought that present plantings are in a "wind corridor" created by air currents flowing between Guatemala's two largest volcanos. New plantings are being made in the area between present acreage and the ocean in the hope that these lands will prove to be outside the wind corridor.

Bananas grown on the Pacific side are shipped by rail some 300 miles over the volcanic highlands and down to the Atlantic at Puerto Barrios. That is by far the longest rail haul of any division. We shall return to this point in a later section.

Bananera, on the Atlantic Coast of Guatemala, was for many years one of the company's major divisions. Peak production of more than

6 million stems a year was reached about 20 years ago. Panama disease forced successive abandonments and, by 1955, exports had declined to 400,000 stems.

However, a new contract was signed with the government in December 1956 which will result in the revival of production at Bananera. The initial program calls for an investment of at least $5 million to bring 5,000 acres into production. Most of the new production will come from lands created by pump drainage. However, flood fallow will be used to rehabilitate some lands formerly planted in bananas. If the initial program is successful, it might be expanded in the future. It might be possible to build new banana acreage by silting. And success in flood fallow might make it economical to rehabilitate a larger acreage. In addition, the company was in the process at the close of 1957 of giving the government 110,000 acres of land on the Atlantic side for use in a resettlement program.

Contract Operations

In 1955, the company was purchasing bananas from independent operators who had 10,700 acres in bananas. As in other areas, United provides sigatoka control and other services and buys acceptable banana stems at a fixed price. About 10,000 acres consist of land on which bananas are being grown as shade for new coffee trees. However, the inroads of Panama disease have been reducing the amount of contract production near Tiquisate.

Standard Fruit has a substantial contract-purchasing operation in the area around Retalhuleu (north of Tiquisate on the Pacific Coast). In 1955, Standard exported 400,000 stems. However, reports are that Standard hopes to have 10,000 acres under contract by 1960 (as compared with 6,200 in 1955). The usual contract obligates the Standard Fruit Company to provide spray, technical and financial assistance, and to buy acceptable bananas at stipulated prices, and the farmers must sell exclusively to the company. Thus, the terms are comparable to those in United Fruit contracts with independents.

Land-Use Problems

Experience in Guatemala emphasizes in dramatic fashion some of the points made earlier about the importance of making the most effective use of abandoned banana lands. United Fruit donated to the government a large tract of almost 100,000 acres on the Pacific side (of which about 10,000 acres consisted of good banana land) to support the government's resettlement program. Most of this was un-cleared land and Point 4 experts estimated that it would cost around $150 per acre to clear the land and provide the necessary roads and other facilities to move farmers onto the land. In addition, each farmer was expected to take on credits of $1,000 to $1,500 to cover the cost of seed, equipment, and other expenses of starting operations. In all, the investment per acre was estimated at $800 to $1,000.

An investment of this magnitude represents a considerable drain on the supply of investment funds in Guatemala. When you consider the fact that the program calls for the establishment of 1,200 families in the resettlement area, it is clear that the effort involved, while most commendable, can make no more than a small dent in the problem of agricultural development in the nation as a whole. And it seems equally clear that every effort should be made to make the most effective use of any abandoned banana acreage, in Guatemala or else-where, to avoid the heavy capital costs of opening up new and un-cultivated areas.

International Railways of Central America

United Fruit's relationships with the International Railways of Central America (popularly known as IRCA) constitute a major— and perhaps *the* major—source of irritation surrounding the company's operations in Guatemala. In view of the considerable publicity these relationships have received, not only in Guatemala but also in the United States (as a result of a minority stockholders' action in the U.S. courts), it may be useful to set forth our findings about IRCA. In an important sense, the developments over the years provide an interesting case study of some of the problems encountered by a large foreign company in carrying out its business.

Without going into the complete history, the origins of IRCA can be sketched this way. Set up, largely with British capital, IRCA was a part of Minor Keith's ambitious plan to develop a railway net-work covering all of Central America. By the early 1930's, IRCA's rail lines extended from Puerto Barrios on the Atlantic Coast over the central mountain ranges to the Pacific plain, and a connecting line ran into El Salvador. At the time, the nation was better served by rail than any of the neighboring Central American nations.

In 1933, however, the IRCA was virtually bankrupt. It had several million dollars in obligations coming due in the near future and no liquid funds available to buy new equipment. Moreover, the contract signed between the government and United Fruit to establish banana plantations at Tiquisate included a provision obligating the United Fruit Company to build a port on the Pacific Coast. No satisfactory port existed, and IRCA derived a major portion of its gross revenues and an even higher proportion of its net revenues on the long-haul business it received from transporting coffee and other products from the Pacific side to the nation's major trade outlet at Puerto Barrios on the Atlantic. Construction of a Pacific port would have led to bankruptcy and subsequent deterioration of the IRCA. A Pacific port would have benefited shippers on the Pacific side (though not as much as might be thought off-hand, because ocean freight rates are so set as to equalize the total cost to the Guatemalan exporter of rail and ocean shipments via either coast). On the other hand, deterioration of railway service would have handicapped the rest of the nation.

In this situation, IRCA officials had no recourse other than attempting to induce United Fruit to ship bananas from Tiquisate over the 300-mile run to Barrios. They demonstrated that such a long haul was feasible and economical. United Fruit then undertook the task of saving IRCA from bankruptcy and probably ruin by providing financial aid and by getting the government to release the company from the obligation to build a Pacific port. Governmental approval was secured. In 1936, United Fruit put up $2.6 million to pay off IRCA's obligations in return for a 3.5 percent note for $1.75 million plus 186,000 shares of common stock. That stock acquisition, plus the 17 percent which United held before 1936, gave the company 42.6 percent of the stock in IRCA.

The United Fruit Company has also invested $5 million in banana cars and locomotives (or much more than the cost of a Pacific port) to supply a major part of the rolling stock available to the railway. These cars and locomotives are used by IRCA to haul other cargo when they are not transporting United's cargo. Banana haulage accounted for only 9 percent of IRCA gross revenue in 1955 (the peak postwar ratio was 13 percent in 1953), so that United's equipment is used much of the time to transport coffee and other cargo.

Under the 1936 agreements, United Fruit handles the spotting of cars and the pickup and makeup of trains on its own rail lines. Completed trains are delivered to IRCA at Tiquisate. United agreed to pay $60 per car of bananas moved over IRCA lines to Puerto Barrios; the rate has been increased in later years to $90. United receives rentals from IRCA equal to 4 percent of the book value of railway equipment (5 percent on diesel locomotives). These rentals are less than half the cost to IRCA of financing equipment purchases on its own.

And, in fact, the inherent risks of banana haulage might make it hard for IRCA to get financing without a firm agreement with United Fruit.

Consequently, it would appear that the 1936 agreement was a lifesaver for IRCA. It may also have been beneficial to the Guatemalan economy by helping to keep in being a railway artery that served to move both imports and exports at lower cost than in neighboring nations, and at a lower overall cost than would have resulted if a Pacific port had been established.

Nevertheless, the arrangement was bound to create misunderstanding and doubts on the part of the public. It set up a special arrangement for United's bananas, with the company paying $60 per banana car moved while competitors paid $130. A part of the differential could be justified by the fact that the rental paid by IRCA for company-owned equipment was lower than conditions would have justified. Moreover, the company spotted the cars and assembled complete trains for IRCA to haul, whereas service to competitors involved much shunting about of freight cars and assembly of individual banana cars into trains. The determination as to whether the spread in the rates charged United and those charged competitors was justified by cost differentials is a most complex and technical task.

However, even if it were completely justified, the special arrangements made for United's bananas was certain to arouse public suspicion and create misunderstanding. It would have been far better public relations to have set a uniform rate for all bananas and adjusted IRCA rental payments to cover the full cost of the use of United's equipment. The company's investment in IRCA has been a major handicap in its dealings with the government and in its reputation with the general public. Every time a train is late, or a rate raised, or a passenger train shunted to a siding to let a banana train by, the public blames United Fruit. There is a widely held belief that rates are far too high and that the railroad yields huge profits. Actually, rates averaged 5.11¢ per revenue ton-mile in 1955, lower than rates in neighboring nations, and IRCA's net earnings averaged nine-tenths of 1 percent of its invested capital in the 1951-55 period. Yet the belief IRCA does not serve the national interest persists.

With the benefit of hindsight, it would seem that the company should have sold its interest in IRCA years ago. In addition to the continuing criticism emanating from Guatemalan sources, the position of United as both an important stockholder and customer of IRCA has been attacked by other minority stockholders of the railroad as prejudicial to their interests. (A group of minority stockholders, virtually all of whom are U.S. citizens, are suing on grounds that the amount charged on United Fruit bananas was unjustifiably low. A Referee appointed by the New York State Courts has handed down a $5.5 million judgment in their favor which the company has stated it will appeal.) Meantime, Guatemala is building a new highway system which will parallel IRCA. Over the long run, the growth in the national economy may provide enough traffic to enable the railway to secure an adequate volume of traffic. The immediate effect, however, will be to take traffic away from the railroad. Thus, it may be difficult for the company to dispose of its holdings in IRCA.

Contribution to the Economy

United Fruit owns or controls less than 2 percent of Guatemala's land area. Acreage actually in use by the company or its

Chart XIX
Sources and Uses of the United Fruit Company Contribution to the Guatemala Economy in 1955

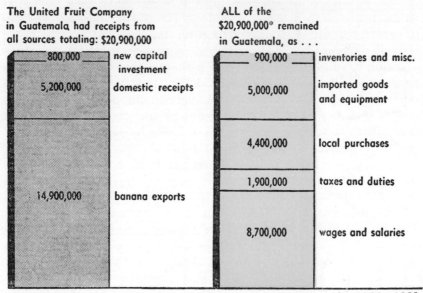

The United Fruit Company in Guatemala had receipts from all sources totaling: $20,900,000

800,000	new capital investment
5,200,000	domestic receipts
14,900,000	banana exports

ALL of the $20,900,000* remained in Guatemala, as . . .

900,000	inventories and misc.
5,000,000	imported goods and equipment
4,400,000	local purchases
1,900,000	taxes and duties
8,700,000	wages and salaries

*No dividends were paid by U. F. subsidiaries in Guatemala for either 1954 or 1955.

168

contractors amounts to slightly less than 1 percent of total agricultural land. The company's total contribution to the economy, including its purchased fruit, amounted to $20.9 million in 1955, a figure that was about 5 percent above the average contribution in the five years 1951-55. Total agricultural output was estimated at $200 million in 1955. Thus, United Fruit's contribution equalled 10 percent of the total—or 10 times as much per acre as the national average.

As compared with coffee, the nation's largest crop, United's contribution per acre is three times output per acre in coffee. Output per man-day worked on United's plantations was two to three times the average on coffee farms. The average daily wage on coffee farms was $1.10 to $1.25 as against $2.25 to $2.60 on United Fruit farms. Investment per acre (at today's prices) would run to $275 to $390 for coffee as compared with $1,200 to $1,500 for United's bananas.

The company's exports contributed $14.9 million to foreign exchange receipts, or almost 14 percent of the total. It paid $1,860,000 in taxes, 2 percent of total government revenues and 2.5 percent of central government revenues. In general, therefore, United's operations have made a substantial contribution to the Guatemalan economy. The amount of money remaining in the nation as a result of the company's operations is substantially greater than the economic contributions made by comparable local activities.

ECUADOR

IN THE PAST DECADE, Ecuador has experienced a phenomenal growth in banana production. In 1947, exports amounted to about 2.7 million stems and bananas were a minor factor in the local economy. Then the government started building roads from the central highlands down into the fertile coastal plains. At that time, sigatoka was not a problem in Ecuador. Thus, bananas could be planted in the exceptionally fertile tropical lands merely by cutting away the jungle, and grown at costs per stem far below the costs in Central America where extensive disease control and irrigation systems had to be installed. Bananas offered the ideal cash crop to support the opening up of Ecuador's coastal plain.

By 1955, there were an estimated 284,000 acres planted to bananas on more than 40,000 farms. That is more than twice the entire acreage United Fruit had in bananas in all its divisions throughout Central and South America. Ecuador exported 23.9 million stems in 1955 —almost nine times the total exported in 1947. Bananas accounted for almost three-fifths of the nation's exports and were three times as important as coffee, which up to that time had been the leading export.

Thus, the development of banana production has provided major support to the nation's economic development in recent years. Cropland in cultivation has been increased by more than 10 percent and the basic facilities for further agricultural development in the lowlands have been installed. Export earnings from bananas have given the nation the growth in import potential needed to support general development. Finally, and this may prove to be the most significant fact, the banana boom has opened up Ecuador's Pacific Coast frontier by demonstrating that the nation's greatest asset lies in these fertile lowlands that can produce crops in competition with any other tropical area.

United Fruit Share

United Fruit has played a minor role in this development. The company began to produce fruit in Ecuador in the mid-1930's when it set up a small division at Tenguel. Production rose from 234,000 stems at the end of World War II to 1,284,000 in 1955. In 1955, United's production amounted to only 2 percent of the national total, and exports of company-produced fruit amounted to somewhat more than 5 percent of total banana exports.

In addition to exporting its own fruit, United has been buying bananas from independent producers on the open market. In so doing, it has been one of 25 to 26 exporters, of whom five could be classed as major exporters. Several of these exporters operate sizable plantations. Under marketing practices prevailing in 1955, exporters bought bananas in three ways: (1) The exporter's agent bought bananas ready for shipment at the farm; (2) an independent buyer bought small quantities of bananas from a large number of small farms and usually arranged for shipment to the port where they were sold at shipside; and (3) the exporter bought at shipside bananas which farmers had transported to that point. During 1955, the company purchased 3.8 million stems in the Ecuadorian market. Thus, its total exports amounted to 5.1 million stems or just over one-fifth of the nation's banana exports.

In other words, United Fruit has been a relatively small factor in the Ecuadorian banana industry. In contrast to the situation in Central America or Panama, the company's major business has consisted of purchasing bananas from independent producers in the open market and exporting them to the North American market. Because of the manner in which volume banana production developed in Ecuador, it was in 1955 the only major exporting area where sizable quantities of bananas could be purchased on the open market. The United Fruit Company has operated as just another exporter, although it has been one of the larger exporters.

Problems of Ecuadorian Producers

So long as bananas could be grown easily and cheaply in Ecuador and so long as the world market would absorb increased supplies at good prices, the Ecuadorian banana industry prospered. The extensive blowdowns and floods in Central America in 1954 and early 1955 made it possible to market increasing quantities of Ecuadorian bananas. However, experience during 1955 placed in sharp focus the problems the nation would have to cope with in continuing development of the banana industry. These problems might well be summed up under three headings: production, quality, and marketing.

The production problems are a result of the spread of sigatoka through vast areas of Ecuador in 1955. It seems clear that farmers will have to adopt control measures if they are to produce marketable bananas. This will increase costs and may well rule out production by the very small farmers who cannot afford the outlays for disease control and by farmers operating hilly lands where disease control would be too costly.

Efforts to control sigatoka by use of oil spray have apparently met with success. This method uses only a fraction of the gallonage per acre applied in Central America in the form of Bordeaux mixture. Oil spray can be applied by mobile units drawn by tractors or by airplane and helicopter. Thus, it is possible that the cost of sigatoka control will be significantly lower than present costs in Central America. (This may result in part from the fact that the disease seems to be less virulent in Ecuador—it has not yet become a problem in the Tenguel area.)

However, the advent of sigatoka plus the fact that Panama disease is present should emphasize the importance of high productivity per acre. To stand the cost of disease control, including the amortization of the investment over the period before Panama disease hits, output per acre will have to be increased.

As delivered in world consuming markets, Ecuadorian bananas are frequently inferior in quality to those from other areas. The primary quality problem is one of handling. In contrast to the tender care with which bananas are handled in Central America, most Ecuadorian bananas are piled high on a truck, bounced over unimproved roads often for 30 to 40 miles to the port, loaded on a lighter and then transferred to a ship's hold in an open harbor. Bananas grown in the Esmeraldas region are loaded on rubber rafts and floated down the Esmeraldas River through a series of rapids. In the process of handling throughout Ecuador, bananas are bruised and scraped. The problem is intensified in periods when volcanic dust, which is peculiarly abrasive, blows down from the highlands and falls on banana areas.

As was explained earlier, one of the characteristics of the banana is that the effects of rough handling are seldom apparent until the banana ripens. Fruit that looks perfectly good in its green state in Ecuador is decidedly inferior when it reaches the grocery shelf in the United States. Compared with fruit from Central America, Ecuadorian bananas after ripening show black spots, black streaks and areas, and present a generally unattractive appearance. In many cases, the pulp of the banana is not affected by surface defects. However, the housewife has no way to distinguish between surface blemishes that are no more than skin-deep and those which indicate serious damage. Thus, Ecuadorian bananas will not sell well even at lower prices if plentiful supplies of high-quality fruit are available. Even in periods when supplies of high-quality fruit are relatively short, banana jobbers and retailers will take Ecuadorian fruit only at lower prices.

In addition, Ecuadorian bananas are inferior in size and quality during the dry season since few farms are equipped with irrigation. As farmers take steps to increase production per acre, many of them may turn to irrigation, a step that will also maintain the quality of produced fruit during the dry season.

The major measures that are called for involve the education of everyone concerned in the importance of careful handling of fruit at every stage. Much could be done by relatively simple and low-cost measures to stress the need for care in every step of transportation from cutting to market. The simple act of washing the fruit after cutting, which will be essential for sprayed fruit, might yield a marked improvement in quality. However, surfaced roads may well prove necessary to reduce damage during the journey from farms to ports. A loan from the International Bank for Reconstruction and Development of $14.5 million negotiated in October 1957 will help improve the road system.

Steps to improve the quality of Ecuadorian fruit as it reaches consuming markets would go far to solve the nation's marketing problems. There is no reason why high-quality fruit from Ecuador would

Chart XX

Sources and Uses of the
United Fruit Company Contribution
to the Ecuador Economy in 1955

The United Fruit Company
in Ecuador had receipts from
all sources totaling $15,600,000:

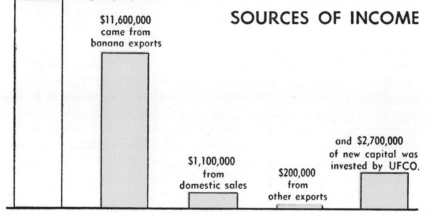

$11,600,000
came from
banana exports

SOURCES OF INCOME

and $2,700,000
of new capital was
invested by UFCO.

$1,100,000
from
domestic sales

$200,000
from
other exports

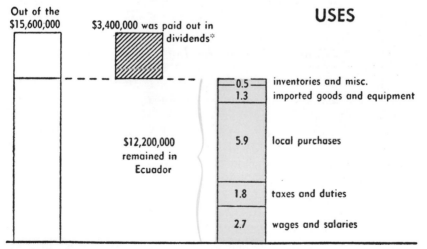

Out of the
$15,600,000

$3,400,000 was paid out in
dividends*

USES

$12,200,000
remained in
Ecuador

0.5	inventories and misc.
1.3	imported goods and equipment
5.9	local purchases
1.8	taxes and duties
2.7	wages and salaries

*No dividends remitted in 1954; 1955 dividends covered both
1954 and 1955 operations.

not sell on a competitive basis in world markets. Emphasis on quality would help lift Ecuador from its present position as the residual supplier in the world market in the sense that Ecuadorian bananas move readily to market only when floods or blowdowns cut production in other areas.

However, marketing procedures within Ecuador may need to be altered before the problems of producing high-quality bananas can be solved. At present the producer assumes the major share of the marketing risk. The price he gets for his bananas depends on the state of the market when he has to sell his fruit. It may be difficult for small or medium-sized producers to finance the costs of measures to control sigatoka and improve fruit handling if they must face the full hazards of the market.

One possible solution would be to work out a marketing pattern along lines developed in Central America and Colombia. The exporter signs a contract with the local producer under which the exporter is obligated to supply disease control, technical assistance, and often financial help, and in return agrees to buy all acceptable bananas at a price fixed once a year (arrangements can also be included to provide a bonus to the grower if market prices rise above specified levels or to reduce the base price if market conditions worsen).

Such a system would help stabilize the Ecuadorian banana industry and would encourage investment to improve the quality of the fruit. It would raise certain problems—small farmers, particularly those in inaccessible locations, could not be brought into a contract system; and production would probably be feasible only in a few of the areas presently in bananas.

Contribution to the Local Economy

United Fruit's cultivated land equaled less than one-half of 1 percent of the nation's total cropland in 1955; its acreage in bananas represented less than 2.5 percent of the national total. The company's contribution to the local economy in 1955 ($12.2 million) equaled about 3.5 percent of the nation's total agricultural production. The return to the local economy per acre of United's cultivated land was four times the national average per acre, and United's banana acreage yielded a return of 34 percent greater than the per acre results from other banana plantings. Moreover, the return to Ecuador per acre of United's banana lands was slightly greater than that from coffee acreage and 75 percent higher than the average acreage in cacao.

United Fruit sales, of company-produced and purchased bananas combined, accounted for 10 percent of the value of Ecuador's total banana production and for 19 percent of its banana exports in 1955. United Fruit exports brought in 9.5 percent of total export receipts from all products. The company had 3,000 workers on its payroll, or two-fifths of 1 percent of the total working in agriculture. The contribution to the local economy per worker was three to four times the output per worker on farms for Ecuador as a whole. United's tax payments amounted to 2 percent of central government receipts in 1955. In contrast, its operations accounted for only seven-tenths of 1 percent of national income, so its tax payments were three times its relative economic weight.

COLOMBIA

THE COLOMBIAN OPERATIONS of United Fruit differ from those in other nations in several notable ways: First, the company's operations are smaller in relation to the total economy than in any of the nations studied in this report. It owns or controls less than a twenty-fifth of 1 percent of all agricultural land and slightly less than 18 percent of all banana-producing land. Its contribution in 1955 amounted to just over 1 percent of the value of all crops produced in Colombia. Second, over 70 percent of the bananas exported in 1955 were purchased from local producers under a contract arrangement that makes the local farmers partners with the company. Third, two local cooperatives compete with United Fruit in purchasing and exporting bananas grown by local farmers. Fourth, Panama disease has never appeared in the area where the company operates for reasons that as yet baffle the scientists. And, finally, the railway over which the company ships fruit has been owned by the government since 1932 and operated by the government since 1947. In a number of farms, trucks moving over black-top roads are used to haul bananas to the main rail lines.

Brief History

The United Fruit Company exported both its own and purchased fruit from Colombia from 1900 to 1942. The wartime shipping shortage forced the virtual abandonment of the company's banana production, and United exported no bananas in the five years 1943-47. The management of United Fruit Company was reluctant to resume operations in Colombia after World War II. Prewar experience had been marred by considerable controversy over payments to local producers, as well as over operations of the Santa Marta Railroad and the docks at Santa Marta.

However, a new contract was worked out with the Colombian government in 1947 which established a new and unique pattern of operations. Under this contract, the company agreed to offer purchase contracts to local farmers and provide sigatoka control and other assistance to them. Purchase contracts obligate the company to take all acceptable fruit at prices mutually agreed upon, to provide disease control and other services, and to handle the marketing of bananas. In addition, the company provides the financing necessary to set local farmers up in banana production and to carry them when their banana crops are destroyed by blowdowns (the major hazard) or other causes. The company also gave up its management contract over the railroad and ceded the wharf at Santa Marta to the government to facilitate construction of a new government wharf.

The Colombian pattern of operations offers a number of important advantages both to the company and to the local economy. The company gets an assured supply of quality fruit with a minimum investment of its own funds. It escapes many of the risks and responsibilities of operating farms and from the responsibilities of operating a railway and a port. The cost of purchased fruit is comparable with that of fruit grown on farms owned and operated by the company.

From the point of view of the local farmer, a contract with the company offers definite advantages. The disease control and technical assistance provided by the company are important in increasing yields and thus earnings. While the company provides an assured market for quality fruit at reasonable prices, the farmer has the option of shifting to one of the two local cooperative marketing agencies if he is dissatisfied with his United Fruit contract. Moreover, the company shares part of the risks both of marketing and of production in that it buys at a fixed annual price and makes loans to rehabilitate farms hit by blowdowns.

During 1955, United Fruit contracted with 225 local farmers operating 12,900 acres of mature banana plantings and producing 3.6 million stems. On the average, local farmers received $260 per acre in gross revenues during 1955 (with United handling disease control, fertilizer and transportation). That was at least 50 percent higher than the average gross return on coffee land where local producers bore all costs.

Chart XXI

Sources and Uses of the United Fruit Company Contribution to the Colombia Economy in 1955

The United Fruit Company in Colombia had receipts from all sources totaling:

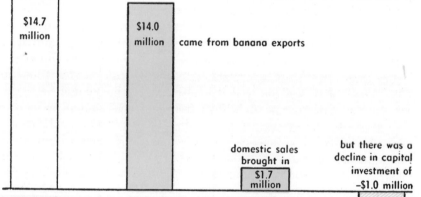

SOURCES OF INCOME

$14.7 million

$14.0 million came from banana exports

domestic sales brought in $1.7 million

but there was a decline in capital investment of −$1.0 million

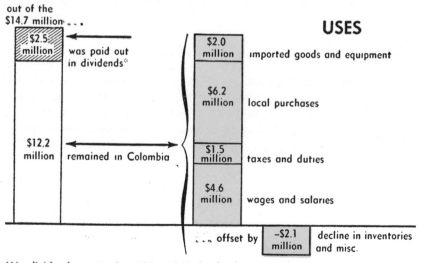

out of the $14.7 million...

USES

$2.5 million was paid out in dividends*

$12.2 million remained in Colombia

$2.0 million imported goods and equipment

$6.2 million local purchases

$1.5 million taxes and duties

$4.6 million wages and salaries

... offset by −$2.1 million decline in inventories and misc.

*No dividends remitted in 1954; 1955 dividends covered both 1954 and 1955 operations.

Possible Future Pattern

Many of United Fruit's present and future problems in other nations might well be mitigated if the general type of contract arrangement with local farmers developed in Colombia could be extended to other areas. Ecuador is an obvious example of an area where the contract system might be extended to the mutual benefit of the company and local producers. In other producing nations, it may prove more difficult to develop a partnership arrangement with local farmers. For one thing, the technical and financial requirements for flood fallow may make contract arrangements impractical.

Nevertheless, the merits of the Colombia contract system are so striking that it would seem that every effort should be exerted to extend it to other producing areas where conditions permit. Obviously, United could not shift overnight into a full-scale contract operation. Yet it may well be that a long-run objective should be to encourage the maximum possible shift from growing bananas on its own plantations to the system of purchasing bananas from local farmers under mutually advantageous contracts. As the nations within which the company operates develop, the opportunities for such arrangements should expand. By adopting a positive policy of encouraging local farmers to grow bananas, United might secure on a broader basis the sort of benefits it now enjoys in Colombia. At the same time, the local economies would benefit by the resulting strengthening in their agricultural base.

Contribution to the Local Economy

Since United owns or controls less than a twenty-fifth of 1 percent of all agricultural land and less than 18 percent of all banana-producing lands, its contribution is bound to be small in relation to the total economy of Colombia. Nevertheless, comparisons with other activities show that United's operations yield real benefits to the nation. Here is how some of the comparatives line up:

1. Output per acre on land owned and controlled by United Fruit is several times the average for the nation as a whole. Value added per acre of United's bananas is more than 3.5 times as great as the average for all cropland and more than 2.5 times the average per coffee acre.

2. Gross return to Colombia from United Fruit operations in 1955 ($12.2 million) works out to $430 per acre as compared with an

average return of $135 per acre for all land planted to crops in Colombia.

3. Value added per United Fruit worker was 2.5 times as great as for all agriculture and 1.5 times that in coffee.

4. United Fruit exports brought in slightly more than 2 percent of the nation's total export earnings and almost three-fifths of foreign exchange receipts from bananas. Each acre of United Fruit or contract bananas produced $700 of foreign exchange as against $288 per acre coffee land.

5. In 1954, when United Fruit tax payments were unusually high, they accounted for three-tenths of 1 percent of total government revenues, or somewhat more than United's contribution of two-tenths of 1 percent to Colombia's national income.

6. Comprehensive statistics on the relative return to people employed on banana farms and those employed elsewhere are not available. In 1955, the average worker employed by United Fruit on a daily wage basis earned $800 per year (the daily rate ranged from $1.60 for unskilled labor to $8.00 for machine operators; if you assume 300 days a year, the average is $2.66 per day). In addition, United paid social benefits which amounted to one and one-third times daily wage payments on the average (not including housing and schools):

	Percent of daily wage
Sunday time	12.92
Holiday time	6.51
Sick time	3.05
Accident time	3.05
Vacation	5.74
Medical treatment	30.30
Ration card[a]	46.60
Shoes and overalls	0.007
Yearly bonus	11.50
Severance pay	11.50
	131.177

[a] Basic food items, sold at frozen prices and below wholesale cost, are as follows: beans (red and white), coffee, flour, lard, onions, potatoes, rice, sugar, spaghetti.

For comparison, the average daily wage on coffee farms ran to $1.70 in 1955. "Usual wages without board" for farm workers are reported to have ranged from 80¢ to $2.00 per day in the 12 Departments for which statistics are available, with nine of the Departments averaging $1.60 per day or less. While comparable figures are not available, it seems reasonably clear that United workers are receiving in wage payments and social benefits double or more the amount received by other agricultural workers.

In summary, the comparative figures support the conclusion that United Fruit's operations make a contribution to the Colombian economy substantially greater than that provided by most local activities. While the company's contribution is relatively small in relation to the total economy of Colombia, it makes a contribution in providing some small diversification in export earnings, and it makes a very considerable contribution to the economy of the province in which it operates. Consequently, it would seem clear that the returns to Colombia from United Fruit's operations are sufficiently great to make it definitely in the national interest to provide continued hospitality to the company.

In Summary

A BRIEF PICTURE of the United Fruit Company contributions to the six nations studied is presented in Table 20. Because of lack of precision in the data, the comparative figures shown are rounded. However, data difficulties are not sufficiently great to vitiate the general conclusion that United's contribution in every nation is substantially greater per acre or per man employed than in agriculture generally.

On a per acre basis, the company's contribution is from two to 12 times the national average in farming. On the basis of per person employed, the company's contribution ranges from two to nine times the local average in farming. Even when measured against export crops, United's contribution per acre ranges from one and three-quarters to five and one-half times that from coffee or cacao or other locally financed export crops.

United Fruit's tax payments are substantially greater as a percentage of government receipts than the company's share in national income, except in the case of Guatemala. And, in view of the fact that virtually all United's land was created from swamp and jungle, its tax payments (which amount to more than 10 percent of government revenues in two of the nations) clearly represent a net gain to the local economies.

Table 20 | Summary of Comparative Measures of United Fruit Company Contributions to Local Economies, 1955

Country	UFCO 1955 banana shipments (million stems)	Contribution by UFCO ($ million)	% of total export receipts	% of cropland owned by or contracted to UFCO	UFCO contribution as % of total agricultural production [a]
Costa Rica.......	6.9	42.0	44	10	20
Honduras........	4.4	27.3	35	2	20
Panama........	8.3	28.3	72	4	30–35
Guatemala......	4.3	20.9	14	1	10
Ecuador........	5.1	12.2	10	.5	3.5
Colombia.......	5.1	12.2	2	.3	1

Country	UFCO contribution per acre as % of national average for all crops and specific local crops [a]	Contribution per worker employed by UFCO as % of average output per farm worker [a]	UFCO tax payments as % of government revenues	UFCO value added as % of national income
Costa Rica........	500 550 (cacao)	200–250	15	8
Honduras.........	1,000 (coffee)	700		
Panama..........	300 (coffee) 1,250	500	4	6
Guatemala.......	1,000		12	6
Ecuador........	250 (coffee) 200	950	2	2
Colombia.......	175 (cacao) 350 250 (coffee)	400 250	2 .2	1 .2

[a] United Fruit contribution is based on export values whereas agricultural production is based on farm costs.

181

Consequently, this summary shows that the company's operations in each of the nations studied measure up to the criteria set forth in the opening section of this chapter. There we stated that for continued hospitality towards foreign investment it must be demonstrated that the foreign investment makes a contribution to the host country's economy that would not otherwise be realized and that compares favorably with that of locally financed activities. The United Fruit Company operations meet these tests fully.

VII.

The Company's Record in Social Welfare

MANY FACTS AND PROBLEMS of a human and social nature that are part and parcel of the banana business usually are not encountered by large companies operating in the United States. Some of these problems arise from facts which have been previously noted.

All of the banana production is carried on in foreign countries and the plantations are usually located in areas that were previously undeveloped and in many cases practically uninhabited. The working force, recruited from local populations, naturally has a somewhat different background than it would have if composed of North Americans. In most of the regions where plantations have been established there were at the start none of the public and private services that in more settled areas are usually provided by the local community, the state, or local private enterprises. Among these are housing, health, education, recreation, places for religious worship, retail merchandising, transportation, and communication. The United Fruit Company has consequently found that provision for the needs of its workers was a part of its obligations. As a result, its overall production program includes many activities and organizational features that have nothing directly or technically to do with the production and shipping of bananas *per se*.

Another set of problems arises from the fact that the company, as a large and integrated enterprise, operates in a number of relatively small sovereign nations. Its program, therefore, not only must be equipped to deal with governments and official agencies, but must be sufficiently flexible to adjust to the varied shades of national public opinion of the several jurisdictions.

It is true that for various reasons, mainly legal, the United Fruit Company carries on its business through a series of subsidiaries operating in the respective countries, but these are known to be controlled by the central organization. In informed and responsible Latin American circles it is also understood that such control and integration of activities is required by the nature of large-scale banana production. The fact that this aspect of the business is not always appreciated in certain sectors of "public opinion" creates a number of problems.

183

Here we briefly review some aspects of the United Fruit program that are oriented toward some of these human and social problems.

HOUSING

ACCORDING TO COMPANY SOURCES, about 60,000 persons were in the United Fruit work force in the six countries here considered in 1956. Free housing is furnished workers and, in most cases, to their immediate families or other dependents who live with them. Several designs are used in workers' housing on the company plantations. For the past several years, a program has been moving forward for the eventual replacement of the older types of labor housing with one-family and two-family dwellings. On those farms and divisions where the latter types of structures have been placed in use, there has been a significant increase in worker morale and sense of community responsibility. Again, according to company sources, the newer type of single-family dwelling units now being built by United cost from $1,500 to $2,000 each. On this basis, new housing for the present work force would require a replacement investment of from $90 to $120 million.

The older standard type of workers' dwelling units on the farms may be described in the following general terms. As previously mentioned, each producing division is divided into a number of farms. On each farm is a "camp" where the work force is housed. The camp usually consists of four lines of barracks *(barracones)*, one on each side of a large and open grass rectangle laid out as a soccer football field. A barracks is a multiple-unit building constructed of sawn lumber, usually painted light gray, and raised on stilts about 12 feet above the ground surface.

In the majority of barracks, the contained dwelling units are occupied by single families, although in some camps one building is reserved for bachelors. Generally speaking, a family has two rooms upstairs, plus a kitchen and wash place to the rear on the ground surface. The ground under the living rooms usually is paved with cement and often the individual families screen this off into separate units that provide each with a third room or lounging place. Toilet and bathing facilities are provided in a separate common building usually located at the rear of each barracks. The roofs of the buildings are usually of corrugated galvanized iron or composition material and are watertight, an important consideration in the tropics.

In the basic plan, a macadam road runs around the outer borders of the central field and in front of the barracks. Often there is a cement sidewalk on the barracks side of the road, and in front of each dwelling unit a small plot that may be planted to flowers. In the older types of barracks, there is no electric light and no running water in the kitchens. Light is furnished by kerosene lamps or candles and water is obtained from a central outside faucet serving a single barracks or several dwelling units. Even the older constructions, however, are systematically sprayed with DDT, which effectively eliminates both the danger and the annoyance of mosquitoes and other insects. The older type of stove is of native pattern, consisting of a wooden platform covered with a thick layer of clay on which a small wood or charcoal fire may be built.

Improved barracks-type design includes electric lights, a water tap and sink in the individual kitchens, screening of one or more of the dwelling rooms, and toilet-bath houses provided with flush latrines and showers. In some camps, there are separate wash houses where the women may do laundry. In all camps, the water supplied to the taps is safe for drinking.

There are many small variations on the basic barracks plan. The most striking is at Sevilla, Colombia, where, because of the good vertical drainage, the barracks are built of brick and on the ground rather than on stilts. Most family units are painted a distinctive color to set them off from their neighbors and the occupants have planted small gardens around the doorsteps.

Present plans calling for the eventual replacement of the barracks-type dwelling with single-family and double-family houses have two basic designs. One is called the "airplane type" because of its appearance from above. It is a two-family dwelling on stilts with a common roofed stairway leading down to the kitchen in back. Each of the dwelling's units has two rooms upstairs, and the space underneath may be walled in to make another room. Each also has its own toilet and shower, and there is a water faucet in the kitchen. It is reported that the workers and their families rapidly learn to take care of the private toilets and that these facilities need less service personnel than the older public facilities of the barracks.

The newest type of worker's house is called "Guatemala type," "T-type," or "breezeway." It is a single-family dwelling built on the ground rather than on stilts, with a cement floor. The living quarters in front are connected by a roofed breezeway to a smaller structure in back containing a kitchen and a small private bath and toilet room.

185

A small fenced garden space is provided at the side. At the Tiquisate division in Guatemala these houses are prefabricated in central shops. One can be erected in about seven and one-half hours and, in 1956, they were being put up at the rate of about one a day. The Sevilla, Colombia, one-family and two-family houses not only are constructed of brick, but are of somewhat different plan, with cement floors and gabled, corrugated, and composition roofs.

Whatever the type of dwelling, the cost of fuel is usually paid by the occupant. During the past few years, the company has made available, at cost or less, small efficient kerosene cooking stoves, and these are rapidly replacing the older wooden-platform kitchen stoves. Maintenance of buildings and grounds is provided at company expense. A sanitary squad regularly cleans up the grounds, collects trash, and scrubs out public toilets and bathing facilities.

Usually a number of other buildings are associated with each camp. Outside the rectangle of the workers' dwellings are located the houses of the supervisory personnel. These are usually single-family structures surrounded by a fenced-in yard. Many camps have a commissary store and a school house. If neither of these is present in a given camp, one will be found at another camp within no more than two to three kilometers' distance. Many camp communities have a workers' club house, for which the company provides the building. And all have some provision for showing movies at least once a week, either in the open air, in the space under the raised barracks buildings, or in the club, school house, or some other roofed space. A dispensary is present, or one is located at some other camp a short distance away. A camp settlement may also include other types of nondwelling buildings, such as sheds and garages for machinery and vehicles, a pumping station, a railroad siding and loading platform, and so on.

The basic patterns of housing sketched above are also provided to workers living in division headquarters and other larger settlements. Although in such centers the dwellings may not always be laid out around a rectangular football field, the basic planning provides easily accessible and large open spaces in all settlements. Nowhere are the workers' dwellings crowded into block after block of solidly built structures, such as are characteristic of many workers' neighborhoods in Latin American cities.

Those familiar with living conditions of workers in the six countries involved would need no elaborate statistical survey to satisfy themselves that the standard set and maintained by the United Fruit Company is, in material aspects at least, definitely higher than that generally available to native workers outside the company installations. And the company standards are constantly rising. One problem, community development and morale, is recognized and will be discussed later.

It was stated earlier that the vast majority of all United Fruit workers in the producing divisions are provided with free housing. A few exceptions should be noted to complete the record. In some of the shipping ports, which are independent local communities, a portion of the labor force, such as stevedores, live in private housing not provided by the company. At various points along the north coast of Honduras are groups of so-called Black Carib Indians who work at least occasionally or periodically for the company but who, while doing so, commute from the independent villages in which they live.

The housing of clerical, supervisory, and executive personnel is equal, in most cases superior, to that available to persons of similar income status in the United States. Except for single persons in lower grade positions, who are usually provided with club-like dormitories, such employees are generally furnished single-family houses surrounded by private yards or grounds. The quality and size of the accommodations rise with the employees' rank in the hierarchy, and this pattern, of course, serves as an incentive for acceptable work and promotion. The dwelling, its basic furniture, its maintenance, and utilities are free, and the yard and grounds are cared for. And, in the higher grades, house servants or an allowance to hire them, and special furnishing are among the perquisites.

Health and Sanitation

The efficiency and stability of a large labor force in the low, wet tropics depend in large measure upon the ability to maintain the people in good health. In addition to the health hazards familiar to dwellers in the temperate zones, the jungle areas from which the United Fruit plantations are carved present the constant threat of malaria, yellow fever, intestinal parasites, yaws, typhus, bubonic plague, and other tropical scourges. Effective measures must be taken to combat them and to control the conditions in which they develop and spread. One of the basic, but often misunderstood, facts is that control of health conditions and treatment of illness must in such situations be both comprehensive and coordinated—provided either by the company or by a government agency. Neither control nor treatment can be left to the individual discretions of the workers or their families and the ministrations of private physicians alone.

These problems were early recognized by the United Fruit Company. In the year of its formation, 1899, the company's first hospital was opened in Bocas del Toro, Panama. Today, an efficient and far-flung medical organization serves all parts of United's tropical installations through hospitals, clinics, dispensaries, and mobile health units. The services of qualified physicians, nurses, and pharmacy personnel are available to all employees. Medicines, medical and nursing care, and hospital treatment are available to spouses and children living on the plantations, as well as to workers on the regular payroll. (Certain types of occasional and temporary workers are not offered the full coverage, except in cases of accident or emergency.) This medical organization is generally conceded to be the largest and best qualified medical service under private auspices in the American tropics.

United's medical service does not carry on an extensive research program in tropical medicine, but it is often in the forefront in the application of new findings. The results are indicated by a few typical figures. In Guatemala, in the company's properties on the Atlantic side, 21.9 percent of personnel were infected with malaria in 1929; this incidence had declined to 0.3 percent in 1955. On the Pacific-side properties, the incidence of malaria fell from 15.3 percent in 1938 to 0.2 percent in 1955. Between 1945 and 1955 in Costa Rica, admissions of malaria patients to hospitals declined by 88 percent in Quepos; by 98 percent in Golfito; and by 99 percent in Limón. Yellow fever, typhus, and bubonic plague are now practically nonexistent; yaws is sporadic, but very rare. Dysentery and other intestinal afflictions are somewhat more difficult to control absolutely, because their incidence depends somewhat upon the personal habits of the people. They have been reduced to a nominal rate, however, through the provision of pure drinking water, sanitary disposal of human excrement and garbage, and the provision of fresh vegetables grown under sanitary supervision.

The general policy calls for medical examination of workers at the time of application for employment. Those with chronic and infectious diseases as a rule are turned down. In some divisions those with early-stage venereal diseases are accepted, but are required to take a free antibiotic treatment. In several centers, workers and their dependents are periodically examined by X-ray and other methods for tuberculosis, and infected cases are placed under treatment. This pattern will be made universal as soon as facilities permit. These and a variety of other measures of preventative medicine are oriented toward the selection and maintenance of a relatively healthy working population.

According to company accounts, its net cost (over and above contributions from wages) for hospital service alone in the six countries in 1955 was over $2,984,000. This does not include interest or depreciation on capital invested in the facilities or the cost of other non-hospital aspects of the program. In addition, the company's records show that the sanitation service cost over $993,000 in 1955. Excluded from this figure are capital funds laid out for camp drainage systems, sewage disposal, and sanitary facilities in housing developments.

In Colombia, comprehensive coverage is given to the worker and his family completely free. In the other countries, workers contribute by withholdings from their wages. In 1955, such contributions of laborers to the company medical program did not exceed 2 percent in any country. (Employees with higher salaries in some cases contributed proportionately more, up to 6 percent in one country.) In some countries, the workers—and the company—were required to contribute small additional amounts to the national social security program. Because of the rise of national social security systems in the various countries, a variety of detailed arrangements between the company and public health services are involved, which it is not necessary to analyze here. In no country, in 1955, was an individual laborer required to contribute more than $5 or its equivalent per month for comprehensive medical service to himself and those members of his family living with him on company property.

All of the nations considered here with the exception of Honduras have enacted national social security legislation aimed at eventually making full medical and hospital services available to all the nations' workers on a contributory basis. If and when such systems become effective, and are extended to workers on its installations, the United Fruit Company will be relieved of the necessity of maintaining its own program, although it will contribute according to the legal rates to the national programs. In an agreement made with the Costa Rican government in 1954, the company offered to turn over its hospital and dispensary facilities to the government, but as of 1957 the national authorities had not exercised this option. The Panamanian social security system was authorized by law in 1954 to extend its services to the two United Fruit divisions in that country but, because of petitions of the company's workers to the President of the Republic, had not done so as of 1957. The labor unions took the position that their members' contributions to the government system would cost twice as much as the company program and cover only the worker, not his family.

There has been no rivalry or criticism of the company's medical and health systems by either organized private medicine or the national social security systems. All of the medical and nursing personnel on duty in the six countries are nationals, although the majority of the physicians have had some of their training in the United States.

EDUCATION

ANOTHER SERVICE usually provided by government elsewhere, which United Fruit has been obliged to carry on at its own expense, is education of the children of its laborers and other employees. Free elementary schools are provided on all producing installations at a total cost to the company in 1955 of $779,000. All of the countries have legislation requiring compulsory elementary education of all children, although the number of years of schooling required varies. Colombia has the lowest legal minimum—two years. The United Fruit Company complies with all legal requirements and in most cases offers more than the prescribed minimum. School buildings are well constructed and equipped, and salaries offered to teachers and administrative personnel are usually higher than in the public schools off the limits of United's properties. In all headquarters settlements and in some other locations, six-year schools are maintained although the legal requirement may be only two or three years.

In several places—for example in La Lima, Honduras—parents have organized secondary schools going beyond the sixth year. In such cases, the company supplies the building and furniture and the teachers are paid from private tuition fees. The company also aids the education of employees' children in the United States. Provided the parents can raise the funds for the first two years, United Fruit pays the last two years of secondary school tuition and provides free transportation from the tropics to the United States or Canada.

The standards of instruction in the company's schools are somewhat higher than those prevailing in the average local elementary schools of the countries concerned. The need for more vocational training in the content of the curriculum is now recognized, however, and present plans include provision of more workshops for boys and domestic science equipment for girls in the company schools.

One problem, not of the company's making, presents some difficulties. This is the fact that national legislation has established minimum ages at which children may be gainfully employed. In no case is the minimum age less than 14. Most of the children are 10 to 12 years of age when they have finished the sixth year of school, and three years younger if they have gone through only the three required years. The result is that there is a gap of several years between the end of school and the time when they can go to work, during which time many children are somewhat at loose ends. Some of these children obtain employment off the company properties where minimum-age laws are frequently ignored by local authorities. But if they remain with their parents on United Fruit installations, the company, in compliance with the legal requirements, refuses to hire them until they are eligible.

Although the United Fruit Company itself has not taken responsibility for adult literacy training, it has actively and sympathetically encouraged private efforts, through the provision of buildings or rooms for night classes with the necessary furniture, blackboards, pencils, and other equipment. In some locations, the labor unions have organized "anti-illiteracy" instruction on a voluntary basis. In others, outside organizations dedicated to this sort of teaching for adults have been of help. The classes meet at night and the workers may attend or not as they wish.

Another type of education which the company has generally encouraged, although not under its own auspices, is the instruction of housewives in more modern and efficient household management than has been their customary heritage. In a Honduran division, for example, a number of social workers supported by one of the United Nations agencies carried on this type of work for a time, with both government and company approval. In other cases, religious workers have occasionally taken part in this sort of work.

In addition to financing its own school program, upon occasion the company also has made substantial financial contributions to schools operated under outside auspices. For example, it contributed nearly two-thirds of the cost of the new $100,000 government school erected at Puerto Armuelles, Panama. In the same division, it contributed in 1954 a dormitory which was turned into a convent and the land on which was built a new secondary school operated by the Maryknoll nuns.

A new program of education just getting into full gear at the time of this writing has to do with labor relations. Heads of labor relations departments in the company's various divisions are called together periodically at some central location for short courses and discussions with top-level personnel from New York and Boston. These meetings are now being implemented by intensive programs of training foremen (*capitanes, capitaces,* etc.) at the "grassroots" level. It is realized that advanced principles of labor relations are of little value if understood only at executive and management levels, and need to be put into actual practice by the supervisory personnel in intimate daily contact with the workers.

AGRICULTURAL TRAINING

THE PANAMERICAN AGRICULTURAL SCHOOL at Zamorano, Honduras, is an educational activity of the company that has nothing directly to do with the education of the families of its own workers and employees. But through it, the United Fruit Company has made an outstanding contribution to Spanish American agriculture. This Escuela Agricola Panamericana was founded in 1942 by Samuel Zemurray, then President of the United Fruit Company, as a practical symbol of the company's appreciation for the collaboration of the Spanish American people.

A good automobile road leads southeast from Tegucigalpa, the capital city of Honduras, and after crossing a mountain ridge at 5,100 feet dips into the broad valley of the Rio Yeguare. The valley has an average elevation of 2,400 to 2,700 feet above sea level. Here lie the neat buildings of the School, made of volcanic tufa in Spanish colonial style. Under the direction, until recently, of widely-famed Dr. Wilson Popenoe, the institution has an attendance of 160 young men between the ages of 18 and 21, selected from applicants all of whom must be Spanish Americans. None of the graduates is allowed to enter the employ of the United Fruit Company.

The boys, who come from various strata of society with agricultural backgrounds, follow a three-year practical, vocational course in all aspects of farming and farm management. About half the training at Zamorano consists of actually working in the fields, gardens, and animal barns—a program intended not only to increase the students' technical knowledge, but also to overcome the traditional Latin American feeling that work with the hands and the soil is demeaning.

Although a few win scholarships for further study in the United States, the great majority return to agricultural work in Spanish America. They are in great demand as agricultural extension agents and also as farm managers.

The School, which has won excellent standing in international agricultural circles, is maintained entirely at United Fruit Company expense. An applicant must have six years of elementary education and preferably about two years of secondary. Once he is accepted, the School pays all his expenses, including travel from his home, clothing, board, room, even haircuts. (The chief barber in 1956, by the way, was the famous Honduran "primitive" painter, J. Antonio Velasquez.) The average cost per student in 1956 was $1,400.

As of 1956, the United Fruit Company had invested over $6.5 million in the School, including cost of land, buildings, equipment, libraries, laboratories, and the cost of operation—which at present runs to about $250,000 per year. The policy has been steadfastly maintained that the School is not for the training or improvement of the company's own personnel, but represents an outright and disinterested contribution to the improvement of agriculture in Spanish America. As Zemurray has said, "This was one way in which the United Fruit Company undertook to discharge its obligation of social responsibility in those countries in which it operates—and even to help others."

The students live in modern dormitory rooms that they care for themselves. It is hoped that they will aspire to something as good or better when they return home. Every day except Sunday they are up at 5:30 a.m. and out doing practical work until 11:30. After lunch and a siesta they attend classes from 1:00 to 4:00 in the afternoon. Then they have two hours for sports, dinner at 6, and must be in their quarters studying from 7 to 8:45. Lights are out at 9 p.m. During the first year, they concentrate on horticulture; on field crops, the second year; and animal husbandry, the third. The classroom studies cover the fundamental principles of tropical agriculture, plus English and simple applied mathematics. At first, the English courses were concerned only with the development of reading ability, because much literature of interest to farmers is published in that language. After the early years, however, the students asked to be taught to speak as well as to read English, and as of now all graduates are able to carry on at least a simple conversation in English.

Zamorano was not designed to be a center of higher theoretical studies or of basic scientific experimentation. It is dedicated to the formation of a growing corps of trained and experienced farmers who will disseminate their knowledge and techniques to their fellow Spanish Americans. Between 50 and 60 students graduate each year.

The company's contributions to tropical agriculture made at the Lancetilla experiment station in the Tela Division of Honduras, have been traced briefly in Chapter VI. That research station was founded in 1925 by the same Dr. Popenoe who formerly headed the School at Zamorano. He had previously established a reputation as a plant explorer with the U.S. Department of Agriculture. The Lancetilla station, with a compound and farm lands of its own separated from the producing banana plantations, carries on experimental plantings and genetic studies of useful or potentially useful plants from all parts of the tropical world with a view to adapting them to various conditions in the Western Hemisphere and adding them to the agricultural resources of Latin America.

Botanical and agricultural research primarily for the benefit of the United Fruit Company takes place at the Research Institute for Tropical Agriculture, located at La Lima, Honduras, with a staff of about 100 scientists.

Commissaries and Food Services

Because producing divisions are located in out-of-the-way places, the United Fruit Company provides for its workers certain consumers' merchandising and production services that in other situations are usually in the hands of local private business. It operates, on all of its producing properties, commissaries which are there in lieu of private grocery stores and other retail outlets usually operated by "small enterprises." To supply these emporia, the company in each country has become a large importer of foreign-made consumers' goods, quite apart from its importations of materials directly concerned with banana production.

The company is also a producer of consumer goods. At one place or another, it is in the dairy business and not only manages extensive herds of milk cows, but also pasteurizing and bottling plants. It is in the meat business and maintains sizable herds of beef cattle, plus the necessary slaughtering and processing plants. In some places it is in the bakery business, and produces bread and pastries. It is in the business of wholesale merchandising and buys large quantities of consumers' goods on the local national market, particularly textiles, clothing, and shoes.

It would be too much to say that these phases of United Fruit's operations are exempt from criticism by local retail business interests, chambers of commerce, and the like. The local business interests do not claim that the company is dishonest, underhanded, or anything of the sort, but they sometimes assert that such activities should be in the hands of local merchants. Company officials agree, at least informally, that such matters should not be the business of an organization whose main interest is the production of bananas. They feel that the company would be better off if it could get out of such consumer services once local enterprise demonstrates that it can fill the consumer needs of company workers efficiently and economically.

For the six countries combined, company accounts show that its total commissary sales have been averaging about $15.5 million per year, which amounts to about 30 percent of their net pay receipts. The commissaries regularly sell a variety of staple items at prices below cost, sometimes under arrangements written into its labor agreements. On an overall basis, however, the company tries to run its commissaries without either a profit or a loss. We have examined the commissary accounts for the six countries over the five-year period from 1951 through 1955. They show receipts and expenditures in almost exact balance for the period as a whole, with profits and losses in individual years never amounting to more than a fraction over 1 percent.

This record makes two things clear. The first is that the wages of United Fruit employees are appreciably upgraded by the privilege exercised of buying so large a proportion of their supplies from commissaries operated on a break-even basis in countries where high retail markups are usual. The second is that the company runs this phase of its operation as an accommodation rather than as a business.

In addition to commissaries, United Fruit maintains slaughter houses like the one in Sevilla where an average of one head of beef is killed per day, about 400-450 pounds of usable meat. Here, as in other installations offering beef, two kinds of meat are provided. "Regular" meat is the product of a beef carcass, including bones, sawed into chunks with a circular power saw. "Cuts" in such cases are purely geometrical —and the customer takes what comes his way. Conventional meat cuts are sold to those who wish to pay a higher price. In Colombia, company cattle herds, including dairy cattle, average about 3,000 head. A new pasteurizing plant was in operation in April 1956, serving the produce of 421 milking cows, milked with machines. The plant makes its own butter for sale. In Colombia, according to the

Labor Code, each worker must be given free work clothes and shoes twice a year, and to each new worker must be given a free machete and shovel, to be returned if he quits within two months. In 1956, the following staples were sold in company commissaries at fixed prices much below those in surrounding independent shops (prices in centavos of Colombian pesos).

Item	UFCO commissary	Ordinary shops
Sugar (lb.)	.11	.25
Potatoes (lb.)	.12	.40
Lard	.65	1.50
Coffee (roasted, ground)	.96	1.10
Flour	.20	.80
White beans	.35	.40
Red beans	.38	.40
Onions	.20	1.50
Spaghetti	.30	1.00

In the Golfito Division of Costa Rica, by agreement with the company, the national government established in 1956 a store for the sale of essential foods. In 1956, the government store was operating in a building rented to it by United Fruit. More are planned, and the company professes itself as welcoming them, so that workers can compare prices. In 1956, prices in company stores and the government *estanco* averaged out about equal, even though the government *estanco* was not obliged to figure overhead as part of the cost to the consumer. By agreement with the labor union signed in October 1955, the company undertakes to sell the following items at cost price: coffee, rice, beans, sugar, lard, flour, powdered milk, rolled oats, kerosene, matches, files, and washing soap. According to the Costa Rican Labor Code, the employer must provide all work tools and replace them when worn out.

At Tenguel, Ecuador, according to an agreement signed in August 1954, the company agreed to sell certain basic foodstuffs at below the cost price in Guayaquil: rice at 20 percent discount; sugar and coffee, 25 percent; oatmeal and lard, 15 percent; all other basic foodstuffs, 10 percent. Every worker here is also entitled to two pounds of meat per week for each member of his family at about one-third the free-market price. In order to allow "free competition" the company permits a free market in Tenguel on Saturdays, which is attended by an average of 50 merchants who come by launch from Guayaquil.

At the Tiquisate Division in Guatemala, the labor union signed an agreement in 1955 whereby, in return for a wage raise, the company was allowed to sell certain basic items at cost, rather than at a fixed price below cost. These are corn, beans, rice, sugar, coffee, lard, and some types of shoes. Here the company supplies meat through a private contractor. Although United maintained a dairy herd of 118 cows and a pasteurizing plant, in 1956 it was producing an average of only 710 liters per day for some 25,000 people. The deficit was made up by imported powdered milk sold in the commissaries.

In both Panama districts certain basic food items are sold at cost, nothing below cost. Here the cost is clearly indicated to the buyers as invoice, plus freight, plus import duties and other taxes and licenses, plus 10 percent for overhead. This itemization of cost to the consumer, at least as of 1956, was not made so clear in other divisions. If it were, some needless criticism might be eliminated.

In Honduras basic food items are sold at cost, including taxes, plus 10 percent overhead.

From the company point of view these retail services and food supply operations are a necessary nuisance borne for the convenience and security of its workers and made mandatory by the general isolation of its farms, and even division headquarters, from established town or urban centers. As of 1956, all workers' purchases were made in cash or on accounts to be settled monthly in cash. The company did not permit the use of scrip or other discountable paper in the settlement of commissary accounts.

IN SUMMARY

THE SERVICES provided by the company can be measured by one or several yardsticks, and one's appraisal of performance would vary widely depending upon which standard of measurement is applied.

The newest type of housing in Tiquisate, Guatemala, would suffer by comparison with the modern living quarters of a Detroit automobile worker. And it would probably come out second best if compared with a new housing development for industrial workers in any of several Latin American cities. But it is by far the best in housing for agricultural workers in the tropics. Even the old barracks-type dwellings are an improvement over the typical hut on stilts to be found in the rural areas surrounding them.

Most problems arise and most complaints are heard from workers living in the old, drab *barracones*. Most of the labor force comes from rural isolated farms in the wilderness where in some cases the nearest neighbors live miles away; therefore, they have no experience in community living. When brought into close contact with other people of the same background, and with shared facilities, difficulties are bound to appear.

The new type of housing attempts to solve these problems by surrounding each family with a greater degree of privacy. The company is carrying out a program designed to replace all of the older structures within a period of 20 years. Unfortunately, this program cannot be carried out with the dispatch that the workers would like to see because of the large capital investment involved. Anything that could be done to step up the program for construction of new, comfortable, gay-colored houses to replace the old, depressing, grey barracks throughout all the divisions would pay handsomely in better performance by the working force and improved material well-being.

Workers sometimes complain of delays in making repairs. There may be some ground for this in cases where normal maintenance procedures have been curtailed because plans for replacing the houses in question by new structures have been approved. There probably have been occasions where the gap between promise and fulfillment of new housing provisions has been longer than called for by the original scheduling.

The workers and their families have not always taken full advantage of the improvements put at their disposal. To move from a primitive shack in the jungle into a cottage with running water and toilet facilities is a drastic change indeed. Unless trained personnel is assigned the task of teaching these rustic people how to make the most of their new surroundings, much of the expense and effort involved can be wasted.

While the buildings and appointments of company hospitals hardly could be expected to rival those to be found in the more modern U.S. health centers, the performance record of the company's medical services commands a very high rating. United Fruit has played a pioneering role in introducing throughout this area effective procedures for protecting the health of a large labor force working in tropical lowlands that present formidable health hazards. The hospital at La Lima can be catalogued among the best to be found anywhere in Latin America.

The general impressions that register most strongly from our review of United Fruit's performance in health, education, housing, and general provision for its workers' welfare can be summarized as follows:

United Fruit's record in all of these fields is substantially better than the prevailing standards for agricultural enterprises in the area. In a number of respects, performance falls considerably short of matching the more advanced standards of modern practice that have been developed in countries like the United States. Despite the evident, and increasingly intensified, effort of management to make improvements, the company has not succeeded in fully disarming local criticism, particularly with respect to housing. Most such criticism comes from those who visualize it as a wealthy and prosperous enterprise beyond limit, and have no realistic appreciation of the pressure upon management to hold down costs from stockholders who have legitimate concern over its relatively mediocre profits showing.

Perhaps the strongest impression is that of the enormous complex of responsibilities that a company like United Fruit has been forced to assume for activities only indirectly related to the business of growing bananas. Faced with the necessity of organizing its production operations in virgin wilderness areas of countries unable to take responsibility for furnishing the normal complement of community services, the company could not avoid taking on multiple activities that range far beyond the scope of the average corporate enterprise. Inevitably, this has involved extra expense, administrative burden, and above all ramification of the difficult problems of human relationships.

There can be little doubt about the direction in which it is desirable to move to free the company from the weight of paternalistic responsibilities. The evolution will necessarily be gradual, but a clear policy leading to the transfer of more and more of these nonbusiness activities to governments and communities will serve the long-term interests of everyone.

VIII.

Labor Relations and Public Relations

THE ESSENCE OF THE PROBLEMS of the United Fruit Company in its relations with Latin American employees, the Latin American general public, and Latin American governments lies in the fact that the company is at present controlled and staffed in its executive branches mainly by North Americans. These people are quite naturally conditioned by value patterns dominant in the United States. In order to carry on the production of bananas in Latin America, they must come to terms with people—ranging from common laborers to presidents of republics—who have been trained in a somewhat different value system.

Latin Americans do not always see things in the same context as their North American opposites. Their area is undergoing a phase of sociocultural and economic development that frequently expresses itself in terms of extreme nationalism and the rejection of anything that, realistically or not, symbolizes for them the suggestion of foreign domination or imperialism.

The basic problem of the United Fruit Company, then, insofar as it concerns Latin American people, is to develop policies under which the company can live with the Latin Americans to the mutual benefit of itself and of them.

LABOR RELATIONS

WITH THE CHANGES—economic and social— which occurred in Latin America during the late 1940's and early 1950's came the realization that the company's labor relations policies should be made uniform in all divisions.

The present system of labor relations offices throughout the United Fruit Company's tropical divisions was standardized early in 1956. These offices were set up after a field study and recommendations had been made by a labor relations expert of long experience who had been retained by the company following a series of difficulties that came to a head in 1954.

A company policy statement issued at the time stated: "Labor problems of the last few years have convinced all of us of the great need to examine our labor relations program. Those recent problems and expensive strikes require us to assure ourselves that we are doing everything possible to avoid discontent among our workers which may result in strikes, stoppages or lowered productivity. . . . All Division Managers realize that our policy of striving for and maintaining the best possible relationships with all our employees is of vital importance. Our thinking and day-to-day labor relations must be modernized and kept up to date. We must recognize that great social changes are in process. It is essential that we develop a fair and constructive policy of dealing with labor."

As a result of this directive all divisions and most districts now have a labor relations officer who devotes full time to the program and the larger administrative centers have fully staffed labor relations offices. Previously in some divisions no such office existed. In others, grievances were handled by the company attorney or the superintendent of agriculture, or perhaps the manager.

The newly established or reorganized labor relations offices process new workers, do the formal hiring, and are required to keep individual employment records for all workers. They are charged also with seeing that close, friendly, personal contact is maintained between the supervisors and the laborers. Similarly, the higher levels of management are directed to seek more frequent personal contacts with the laborers. An effective grievance procedure is set up, channeling through the supervisor and superintendent to the labor office. In most places, the labor relations officer now holds weekly meetings with the representatives of the workers, even when there are no complaints to be heard. The basic directive states: "Under no circumstances should anyone be directly or indirectly hurt because he presented a grievance to the company. Our primary emphasis must be to get rid of the trouble—not the person who reports it."

The labor offices are also responsible for establishing procedures to increase the efficiency of the work force through monetary and other incentives, and for reducing turnover. In some farms, the turnover previously had amounted to 100 percent per year. And in many the great majority of workers finish the agreed-upon task quotas *(tareas)* upon which basic wages are set by laboring only four to five hours per day. "We should encourage higher monthly earnings provided we get increased productivity. A worker with higher earnings is a more satisfied worker who will stay on the job." The labor service is also required to collect data for future collective bargaining—statistical data on wages, monthly earnings, hours of work, cost of living indices, wages being paid by other employers in the area and in comparable industries, etc. And these offices are also charged with inspection of safety and health programs, supervision of motion picture programs, sports, labor clubs, and the improvement of worker morale.

The labor relations offices are subject to control by the manager of each division, but are to be given equal status and prestige with other departments, and are required to work closely with all departments.

Most of the decade ending in 1954 had been marked by a series of strikes and labor troubles on company properties in Guatemala. In that year a long and expensive strike took place in Honduras, where company officials had thought that organized work stoppages were almost unthinkable. In 1955, a large-scale strike at Laurel, Costa Rica, was ended only after the company agreed to make important concessions.

These and other labor troubles brought the realization that labor was organized and capable of inflicting severe damage upon the company interests. Hence, the reorientation of policy. The nature of banana production makes shutdowns far more costly to the United Fruit Company than they are to most industrial enterprises. The product is perishable, ripens continuously throughout the year, and must be harvested and shipped according to very tight schedules. Furthermore, in most sites sigatoka control must be maintained constantly. Any significant stoppage in harvesting, shipping, and blight-control activities—all of which require large numbers of properly coordinated workers—results in serious financial loss, in addition to severe and lasting damage to the company's public relations in the countries in which it operates.

At present, the company recognizes labor unions in all of its divisions, and through its labor relations officers maintains continually open channels of communication with union representatives. Where the law or an agreement with the union requires it, the payroll office collects union dues by checkoff from wages and turns them over to the union. A few details may be given for each country to convey some idea of the variations in the pattern of unionism in the company's several divisions.

At Tiquisate, Guatemala, the union has an executive committee composed of nine secretaries, five of whom are changed each year in elections. It has headquarters in a building on company property that formerly belonged to a workers' cooperative that failed. In addition to the general executive committee, each of the 24 farms in the division elects four representatives to a general council. According to the present labor code, the employer is obliged to check off dues, fixed by the union at 1 percent of wages. Also the law guarantees the jobs of five members of the executive committee during the year that they are "on leave" from the company to serve the union. And, by agreement with the union, the company provides free transportation of union representatives from the farms twice a month to attend meetings at the Tiquisate headquarters. The union here seems to be quite independent of company influence. At the Bananera Division, which has been practically out of production because of Panama disease, there has been no union organization since 1954, although the company representatives state that they are willing to honor an agreement signed in 1953 with the union, once the latter is reorganized. Puerto Barrios in 1956 had an independent union of dock workers, and the railway workers had a union of their own.

In Honduras, labor organization had not been authorized by the country's laws from 1933 until after the strikes of 1954. As of 1956, United Fruit workers were represented by three unions with which the company bargains. The principal union, Sindicato de Trabajadores de la Tela Railroad Company, claimed a membership of 7,000, with dues assessed at 2 lempiras ($1.00 U.S.) per month, collected directly without a checkoff agreement. There is a subsection of this union on each United Fruit farm and in each of its workshops, and each subsection elects five representatives to a central "congress." Seven members of a central executive committee are on the Sindicato payroll, and the company grants them leave of absence while they serve and agrees to rehire them when their union service terminates. The dock workers, in Puerto Cortes, were organized in a separate union claiming 280 members, as were approximately 300 mechanics and machine shop workers.

In 1956, the situation in Costa Rica was complicated by the existence of three unions each competing for the allegiance of company workers: Rerum Novarum (Catholic-inspired), Federación de Trabajadores Bananeros y Anexos (FOBA), and Federación de Trabajadores Bananeros (FETRABA). The first was insignificant in the banana business in 1956. As of that date, FOBA was strongly influenced by Costa Rican communists, and FETRABA was slowly evolving, with many errors caused by the inexperience of its leaders, into an independent democratic union. There is little doubt that there is an active, well instructed, and intelligent communist element in

Costa Rica ready and willing to exploit the labor situation by all possible means and at every opportunity. (One of our consultants had long talks with two of the top leaders.) This indicates the necessity of a high order of labor relations statesmanship in Costa Rica.

In Panama, company officials in both the Armuelles and Almirante divisions refuse to recognize more than one union and have placed effective blocks in the path of other organizations. Both of the company-recognized unions in these divisions are accused by a variety of sources of being "tame" and company-controlled. The weakness of union organization there was acknowledged to one of our interviewers by company officials in Almirante, where in 1956 the union had fallen into desuetude and the company representatives were making efforts to revive it.

In Colombia, the banana workers union is affiliated with the national Colombian Workers' Union (UTC), which in turn is a member of the anticommunist International Confederation of Free Trade Unions (ICFTU) and the Inter-American Regional Organization (ORIT). Relations with the company are very good. The union collects dues of two pesos per month (about $0.40 U.S.) plus an initiation fee of three pesos. It has its headquarters in a building erected and presented by the company, but which is located off company property in a nearby town. The dock laborers in Santa Marta have their own closed-shop union that is not affiliated with any national or international association. It is one of the oldest labor organizations in Colombia and bargains not only with United Fruit and its subsidiaries but also with other banana export groups. There is no social security coverage for the dock workers, and they have brought and lost three lawsuits against the United subsidiary in an effort to force it to pay pensions. In 1956, United Fruit officials were trying to work out a joint plan for pensions in collaboration with the government and the two national banana-exporting groups.

At Tenguel, Ecuador, the union was organized in 1944 by a local small-businessman, a Socialist, who still continues to direct it. The company, to help him, has given him the beer and soft drink concession at the workers' club, since he receives nothing from the union. Dues of 5 sucres (about $0.25 U.S.) are collected by checkoff. Only some 500 workers (of a total of nearly 2,000) belong. The union formerly belonged to the Guayaquil Workers' Federation, but withdrew because of communist influence in that group. It is not currently associated with any larger organization. Although not large, this union is not company-controlled and is quite aggressive in negotiations.

Although some docks and loading facilities are organized on a closed-shop basis, this is not true of any of the banana plantations in the six countries.

Thus, the United Fruit Company recognizes and deals with organized labor unions in all of the six countries in which we made firsthand studies. It has, however, had some misgivings about the possible future implications of a general drive to affiliate the unions with which it deals with ORIT. This organization of affiliated local and national unions throughout Latin America was set up with the help of the AFL-CIO, is supported by the Organization of American States, encouraged by the U.S. Department of State, and is affiliated with the ICFTU which comprises most of the anticommunist trade movement of the world. It was originally organized to offset the influence of the Latin American Workers' Confederation (CTAL) which has headquarters in Mexico and whose policies are strongly influenced by the communists. Before ORIT, Latin American trade unions had nowhere else to go if they wished to unite on a regional basis.

United Fruit's fears concerning ORIT obviously stem not from the latter's anticommunist position, but from the integrated, international nature of the company's operations. If all the local unions with which the company deals were united in ORIT, it is feared that any small labor dispute of a local nature could lead to a general sympathy strike throughout company properties in all countries where it operates, and even interrupt shipments to and within the United States and Canada. This is an understandable apprehension on the part of company policy makers, although ORIT has to date threatened no actions of this type. A dilemma, however, is created for both company and Panamerican policy groups, which deserves attention and should not be too difficult to resolve so that all interests may unite in forwarding ORIT's major aim. Perhaps some assurance might be offered that ORIT will not become an instrument for organizing international sympathy strikes or hot-cargo embargos. Such assurance would go far toward removing such doubts about ORIT as United Fruit and other internationally operating enterprises in Latin America now entertain.

The Labor Force

THE HETEROGENEOUS CHARACTER of its work force raises other labor relations problems for United Fruit. As stated previously, in the six countries we are concerned with the great majority of laborers are Spanish American nationals, with the loyalties and values of such people. However, a variety of ethnic groups is also represented. Since the banana farms were originally located in sparsely settled areas, in each instance practically all of the laborers initially had to be attracted from more thickly populated sectors.

In the Tenguel Division of Ecuador, which is located in the low, wet coastal zone southwest of Guayaquil, 68 percent of the workers in 1956 were migrants from the sierra—the inland, intermountain, high-altitude region. Their move to Tenguel involved a considerable change in climate and customs.

At Sevilla, Colombia, by contrast, most of the workers are from the surrounding coastal region, which, although low in altitude, is here much drier than at Tenguel, and there is little problem of acclima-tization. However, the Sevilla work force is about equally divided between *mestizos* and Negro-mulattoes.

The Panama divisions have the greatest variety of racial and cultural backgrounds among their work forces. The Puerto Armuelles Division in its Panamanian District (another district is located in Costa Rica, but administered from Panama) has a labor force consisting of *mestizos* and Negro-Panamanians in about equal propor-tions, plus some 1,000 Guaymi Indians, and a few San Blas Indians. In the 1920's, the Almirante Division on the Atlantic side was so badly hit by Panama disease that it was thought the company would have to abandon its Panama lands entirely. However, it was finally de-cided that bananas could be grown on the Pacific side and, in 1928, operations began at the present Armuelles Division, an area covered by tropical jungle interspersed with swamps. It was inhabited only by a few scattered families debilitated by malaria, so that labor had to be sought outside. Recruiters were sent into the mountains where the Guaymis live, a population of docile Indians at that time with-drawn from civilization. Many of them do not speak Spanish even today. In the beginning, they were the principal labor force at Armuelles, but now they are used mainly for sigatoka spray work. Gradually the Guaymis are settling down, stimulated by the Labor Code of 1948, that grants all workers a full month's vacation with pay after each 11 months of steady work. Although they are an in-dispensable element of the work force as presently constituted, the company has not yet provided family housing for them; women and children of the men live in barracks built for single workers. Negroes and mulattoes working at Armuelles live in an unofficially segregated company village near the beach, and are the most stable labor element in this division.

The Almirante (Bocas del Toro) Division on the Atlantic side of Panama presents an even more complicated picture. Here the principal elements of the work force are Chiricanos (*mestizos* from Chiriqui Province), about 1,200 Guaymi Indians (locally called *cholos* and *cricamoles*), some old Negro Jamaicans and their descendants, plus an average contingent of about 300 San Blas Indians. In 1956, a literate Guaymi was hired by the company to work with his fellow Indians, teaching them to save their earnings, to keep time, and to stick to one name. A source of seriocomic annoyance, both here and at Armuelles, is the fact that the Guaymis choose whatever English name tickles their fancy and think nothing of acquiring a new one every week. The Guaymis here have their own little farms in their home territory and tend to come and go to their banana plantation jobs somewhat irregularly. They are steady workers, however, when sober.

The San Blas or Kuna Indians constitute another significant element of the labor force. They live a semi-independent life on islands in the Gulf of Darien and the mainland fringe facing it. They are tribally organized under their own chiefs and headmen. The San Blas men join gangs or cuadrillas at home which are sent to Almirante, usually for six-month periods, under the supervision of their own leaders, who are responsible for their work and good behavior. In 1955, 386 completed their six-month contracts with the company. Through agreement instigated by their tribal authorities, half their pay is given to them while on the job and the other half at the time they leave for home. This deferred pay allotment for the 386 men in 1955 was $72,391.01, or an average of $187.54. The highest liquidation figure was for one group of 27 who collected an average of $245.62 apiece. The company provides a bunk house and a cook for each gang, and also pays the expenses (about $100 a visit) for occasional trips of one of the tribal chiefs who comes to the plantations to see how things are going with the men and to report back to the tribe upon their welfare.

In the Golfito Division of Costa Rica practically all the workers are whites or *mestizos*, about 70 percent Costa Rican, the remainder Nicaraguan. Labor turnover here and at Laurel (a Costa Rican district which is attached to the Chiriqui Land Company subsidiary and is administered from Panama) tends to be heavy. Many of the workers have small farms of their own in the interior, and come to the plantations only a few months each year to make some extra cash. The bulk of the labor on the Division at Limón on the north coast—now closed as a banana operation but still producing cacao

—was Negro or mulatto. The government refused the company's offer to resettle these workers on the Pacific Coast when it opened new banana divisions there on the ground that it would upset the racial pattern of the country and possibly cause civil commotion.

About 20,000 workers make up the labor force in the Honduras Division. The great majority are Honduran *mestizos,* but about 15 percent come from other Central American countries, mainly El Salvador. In the vicinity of Tela there are many Negroes, most of them descendants of West Indians imported in the early days of the development. Also scattered along the coast are several villages of Black Caribs, who work for the company mainly as stevedores when they have the opportunity. They also carry on some farming and fishing independently and provide their own housing. A few Indians from the interior have joined the work force, but they are acculturated to Honduran ways, speak Spanish, and wear European-type clothing. The bulk of the labor force here is stable, and there is little seasonal migration.

On the Guatemalan plantations, practically all of the labor force by 1956 consisted of Guatemalan *mestizos (ladinos),* settled down with their wives and families. Formerly there was a heavy turnover of highland Indians who came to the plantations for a few months to earn extra cash. At Puerto Barrios on the Atlantic side, a high proportion of the dock workers are English and Spanish-speaking Negroes, mainly from neighboring British Honduras.

In view of this variety of backgrounds among the workers, with the difference in languages, traditions, customs and levels of culture that are involved, one can understand that labor relations officers and other management personnel require a considerable range of knowledge and sympathetic understanding to achieve results in winning the loyalty of the workers to the company, increasing their motivation for productive effort, and minimizing frictions between its worker groups.

One further factor in the social changes affecting the problems of labor relations needs to be mentioned here. This is the fact that all the governments in recent years have established labor codes or other legal labor regulations which guarantee certain rights to the workers, whether they are organized or not. The company attempts to obey the laws in all cases, but has recourse to the courts and other established media of appeal against decisions it considers unjust.

Among the reasons for the rather tardy establishment of the present modernized labor relations program was the feeling in the company

EMPLOYEES
AND THEIR FAMILIES

About 60,000 persons in 1955 worked for United Fruit in Colombia, Costa Rica, Ecuador, Guatemala, Honduras, and Panama. Together, they received approximately $53 million in direct wages and $8 million in fringe benefits. Added to this were free housing and the provision of supplies at break-even commissaries which stretched take-home pay. The company spent a further $4.25 million on schools, hospitals and infirmaries, welfare programs, and sanitation services. The places of worship, recreational facilities, and athletic fields and equipment provided for United's workers are upon a scale matched by few, if any, locally owned agricultural enterprises. And many of the company's community services to workers are also available to members of other settlements that often grow up on the fringes of company divisions.

WORKERS' CHILDREN enjoy their introduction to the outside world through movies.

EMPLOYEES of United Fruit celebrate a fiesta.

HOUSING

Free housing is furnished for the vast majority of workers on United Fruit farms and, in most cases, their immediate families or other dependents. Adjustment of workers to community life often is difficult since most of the labor force comes from isolated farms, where the nearest neighbors often live miles away.

SEVERAL HOUSING DESIGNS are used on company plantations. Not all are ideal, but all are a great improvement on anything found on farms in surrounding areas (as illustrated by houses at right), and a program is moving forward for eventual replacement of the older multiple-type housing on company plantations.

WHERE NEW single-family housing has been constructed, worker morale and the sense of community responsibility have significantly increased. These houses have roofed breezeways, private baths and toilets, electric lights, and gardens. Some are of brick. Where old-style barracks still exist, the worker's family usually has two rooms upstairs, plus a kitchen and wash place to the rear of the ground level and a paved space for additional activities. Toilet and bathing facilities are in a separate common building.

SEWING MACHINES made possible by better-paying jobs, access to well-stocked markets, and the convenience of electricity, running water, and the kerosene stoves now widely used on United Fruit farms make housekeeping somewhat simpler than in many rural areas of host countries, as seen at right.

THE HOUSING of clerical, supervisory, and executive personnel is equal, in many cases superior, to that available to persons of similar income status in the United States. The dwelling, its basic furniture, its maintenance, and utilities are free, and the yards and grounds are cared for.

United's first hospital was opened in 1899; today its medical organization serves all parts of its tropical installations through hospitals, clinics, dispensaries, and mobile health units.

THIS COMPANY HOSPITAL has 300 beds divided among private and semi-private rooms and wards, X-ray equipment, and a complete laboratory.

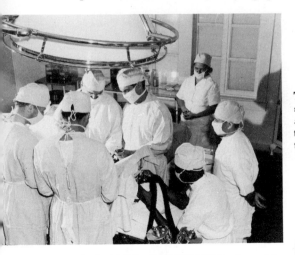

THE MEDICAL AND NURSING personnel on duty in the six countries are all nationals, although the majority of the physicians have had some of their training in the United States.

WORKERS CONTRIBUTE, by withholdings from wages, for comprehensive medical service for themselves and members of their families living on company property in all six countries except Colombia, where comprehensive coverage is completely free.

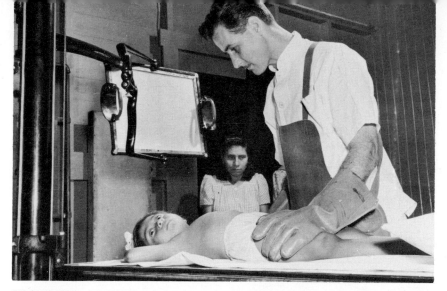

IN SEVERAL CENTERS, workers and their dependents are periodically examined by X-ray and other methods for tuberculosis and infected cases are placed under treatment. These, pre-employment examinations for chronic and infectious diseases, and a variety of other preventive measures are oriented toward the selection and maintenance of a healthy working force in traditionally disease-ridden tropical environments.

VISITING NURSES from United Fruit hospitals and dispensaries make daily calls on convalescent patients.

THE JUNGLE AREAS in which United's plantations are developed present a constant threat of malaria, yellow fever, intestinal parasites, yaws, typhus, bubonic plague, and other tropical scourges. One of the measures taken to combat such diseases and control conditions under which they develop and spread is the spraying machine, constantly at war with the mosquito.

EDUCATION

Free elementary schools are provided on all producing installations. Although the legal requirements in the host country may be for only two- or three-year schools, six-year schools are maintained in all headquarters settlements, and in some other locations.

WELL-CONSTRUCTED SCHOOL buildings are better equipped and the salaries of teachers and administrative personnel usually higher than in the public schools off the limits of United's property. Most teachers are nationals of the host countries.

STANDARDS OF INSTRUCTION in the company's schools are somewhat higher than those prevailing in the average local elementary schools. However, the need for more vocational training is now recognized and present plans include the provision of workshops for boys and domestic science equipment for girls in the company schools.

PARENTS HAVE ORGANIZED secondary schools going beyond the sixth year in several places and, in such cases, United Fruit has supplied buildings and furniture. Also, the company has encouraged private efforts to undertake adult literacy training through the provision of buildings or rooms for night classes with the necessary furniture, blackboards, and other equipment.

COMMISSARIES

Because producing divisions are located in out-of-the-way places, United runs commissaries in lieu of private grocery stores and other retail outlets. The company stores regularly sell a variety of staple items at prices below cost but, on an overall basis, United tries to provide commissary services without either a profit or loss. Total commissary sales have been averaging about $15.5 million a year.

AS STOREKEEPER, the company buys large quantities of consumers' goods in host countries—particularly textiles, clothing, and shoes.

TO SUPPLY its stores, United also has become a large importer of foreign-made consumers' goods, quite apart from its importation of materials directly concerned with its banana production. And it not only maintains dairy and cattle herds but also operates pasteurizing and bottling plants, slaughtering and meat processing plants; and in some places it bakes breads and pastries.

MANY CUSTOMERS at the commissaries are more accustomed to buying in open-air markets than in modern retail stores, and to such activities as weaving their own cloth and roasting coffee beans at home.

RELIGIOUS
AND SOCIAL ACTIVITIES

The great majority of workers in areas where United operates are Roman Catholics. Church buildings for Catholic services are provided at company expense and, in some instances, financial aid is given to the priests. For members of other organized sects, space for services is given in schools or other appropriate buildings.

AT THIS DIVISION CENTER, a Franciscan friar works with Boy Scouts.

HOUSING in practically all divisions is built around large athletic fields, and workers are encouraged to form sports clubs and committees. Athletic fields are built and playing equipment usually provided by the company.

WORKERS' CLUBS are built in accessible locations in all divisions. Provided by the company, they usually have a dance floor, tables for games, a snack-and-drink bar; and free movies are shown at least once a week in all workers' settlements. Usually, the members choose their own officers and committees.

THIS SWIMMING POOL, at a club maintained by the company, is convenient to employees' housing seen in the background.

CULTURAL CONTRIBUTIONS

In return for the hospitality of countries in which it operates, United Fruit has made a variety of contributions to Latin American culture.

ONE OF THESE was the restoration of the ancient city of Zaculeu in western Guatemala. Started in 1946, the site was formally turned over to the Republic of Guatemala in 1949 for the permanent enjoyment of the public and for use by students of Mayan civilization.

ANOTHER EXAMPLE is found in the National Museum of Costa Rica in San Jose. This 19th century institution was refounded in 1948 when the government provided an old fort as a site and individuals and groups—including United Fruit—contributed funds, art objects, and labor.

that its policy of high wages and fringe benefits through the years had made such a setup unnecessary—its workers were already better paid and better treated than labor of similar skill and training employed elsewhere in the countries involved.

At present, the company everywhere has a guaranteed minimum daily wage for common, unskilled labor which in every case is substantially higher than the wages paid to other agricultural workers in the several countries. Such workers may be paid by the hour (spray work is usually so compensated), but more usually by the task (*tarea* or *destajo*). The United Fruit Company laborers have been and are better off from the materialistic point of view than other similar workers in their respective countries. But even Spanish American laboring people apparently do not "live by bread alone." The realization of the wider range of workers' wants and aspirations as clearly expressed in the new United Fruit labor policy is an important forward step.

Not the least of the problems of the new policy of dealing with labor unions is the fact that there is a shortage of experience and training among potential labor leaders of a democratic or free-enterprise orientation. Some of the best informed and most practiced labor union men are communist-oriented and have received training behind the Iron Curtain. They know how to organize and administer a union, how to "negotiate," and how to propagandize their followers against the United States and the United Fruit Company as symbols of "capitalism." Even many of the noncommunist leaders are still dominated by the older European notions that management-labor relations can only be characterized by constant struggle and conflict. The newer philosophy, that collective bargaining is directed toward finding a common ground of higher production and the sharing of its benefits by both sides, has not been widely diffused as yet in the area. Under Point 4, scholarships were set up for the training of selected Latin American labor leaders in Puerto Rico. The United Fruit Company has been cooperative in granting leaves of absence and guarantees of re-employment to its men who have been chosen for such scholarships.

COMMUNITY DEVELOPMENT AND MORALE

FOR MANY YEARS, the company has promoted an active sports program for its male workers. As previously mentioned, the dwelling units of practically all farms are laid out around a large rectangular soccer football field. Under the current labor relations policy, the sports program is being reinvigorated, with more encouragement given to worker initiative in forming sports clubs and committees, arranging schedules, and so forth.

Formerly, four newspapers were published and given away free to workers and employees; at present there are three, and it is a matter of discussion how long they will survive. The papers are *El Pacifico* in Costa Rica, with a circulation of 10,000; *Nuevo Tiempo* in Guatemala, circulation, 13,000; and *Chirilanco* in Panama, circulation, 15,000. The relative lack of success of the company newspapers may result from two factors. On the one hand, many workers are unable to read well enough to appreciate the publications. On the other, the editorial policies tend toward printing personal items and local sports news with little attention paid to other events of more vital interest to the workers.

Serious consideration has been given to the possibilities of setting up some sort of home-ownership plan for workers, as a means of increasing their stake and sense of pride in the community. However, so long as Panama disease forces the periodic abandonment of farms and moving of workers to new locations, any such plan seems to be impracticable. As more and more workers are housed in one-family and two-family detached units, it is believed that some of the same results will be shown that could be expected from home ownership.

The company provides the buildings for workers' clubs which are scattered about all divisions in accessible locations. The club usually has a dance floor, tables for card playing, and a snack-and-drink bar. Usually the members choose their own officers and committees. Free movies are shown at least once a week in all workers' settlements, and they are open to women and children as well as the workers themselves.

Church buildings for Roman Catholic services are also provided at company expense and, in some instances, financial aid is given to the priest. The great majority of workers in most locations are Roman Catholic. For members of other sects space for services is given in school houses or other appropriate buildings, provided the sect is organized and responsible.

Various other plans for increasing morale and a sense of community solidarity among the workers are being discussed by the management. Among the possibilities is the employment of community development workers who would help the women to practice higher standards of housekeeping and to plan better balanced menus. Diseases caused by vitamin deficiency are among the very few health problems of workers and their families that remain unsolved. Another possibility is the encouragement of voluntary committees or other organizations which would enlist the interest and personal cooperation of the workers in community affairs, such as fiestas, beautifying and keeping the grounds clean, the promotion of night schools and secondary schools, the development of savings plans, and so on. Community development and the enhancement of worker morale are among the responsibilities of the reorganized labor relations departments.

PUBLIC RELATIONS

A PUBLIC RELATIONS MAN with long newspaper experience in the United States and in Latin America in 1951 was retained to make a survey of the United Fruit Company's use of the mass media and its access to influential sectors of public opinion in the countries where it operates. As a result of this study, a public relations department for Latin America was established in 1952, with headquarters in San Jose, Costa Rica. It is headed by the same expert who made the survey in 1951. The assistant director, also an experienced bilingual journalist, is located in Guatemala City. In each of the other four countries a local journalist is attached to the headquarters staff as a public relations man. The public relations staff is directly responsible to the president of the company in Boston, rather than to the local division managers, although close liaison is maintained with the latter.

As the director of Latin American public relations for the company has stated, "Public relations is a preventative process, not a cure. It must operate on a base of long-established and persistent dissemination of correct information, through every possible medium. Every action of every employee of the company is a form of public relations, good or bad."

Previous to 1952, press contacts and other public relations were usually handled by the division manager or one of his deputies who had no professional standing or experience in this field. By 1956, the public relations department was operating through a number of media. Close contact was maintained with reporters and editors of local and national newspapers in order to help them get material for their own stories about company activities. It was made clear that United Fruit would not pay for complimentary articles appearing in the news columns, but that its staff would do everything it could to assist newsmen to get the facts. The company established its own news and picture service, which was distributed free to publications in the countries where it operates and to a selected list throughout Latin America. In 1955, a total of nearly 1,000 such items were printed by the publications to which they were sent.

Formerly, paid advertising space in local media usually carried only the company's name, together with an announcement or greetings. The new policy involves specially written advertisements that give information about the company's operations.

Informative pamphlets produced and distributed by the public relations department are of two kinds—annual reports of the operating subsidiaries and educational publications. The first are distributed to government officials and the general public and are designed mainly to show company contributions to the national economy. The educational pamphlets are planned to promote a better knowledge of company operations among the public, but are especially aimed at school children—the coming generation upon whose opinion the future reputation of the company will depend. In 1955, some 4,000 copies of a pamphlet about Golfito were distributed to the 1,747 public schools in Costa Rica, as well as to public libraries and reading centers. A contest was held for compositions by school children based upon the pamphlet and seven winners were selected, one for each province of the country. They were given a free trip to Golfito in March 1956.

Another successful method of promoting understanding of company problems is arranging for study trips to the plantations. The usual procedure is to invite a group of influential journalists, administrative officials, legislators, and lawyers to take a two-day or three-day tour through the company installations in the country. These are not pleasure junkets, but carefully planned studies of problems and policies based on firsthand observation by the guests. Since the plantations in all cases are located in areas remote from the capital cities, many of the guests on these tours have never before seen them, but have based their opinions of the company on rumors and often biased propaganda. A special effort is made to answer all questions frankly and to help the visitors to see anything they ask to see.

The new policy of public relations also aims at more personal contact between working company officials and national citizens. Speeches by managers and superintendents before luncheon and other clubs have been one means to this end. In a few instances, conferences or seminars have been arranged between company officials and local leaders.

Other public relations programs include short news or sports features on the radio under company sponsorship; display boards with photographs of company activities set up in hotel lobbies, store windows, and other public places; cooperation with newsreel crews; and the three company newspapers for its workers, previously mentioned.

In view of the vast amount of criticism and propaganda hostile to the company which circulates throughout Latin America, any public relations program has a heavy burden to carry. The present policy is directed toward winning the confidence of the public and the molders of public opinion and opening up channels of communication to them. It would be desirable to check its effectiveness periodically through polling or survey techniques or some other reliable method of public opinion study. It might also be bolstered by some intensive field studies of the sources of complaint and criticism and of the "image" of the company held by its critics.

In the meantime, the public relations department continues to put the facts as it sees them before the public and trusts that in the long run the truth will have an impact. In earlier days, public opinion in Latin America could perhaps be ignored, but over the years a constantly increasing proportion of the public in each country has become accessible to the mass media. It is essential that the United Fruit Company's side of the story be heard if it is to continue to carry on its production in a harmonious fashion in the host countries.

One aspect of public relations needs to be mentioned. This is the isolated and not very well publicized contributions it has made to education and culture. The Zamorano Agricultural School, for example, has been shown to have a strong and beneficial effect upon Latin American agricultural circles, at least. Mention should also be made of the company-financed excavation and restoration of the ancient Maya archaeological site of Zaculeu in Guatemala. Both of these projects were undertaken at the instigation of Samuel Zemurray.

RELATIONS WITH GOVERNMENTS IN HOST COUNTRIES

IN THE BANANA-PRODUCING REGIONS here considered, the United Fruit Company must deal with six separate national governments. Many other North American concerns that do business across international frontiers in Latin America are able to deal with their relatively minor government relationship problems in a more or less routine manner. But the United Fruit Company has special problems for a number of reasons.

In at least three of the countries—Guatemala, Honduras, and Costa Rica—the company, in its own name and through its subsidiaries and affiliates, is the largest single landowner, the largest single business, and the largest corporate employer of labor. In Panama, although the company is overshadowed by the Canal and its adjuncts, it is otherwise the largest single business and, until the United States-Panama treaty of 1955, its annual payments in taxes to the Panamanian government were nearly 10 times those made by the United States as rent for the Canal. In Colombia and Ecuador, the United Fruit Company's business assumes far less weight in the national economies, but it is still large enough to be conspicuous.

Another problem arises from the fact that everywhere except at Sevilla, Colombia, the ravages of Panama disease require the company to control large areas of reserve land, some of which may not be in cultivation at any given time. This requirement runs counter to various laws and regulations intended to prevent the monopolization of land and its withdrawal from cultivation. Therefore, special arrangements have to be worked out between the governments and the company.

Furthermore, in the past, the company has obtained concessions very favorable to itself from governments. At various times and places these have involved land at very low prices, exemption from certain taxes and duties, relaxation of some regulations, and so on. In some cases, these concessions have been severely criticized and have become political issues within the countries. Government officials negotiating with the company are subject to attack on the grounds that they are "allowing a state within a state," or "ceding the national territory to a private enterprise." There is little general recognition of the fact that the extraordinary obligations assumed by the company—in its higher than ordinary tax payments, its provision of basic utilities and services, its not infrequent loans or advance tax payments to governments and the like—generally outweigh by a wide margin the value of any so-called concessions written into its agreements.

As the various countries develop economically and socially, new political pressures appear. The rise of the labor movement has already been mentioned. National businessmen, chambers of commerce, and distributors want to know why they should not have the business that is handled through the company commissaries. Local travelers and shippers want the company railroads to be operated as a public utility for their convenience. The list could be multiplied.

214

As a result of all these and other problems, United Fruit representatives in the field occasionally fall into a self-pitying mood in which they feel that the company serves merely as a large and conspicuous punching bag for any local elements in need of venting a bit of spleen. However, the United Fruit Company has so far shown itself generally able to take care of itself—with the occasional moral support of the U.S. State Department.

The most serious recent difficulties with a Latin American government occurred in Guatemala during the communist-influenced regime of President Jacobo Arbenz Guzman (1951-54). The crisis came as a culmination of a series of disagreements dating back almost a decade. In 1954, the Arbenz government, acting on the legislative authority of its Agrarian Reform Law expropriated some 178,000 acres of United Fruit Company lands and, following the letter of the same law, offered to pay for them with 25-year bonds, to the amount at which said lands were entered on the tax books, about $525,000. The company promptly presented a claim for $15 million which, it said, was the true value of the lands, and was supported by the State Department. Why, then, replied the Guatemalan government with a logic that studiously ignored any reference to the prevailing pattern of property tax valuation appraisals, was not the company paying taxes on this valuation?

The whole issue of expropriation was dropped after the success of the Liberacion, led from Honduras by Colonel (later President) Carlos Castillo Armas—who was assassinated in August of 1957. It has been widely rumored, throughout Latin America, that the United Fruit Company played an important part in organizing and financing Castillo's overthrow of the Arbenz regime. The available evidence indicates that it had no part in it. The company had its hands full in other affairs, and the attribution to it of the conception, financing, and management of such a plot is perhaps paying the United Fruit Company too high a compliment. However, the chain of events in Guatemala illustrates the sort of political problems United Fruit must be prepared to handle.

Following 1954, the company has developed a new approach with respect to its relations to Latin American national governments. In general this might be described as a "partnership" relationship, as reflected by the statement of one of the national presidents who said: "We feel that we are now in partnership with the United Fruit Company." Ecuador is the one country in which the United Fruit Company is operating without a general contract agreement with the central government. This not only reflects United Fruit's confidence in the political stability and good faith of Ecuador in dealing with foreign capital but demonstrates that it is possible to build up such confidence on both sides through a record of mutually beneficial relationships maintained over a period of years.

It is possible that the future will see a general evolution toward the abolition of special contracts between foreign-owned corporations and sovereign governments, except where specific permits are required by law for a public-utility type of operation. However, because of the record of political instability in some of the countries, the company feels that the added protection of a written document is essential. One of the features of its newer contracts is the provision that the company pay a 30 percent income tax to the local government. Corporate income taxes are a relatively new institution in most of the six countries. The fact that they now derive such considerable revenues from a tax on the profits of United Fruit subsidiaries operating within their borders gives them a new awareness of enlightened self-interest in having these subsidiaries operate profitably. From the company point of view, of course, there is genuine advantage in paying locally all income tax assessments that are levied upon a nondiscriminatory basis. Not only are such payments deductible from what would otherwise be collectible in the United States, but also the good will derived from a local stake in company operations is evident.

IN SUMMARY

THE HISTORY OF UNITED FRUIT, as we have stated, is not a straight success story. Its signal contribution toward converting the perishable banana into an important item of world trade was a difficult and complicated endeavor. Many mistakes were made before experience helped find the road to success, and the company—although at times one step behind instead of a step ahead— has always shown great sensitivity to the need for keeping abreast with the times.

The 1954 strike in Honduras intensified the company's awareness of great social changes that were in process throughout Central America, one of which was the rise of the organized labor movement. A need was felt to re-examine the company's labor relations policy. After a survey by experts, a modernized labor relations program was put into effect and a system of labor relations offices took over a task formerly administered as a part-time responsibility of company lawyers, superintendents of agriculture, or managers. It would be less than fair to regard the change as a reform measure representing a complete reversal of a formerly benighted company attitude towards labor. Primarily, the new procedures provided a professional approach through which the company now deals with its workers in modern terms. It replaced a generally paternalistic and benevolent policy under which the workers for years had received high wages and fringe benefits.

One of the drawbacks in the new labor relations policy is the shortage of field personnel with sufficient experience and training to digest, and interpret in terms of local values, the excellent directives sent out from expert sources in the United States. The remarkable progress that has already been made in spite of this fact is a credit to the sensitivity and understanding of men of good will turned labor relations experts with little or no previous experience.

One of the weakest points of the whole company setup still is the inadequacy of communication between the company and the individual worker. The fragilely elusive factor that, for want of a better name, may be termed the human touch is not something that can be established by pronouncements from headquarters. It depends importantly upon the personality of the company's management representatives in a given area as well as upon the temper of local labor leadership. In some divisions, the directing management has been able to instill a general feeling of mutual confidence into the day-to-day relationships between workers and supervisory staff. In others, although the same general policy codes and practices apply, there is an atmosphere of arms-length aloofness that often magnifies rather than dispels the issues inevitably arising in worker-management relationships.

It is an excellent idea to publish company papers for free distribution among all workers. Unfortunately, those that are being published are less than effective because they are so generally limited to publishing social news and other superficial items conveying the false impression that life on a banana plantation is one continuous happy holiday. There is some lack of psychological insight into the worker's minds; seldom is an attempt made to discuss seriously the problems and issues that are of basic importance to both worker and company and to the climate of their relationship. It almost appears that there is a conscious effort to avoid such discussion.

Neither has the company yet been successful in adequately telling its story to the communities in which it operates or to the world at large. The many positive aspects and valuable contributions to the

217

economies of the host countries are seldom heard over the loud clatter of charges, most of them false or exaggerated, from the very vocal opposition. Some publications have been issued in the past, in most cases written without sufficient imagination and in too dry a style to win general attention to the genuinely amazing story that the company has to tell. But in this field, also, there are signs of improvement.

In sum, the United Fruit Company is faced with the formidably difficult task of finding a way to make the image of United Fruit that exists in men's minds conform, in at least reasonable measure, to its genuinely impressive performance record. It has made progress in this direction in recent years, but there is still a long route to be travelled. There is no magic formula beyond unremitting effort applied with patience, sensitivity, and imagination.

IX.

Summary and Outlook

We HAVE ARRIVED at the scholar's lonely point of no return— where we no longer can take refuge in the hypnotically comforting process of assembling additional data but must discharge the harsh responsibility of saying what the record means.

Our assignment was to appraise the operations of the United Fruit Company as a case study of an important direct private investment abroad by a U.S. business interest. We accepted it with full awareness of the degree to which this company's name has become an emotion-charged symbol in an old and continuing controversy over the virtues and deficiencies of this form of investment as an instrument for forwarding the development process in economic frontier areas. Accordingly, we have tried to provide objective measurement data as a substitute for subjective judgments wherever it was possible to do so.

A fairly extensive literature exists dealing with banana production and distribution in general and with United Fruit operations in particular. Yet there seems never to have been a serious attempt to measure the overall value of this crop in world trade, let alone to determine what portion of this value was left in the countries of production and what portion was claimed by foreign investment interests committed to production and/or engaged in distribution. Accordingly, there has been, up to now, no valid basis for making an informed judgment as to what banana growing has contributed to the producing economies. Lacking this, there was no way to compare the profitability of banana growing to producing countries with that of other economic activities in which they engage, either with or without the participation of foreign capital. But, as set forth in Chapter II, we believe that only if it can be clearly demonstrated that activities set up largely by foreign interests can be shown to yield greater returns to host countries than could be realized in their absence will a solid case for extending hospitality to such foreign investment be established.

The work that we have done furnished a basis for evaluating at least the general dimension of the world banana trade and for appor-

219

tioning the incidence of costs and mark-ups for the successive steps in production and distribution. With respect to the considerable but shrinking proportion of world banana exports handled by the United Fruit Company, we have been able to provide a very precise breakdown from the full access to its accounts that was provided by the company.

There can be no reasonable doubt that the United Fruit Company should be given major credit for developing to its present dimension the international trade in bananas. Despite characteristics that would place the banana among the least likely candidates for high ranking as a world trade item—its exceptional susceptibility to disease and disaster in growing, to deterioration or complete loss under anything less than meticulously tender handling upon the most demanding schedules of distribution logistics, and to the fact that no processing methods have been devised to permit any considerable portion of the world crop to be marketed in a form other than as a fresh fruit—the volume of bananas shipped in international trade exceeds that of any other fruit and decisively dwarfs that of all other fruits of exclusively tropical habitat. In the United States, the largest import market, bananas now represent about 1 percent of the total national diet measured on a weight basis. The United Fruit Company, since its incorporation in 1899, has played the leading role of pioneer in almost every stage of development that has made this trade feasible—from large-scale plantation production, through disease control techniques, land and ocean transport, and sales promotion. Without the United Fruit Company's initiative, it is highly unlikely that the world trade in bananas would have developed to anything approaching its present dimension.

MAJOR FINDINGS OF THE STUDY

THE MOST IMPORTANT MEASUREMENTS and valuations supported by this study may be summarized as follows:

World Banana Trade in 1955: Measurement of Overall Dimension and its Worth to Producing Areas

1. The value of the 1955 commercial banana crop of the world *at retail level* was between $1.3 and $1.5 billion.

2. Only about 25 percent of the stem total was shipped across national boundaries and thus entered into international trade. But consumers in importing countries paid almost $1 billion ($976 million according to our estimate) of the total retail bill. Thus, the creation of temperate zone markets for this tropically grown fruit has increased the retail value of the entire commercial crop by from two to three times, since a banana to consumers in the United States, England, or Germany is worth about six times what it brings when sold to consumers in Guatemala, Panama, or Ecuador.

3. North America and Europe combined provided all but a small fraction of the world market for export bananas. The United States-Canadian market was the outlet for 54 percent of all banana shipments and Europe for about 37 percent. Together they absorbed some 91 percent of world banana exports.

4. We estimate that the overall capital investment (upon a depreciated book value basis) committed to all phases of production, transport, and distribution of bananas moved in world trade for 1955 was of the order of $1.5 billion, of which not more than 6 percent, or $90 million, was supplied by investors native to the countries of banana origin. (See Chapters III and IV for derivation of this estimate.)

5. Despite this very low capital commitment of interests in producing areas, the return from banana exports realized by the economies of producing countries amounted to approximately $263 million in 1955, or 27 percent of the retail value and over 72 percent of importers' landed cost in the area of distribution. (See Chapters III and IV.)

6. Of each dollar spent by North American consumers for bananas, 25¢ represented the expenses and mark-ups of retailers; 24¢ covered jobbers' costs (including inland transport) and margins; 24¢ the ocean transport, unloading, wholesale selling costs and the profit return of "importers" on all of their integrated operations, including their growing and purchasing activities in countries of origin, and 27¢ the net accrual to the economies of the producing countries. The 27 percent return of retail selling price to producing economies is about in line with the 37 percent of retail price that is realized by farmers in the United States on their produce, when allowance is made for the 10¢ out of the consumer's banana dollar that goes to ocean transport.

7. On a stem basis, United Fruit handled 59 percent of North American imports in 1955, and 10 percent of Europe's imports, or 28 percent of the world total. From 1900 to 1909, the company had handled from 72 to 85 percent of shipments to the two major importing areas, and it never handled less than 50 percent until the outbreak of World War II. Since 1939, its relative competitive position has consistently declined, principally because of failure to hold its previous position in the European market. The company's relative share of the North American market, while holding comparatively steady since 1910, has fallen markedly below the 77 percent average that it held for the first 10 years after its initial incorporation (Chapter III).

8. Six Latin American republics (ranked in order of the value of their 1955 banana exports), Ecuador, Costa Rica, Panama, Honduras, Colombia, and Guatemala, accounted collectively for 60 percent of world banana exports in 1955, and were the source of 92 percent of North American imports of this commodity (Chapter IV).

9. It is in these six countries that the United Fruit Company's banana procurement operations are centralized. They were the source of 95 percent of all of the bananas that United Fruit grew or purchased for shipment in 1955, and 60 percent of all of their total shipments for the year were handled by United Fruit.

10. From our study of banana prices and the combined effect of price-times-volumes imported by the major North American market since 1940 (see Chapter V), it is evident that this trade has been markedly free of the violent fluctuations in returns realized by producing countries that have been widely attributed to export businesses based on primary commodity shipments.

10a) Average annual prices for banana imports over the entire period have shown a remarkably consistent upward trend, generally in line with but somewhat more regular than prices of domestically produced fresh fruits in the North American market. In the few years that show a lower price for banana imports than in the immediately preceding year, the decrease has been too small to have a significant effect on the fortunes of the supplying countries.

10b) When the total impact upon the exchange earnings of the producing countries is measured by multiplying sales prices by volumes shipped, it will be seen that in only two years of the measurement period was there sufficient falloff in revenues to impose any considerable strain upon balance-of-payments yields to banana-producing countries. In these two years, 1942 and 1943, the cause was clearly the withdrawal of shipping facilities incident to the submarine blockade of World War II rather than any influence attributable to the supply-demand situation in the banana market as such. North American banana sales in 1955 amounted to three times the value of such sales in 1940, and the rise in banana prices over this period was sufficient to allow selling countries to buy 45 percent more of United States exports of manufactured goods in 1955 than they obtained in 1940 for a given volume of banana exports.

10c) Although European banana prices have been more volatile than the North American, the greater postwar volume increase in European imports has been more than sufficient to compensate for the decline in prices per pound that recently has taken place in this market from the highs registered there from 1946 through 1952. In no year from the end of the war through 1956 has the total value of Europe's banana imports been appreciably lower than in the immediately preceding year, and in all but two of these years substantial gains have been registered. When European sales are combined with North American sales, it is evident that the postwar trend of producing countries' return from banana shipments has been one of dramatic increase unmarred by any years of substantial setbacks.

10d) This remarkably steady growth trend in producers' realization from banana exports as a whole has not been comparably consistent for all banana-exporting countries considered individually. As our study has shown, the incidence of such disasters as floods and blow-downs has seriously cut into the export volume of particular countries from time to time. Even when this has occurred, the impact upon the economy of the country affected has been far less than might logically be inferred. As has been illustrated in the accounting presented in Chapter VI of the impact of the 1955 flood in Honduras, the brunt of the losses from such interrupted shipments tends to fall most heavily upon the foreign-investment interests that are so heavily involved in this trade. In this case, it was estimated that only one-fourth of the total loss from a halving of United Fruit's normal shipments actually represented decreased payments within the Honduran economy.

While we have not pushed our investigation far enough to state with assurance that these allocations are typical, there is at least a strong inference that among the advantages accruing to host countries from hospitality afforded to foreign investments is the fact that such investments shoulder a share of loss-risk proportionately much larger than the share in profits that they claim. This factor would appear to be one of the more glaring omissions in a literature dealing with foreign private investment that generally has been characterized by the absence of any measurement discipline.

10e) On the negative side of the stability picture, it must be recorded that banana production for export has not proved to be a uniformly enduring revenue earner for all nations which have engaged in it. Among Western Hemisphere countries, Cuba, Jamaica, Mexico, British Honduras, Nicaragua, Dutch Guiana, and the Windward Islands bear witness to the fact that it is possible for such a trade to be developed upon a significant scale and then to shrink to a small fraction of its previous dimension or disappear entirely. Within certain other countries, its locale has moved from one area within national boundaries to another. The incidence of decimating banana diseases has been the dominant factor influencing such disruptively costly shifts.

There are, however, certain hopeful signs to indicate that banana culture for export is outgrowing its itinerant stage. Effective methods for keeping sigatoka under control are now in general use, and even the hitherto inexorably lethal march of Panama disease may be thwarted through flood fallowing or, at worst, through the planting of resistant variety strains. The scientific methods for combating these and other banana diseases and blights have been introduced through the initiative of the United Fruit Company and other large producers. Much still remains to be done to check these methods; and if they prove to be less than fully effective, to mitigate the wastefulness of chronic abandonments of banana acreage, a problem to which we shall revert later in this chapter.

We are confident that the above listed findings are substantially proximate for the world banana trade as a whole, although the totals have been derived from intensive studies only of the North American distribution system (a 54 percent sample of the world trade in bananas) of the listed six-country producing area (a 60 percent sample of the export market) and of the United Fruit Company (a 59 percent sample of North American importers' operations and a 28 percent sample of world importers' operations in 1955) checked against such overall data on world banana production and trade as exist. The inescapable conclusions are:

- That the world banana trade is overwhelmingly the creation of foreign private capital investment from the major importing centers.

- That these same private investment interests have supplied the initiative and the technology upon which the present dimension of the world trade in this commodity has been built.

- That the benefits accruing to the local economies in the produc-

Chart XXII
Foreign and Domestic Shares
in the Banana Business
of the Six Countries in 1955*

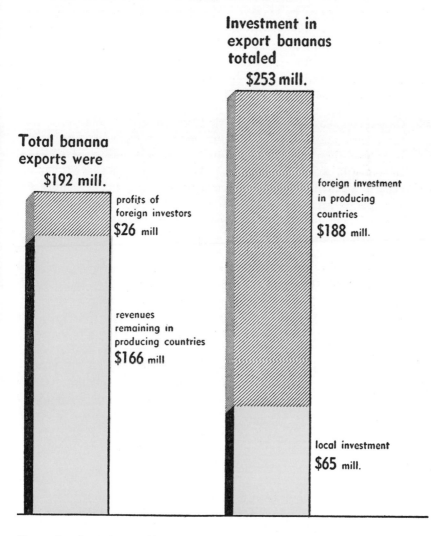

Investment in
export bananas
totaled
$253 mill.

Total banana
exports were
$192 mill.

profits of
foreign investors
$26 mill

foreign investment
in producing
countries
$188 mill.

revenues
remaining in
producing countries
$166 mill

local investment
$65 mill.

*Data taken from chapter IV.

ing areas are about four and one-half times larger than their proportionate contributions to the total capital investment upon which the establishment and maintenance of this significantly important segment of the world food trade depends. Upon almost any criterion of reckoning, this constitutes a remarkably good bargain for capital-poor countries faced with the problem of financing an expanding economic development. Most scholars who have worked in the development field calculate that anywhere from $2.00 to $4.00 of capital funds normally are required to increase the annual production of an area by $1.00. Because the major burden in furnishing the capital needed for the production of bananas for export has been borne by outside investors, the producing countries have been realizing $1.00 of return for a commitment of their own scarce capital amounting to only about 34¢.

● On every measurement basis that we have been able to devise, the return realized by producing countries from banana exports is extraordinarily high compared with any other agricultural endeavor in which they engage. Acre for acre employed, banana exports yielded to the local economies at least three times the average return from croplands as a whole, and about five times as much per agricultural worker employed. Banana exports earned them from two and one-half to three times the foreign exchange realized per acre upon coffee shipments, the largest gross export for the area as a whole. When account is taken of the fact that comparatively little local capital had to be employed to realize the far higher and much more stable per acre returns from bananas, the preponderant advantages of offering hospitality to foreign private investment in this field are irrefutably evident.

United Fruit Company Contributions to Countries of Production

With respect to the United Fruit Company as a business entity, we are able to measure with precision and in considerable detail its economic impact upon the six countries in which all but a small fraction of the bananas it handles are produced. Since (as set forth in Chapters V and VI) the company produces a variety of other crops in the six republics and none yields a profit to the company that is comparable to that realized from its banana operations, the net return to the local economies from its combined activities is higher when related to its total business than for banana operations alone.

Our accounting of the total impact of all business that United Fruit conducts in the six countries may be summarized as follows:[1]

1. The total invested capital of the United Fruit Company in its subsidiaries operating in the six countries amounted to about $159 million.

2. The current account receipts of these subsidiaries were slightly over $150 million ($122 million from exports and $28 million from local sales). Current account expenditures totaled $122 million. The profit of the subsidiaries upon current account operations was thus about $28 million. Of this, something under $18 million was transferred in the form of dividends to the parent company.

3. Upon capital account, the subsidiaries had expenditures of about $17 million. These were paid for by the $10 million of current account earnings retained by the subsidiaries, and by new company investment commitments to the area of almost $7 million.

4. The six local economies received the direct benefit of the combined current and capital account expenditures totaling $139 million— about $103 million in the form of direct expenditures for wages, taxes and local purchases of goods and services, and $36 million of items purchased abroad that were imported and put to use in the area.

5. Thus the total realized benefit accruing to the economies of the six countries amounted to about 92 percent of the income of the United Fruit subsidiaries operating within their borders, from exports, local sales, fees, and miscellaneous earnings combined.

6. The dividend income drawn out by the United Fruit Company of something under $18 million amounted to about 12 percent of the subsidiaries' total sales and to about 11 percent on the depreciated book value of its investment in these subsidiaries.

7. On the very important consideration of the effect on balance of payments, the subsidiaries' foreign exchange contributions to the local economies (that is, the total of export receipts and new capital commitments minus foreign materials and merchandise imports added to dividends transmitted) amounted to almost $76 million, or to about 62 percent of their total exports.

8. When the United Fruit Company's contribution to local econ-

---

[1] For this accounting, we have used the combined average of all operations of the subsidiaries in the six countries for 1954 and 1955. As explained in Chapter V, advanced tax payments made by certain of the subsidiaries in 1955, and the fact that dividends for both 1954 and 1955 were transmitted in the latter year, would make an accounting based on the 1955 operations alone something less than fairly representative.

Chart XXIII
United Fruit in the Six Countries*
1954-55

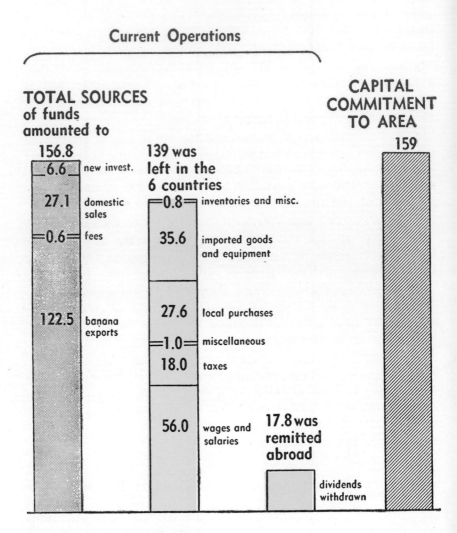

Current Operations

CAPITAL COMMITMENT TO AREA

TOTAL SOURCES of funds amounted to

156.8

6.6 — new invest.

27.1 — domestic sales

0.6 — fees

122.5 — banana exports

139 was **left in the 6 countries**

0.8 — inventories and misc.

35.6 — imported goods and equipment

27.6 — local purchases

1.0 — miscellaneous

18.0 — taxes

56.0 — wages and salaries

17.8 was **remitted abroad**

dividends withdrawn

159

*Figures in MILLIONS OF DOLLARS

omies is compared to the overall record of U.S. direct private investments in Latin America as a whole, as developed in studies made by the U.S. Department of Commerce, its comparative showing is definitely above average. This is particularly true with respect to its foreign exchange contributions, as cited immediately above. When compared with other U.S. direct private investments in agricultural enterprises, the United Fruit record is outstanding upon every comparative count.

9. When the realization of the combined six-country economies from United Fruit operations is compared with the return from their domestically financed and operated enterprises, the contrast is even more striking.

9a) On the measurement of yield per acre of land put to agricultural use, the return from land owned or contracted to the United Fruit Company was more than 20 times the average for all other improved agricultural land in the area as a whole, and from United Fruit *cropland* it was three times the average from all other cropland.

9b) On the measurement of yield per worker employed in agriculture, the returns from United Fruit operations were about five times the average for the six countries. In all cases, the wages paid by the United Fruit Company were substantially higher than the average for agricultural employees.

9c) From its employment of one-fourth of 1 percent of all improved agricultural land in the six countries, and from 2 percent of their combined croplands, United Fruit operations have accounted for about 12 percent of total foreign exchange earnings, agricultural and non-agricultural combined, for the area as a whole.

9d) For the five republics other than Colombia (where the United Fruit operations are of insignificant weight in the economy as a whole), the taxes paid by United Fruit amount to more than 6 percent of total central government revenues. The company's total tax payments in the six countries (to central and local governments combined) have been running in recent years to a sum that about equals its dividend withdrawals from profits earned in the area.

By every economic measure that we have been able to apply, the contribution of the United Fruit Company to the economies of the six countries is enormously advantageous when regarded from the viewpoint of their national interest. The fact that it has been leaving within the production area more than $7.00 for every dollar in profits withdrawn is an impressive but perhaps not the most important factor

229

in determining the degree to which these host nations have gained by offering it their hospitality. Of even greater significance is the fact that the enterprise which the United Fruit Company pioneered, and for which it has played a continuing leading role in developing large temperate zone outlets, is one that is enormously productive compared to any other agricultural pursuit in which these countries engage. Because successful banana production and distribution in international trade requires far heavier investment commitments than most other agricultural products, it is doubtful that the trade would have developed to anything like its present stature if even the production end had depended upon the local financing that capital-poor countries could provide. Since the United Fruit Company furnished the major capital and technological requirements for the establishment of this type of agricultural enterprise, its operations in the six countries have yielded a return to their economies several times larger per acre of land and for each agricultural worker employed than any agricultural activity developed through local initiative and capital financing. And the growth trend in national realizations from United Fruit operations has been far more stable than those obtained from the general agricultural exports of the countries from which it operates.

From the studies of capital-output ratios that have been made in various parts of the world, it is difficult to conceive of any activity—agricultural, extractive, or industrial—organized upon the basis of capital supplied from their own resources that would have yielded these countries a comparable economic return per dollar of national investment.

The United Fruit Company has made numerous additional contributions to the progress of economic development in the six countries that are less amenable to precise measurement. Its enterprise has opened up vast areas of low, hot, humid, and heavily forested terrain that otherwise might have remained closed to settlement and productive use for many decades at best. It has supplied the basic facilities —roads, railways, port and communication facilities, electric power establishments, hospitals, and schools that have made this possible. It has introduced modern scientific agricultural methods and equipment, and has trained hundreds of thousands of the local inhabitants in their use over the span of its existence. It has pioneered in the introduction of the health and sanitation measures without which operation in the banana-producing areas is virtually untenable. It has played a leading role in the introduction to the area of new crops such as African oil palm, abaca, and a variety of timber species that have been far more profitable to the local economies than to itself. It has vastly improved the available planting stock and cultural procedures in planting and maintaining others, like cacao, and has contributed to the improvement of tropical agricultural practices in the area of its operations in literally hundreds of other ways.

Upon all *strictly economic measurements* that can be applied, the suggested test for justifying the worth of a foreign private investment to host countries—by clear demonstration that it brings them greater gains than they could have hoped to achieve without it—is answered in terms too conclusive to admit debate. The analysis and summary tables presented in Chapter VI show that the conclusion holds not merely for its overall operations but for every one of the six countries on which its core activity of banana production and procurement is based.

It is appropriate to turn next to the evidence produced by our case study of the United Fruit Company upon the second major test suggested for judging the worth of direct private investments abroad. The thesis set forth was that the continuing flow of private capital funds to investments in economic frontier areas depended upon the realization of earnings sufficiently higher than could reasonably be expected from investment at home to compensate for the trouble and risks inherent to such venture capital commitments.

Appraisal of the United Fruit Company as an Investment

The evidence, as set forth in Chapter V, makes it very clear that the United Fruit Company, far from earning sufficiently high returns to compensate for the risks involved in committing three-fourths of its capital to areas of low economic development and high political instability, has fared less well than the average U.S. enterprise of its general size based primarily upon operations and investment in the home market. Our findings upon this score may be summarized as follows:

1. At the end of 1955, the United Fruit Company—with total assets of $390 million, a stockholders' equity of $350 million, and with gross sales of $288 million—ranked somewhat above the average size of the 500 larger corporations in the United States. There were, however, scores of corporations in the list of a size that, compared with United Fruit, reduced the latter to pygmy-like proportions. At least five of United Fruit's own chain-store customers had total sales much higher than its own.

2. Since it was organized in 1899, the profits after taxes of the United Fruit Company have averaged under 13 percent on net assets. We do not have a comparative base extending back that far, but the 13 percent average for its entire history may be compared with the 14.9 percent average return on net assets shown for 1,843 leading U.S. manufacturing corporations in 1955 in a tabulation made by the First National City Bank. For that year, the comparative showing of the United Fruit Company was 9.8 percent. From 1928 through 1955, the average profits of United Fruit were 11.1 percent on net assets, a trifle higher than the average showing for the National City Bank's total list of larger manufacturing corporations and a trifle lower than that of its list of larger trading corporations. Needless to say, the level of United Fruit's profits has run consistently far below the rates that are considered tenable for local business enterprises in the Latin American communities where its procurement operations are based.

3. On the more important factor of growth in earnings and capital appreciation, the record of the United Fruit Company is definitely substandard. The average annual earnings for the 50 industrial corporations included in the Standard and Poor's list increased three and one-half times between 1946 and 1955, and the average prices for their stocks by three and one-third times over the same period. By comparison, United Fruit Company earnings declined by more than 15 percent over this period, and there was no substantial appreciation in the price of its securities upon the New York Stock Exchange.

4. There is a fourth finding from the evidence assembled in Chapter V, that is not strictly relevant to the question of comparative profitability but that is germane to the widely held Latin American preconception that a few North Americans are growing rich from a trade based upon an item of their production. In comparison to its size, the ownership of the United Fruit Company is exceptionally widely diffused among U.S. corporations. The company has almost as many separate stockholder accounts as it has tropical employees. The dividend check paid to the average stockholder in 1955 amounted to $360 upon 120 shares, compared with the average $942 wage payment to each of its 80,000 employees in the tropics. Even the 141 largest shareholders received dividends averaging just above $50,000 each, and many of these went to trust funds shared by a number of individuals.

The conclusions from this part of our economic accounting are clear. As a case study of U.S. direct private investment abroad, the United

Fruit Company record is one that does not fully measure up to the second criterion of performance that was set. Although earnings have been large enough to justify a continued effort to maintain and expand the company's operations, they have not shown consistent profits at a level that would encourage other foreign investors to emulate its example. This may explain why U.S. investors generally have had so limited an interest in foreign agricultural enterprises. It assuredly accounts for the fact that virtually no Latin American investors have availed themselves of the opportunity to purchase United Fruit Company stock that has been traded at so considerable a volume on the New York Stock Exchange that they might easily have acquired a controlling interest had they so elected.

It is conceivable, of course, that local investors in producing areas would have shown more interest if an opportunity had been offered to invest in United Fruit subsidiaries operating in their several countries rather than in the stock of the corporation as an integrated whole. The concept of joint foreign-domestic investment in subsidiaries, with local representation on their boards of directors commensurate with their investment interests, is one with such evident appeal that we have given it careful consideration. Such an arrangement would dramatize the local stake of each producing country in the operations conducted within its borders. It would provide the United Fruit Company with powerful allies to dissipate the prevailing sentiment that its activities are essentially of foreign rather than domestic concern. It would conform to the growing sentiment that favors the joint foreign-domestic investment pattern.

Very reluctantly, we have concluded that despite its general merit this procedure would be of dubious practicality for application to the particular operations in which the United Fruit Company engages. The historic pattern upon which continuing, as opposed to ephemeral, operations in banana production and distribution have evolved is one that seems to demonstrate the preponderant advantages of integrated organization based on multiple sources of supply. The whole trend of the United Fruit Company and of other major participants in the trade has led in this direction and promises to continue. The high incidence of periodic disasters from floods, blowdowns, and chilling, not to speak of the progressive incursions of Panama disease, that cut deeply into the annual shipment levels of a given area and drastically alter yearly production costs, have placed a high premium upon stability that can be achieved only through treating multiple supply sources as a pooled operation with an averaging of costs.

It is difficult to see how the conflicting interests of separate stock-holder groups for the individual subsidiaries could be satisfied under such integrated operation. For example, the local stockholders in a subsidiary that showed comparatively low costs and high profits for several successive years would be hard to convince that an important expansion of its operations was not justifiable. The parent company, however, might be far more impressed by its long experience demonstrating that differential costs among producing areas are habitually inconstant. On this basis, it would be loathe to commit too many of its investment dollar eggs to one production-area basket. Similar conflict-of-interest issues would be generated by almost every subsidiary-parent company transaction. The complications arising from autonomous joint capital investments in the several subsidiaries as opposed to unified investment in the integrated operation would almost certainly outweigh the advantages achieved.

The United Fruit Company Record in Social Welfare, Labor, and Public Relations

Obviously, the direct economic impact of a foreign investment enterprise upon the areas of its operation is only one of the ways in which its influence may be appraised. A corporate entity, whether it operates at home or abroad, is in effect an individual, created by legal fiat, subject to obligations and afforded privileges and immunities, as prescribed by the prevailing law. Its overall responsibilities include performance as a good citizen of the areas in which it operates.

In Chapters VII and VIII, we described the general scope of the company's activities in such fields as the provision of housing, health and sanitation, education, club and recreational facilities, commissaries and food purveying, and a variety of other community services for its workers. We have reviewed also its labor and public relations policies and procedures. Our general findings in this field may be summarized as follows:

1. In the six countries of our firsthand study, the United Fruit Company in 1955 paid out approximately $53 million in direct wages and $8 million in fringe benefit payments to 59,600 employees on its payrolls. It spent a further $4.25 million on schools, hospitals, and infirmaries (on a net basis), welfare programs, and sanitation services —all of which were of direct benefit to its work force. Thus, for the six-country area, the labor cost per company employee averaged almost $1,100 without any allowance for the rental value of the

living quarters provided for employees by United free of charge.

2. In addition, the company's books show a net cost to it of about $1.2 million on staple commodities that it sold to its employees at prices below cost. Since its total commissary operations in the six countries have been run on a break-even basis with both costs and sales revenues averaging around $15.5 million per year over a five-year period, there is no reason for the loss-item portion of this business to be segregated. It is apparent, however, that the commissary privilege, through which the company's workers have spent about 30 percent of their net pay receipts for living necessities on which they have paid no distribution markups, has substantially stretched the value of their take-home pay. And this take-home pay, as already noted, is uniformly higher than the going rates in the area. There is an added bonus through the general company practice of making available garden plots upon which its workers are encouraged to grow foodstuffs for their own tables.

3. As our review has shown, the United Fruit Company record with respect to its furnishings of hospital, dispensary, and sanitation services has been generally excellent when measured by the objective standard of the health records of its employees. In this field, the company has pioneered in the difficult task of making traditionally disease-ridden tropical environments safer places in which to live and work, and complaints about its performance on this score are remarkably infrequent from any source.

4. With respect to the provision of educational facilities, United Fruit usually goes well beyond what is required by law, but its performance here is less outstanding than in the fields related to health. Its schools are better equipped and manned than the average for surrounding rural areas and, in some cases, provide a longer period of instruction than the prescribed minimum. There is, however, a serious problem raised by the gap of three to six years that, under prevailing laws, exists between the normal completion of compulsory school requirements and the minimum age for the granting of work permits. There is also a largely unfulfilled need for vocational and domestic science instruction that applies to the United Fruit Company schools in common with the rural school system as a whole. The company recently has taken some steps to provide more of this type of instruction. It also materially assists in providing opportunities for the continuing education of its employees' children in the United States and Canada, and has invested some $6.5 million of capital in the establishment of the Escuela Agricola Panamericana in Honduras. This excellent school provides practical, hands-in-the-dirt training to about 160 pupils selected from many Latin American countries. The company pays all of their expenses for a three-year course that covers horticulture, field crop production, and animal husbandry, and it strictly adheres to the rule that none of the graduates shall enter into United Fruit Company employment. By this provision, it gives assurance that the School is intended to serve the general interests of Latin American agriculture rather than forward the company's own advantage.

5. On all of its establishments within the six republics, the company provides for its workers places of worship, clubs, recreational facilities, and athletic fields and equipment upon a scale and of a standard that are matched by few, if any, locally owned agricultural enterprises. To an important degree, its railroads, ships, radio communications, electric light and power facilities, and commissaries serve a wider community than its own employee group. In many cases, this is true of its hospitals and other amenities as well. Its general record of performing services of benefit to the communities that always tend to grow up on the fringes of company divisions is excellent. On a number of occasions, the company has even helped central governments over difficult financial emergencies by making advance payments on prospective taxes, a procedure that generally would be accepted as beyond the call of normal duty.

6. In the important field of housing, the company record again is good to excellent if viewed in the perspective of prevailing standards. The accommodations furnished to United Fruit workers free of charge generally are far better than anything to be found on farms in the surrounding areas. But this, in itself, is less than an unqualified endorsement, since the housing of the great majority of agricultural laborers in the six countries is deplorably substandard. The newer single-family houses that the company has been building upon a systematic replacement program would qualify as good under almost any standard. But the pace of the replacement program is necessarily limited by what the company can afford. The cost of the new single-family dwellings runs from $1,500 to $2,000 per unit, so that more than $100 million is involved in the rehousing of all of its employees in the six countries alone. This sum is equivalent to five or six years of the company's total dividend transmittals from the area at the rate that has prevailed in recent years.

Meanwhile, the major part of its agricultural laborers still are housed in barracks-type structures partitioned off into family-unit divisions. At their worst, as exemplified by some of the older buildings at Tenguel in Ecuador and Almirante in Panama, such accommodations are somewhat grim. At their best, they represent a huddled pattern of living that is in accord neither with a rural environment where space is not a luxury nor with the deeply rooted Latin American sentiment for family privacy. The multiple dwelling units are being replaced by single family units at a rate of about 5 percent each year. It is difficult to see how a faster pace than this could be provided on the current earnings record. There are, however, complementary measures through which the situation might be improved at far less cost. One of these might take the form of an intensive educational effort to encourage workers to exert their own initiative toward better standards of housekeeping and household improvements. A relatively inexpensive program of recognition and rewards for the best kept and most attractively decorated or landscaped dwelling units might serve to awaken a competitive pride that could achieve much to relieve the present somewhat drab standardization in workers' living quarters.

7. Relations with labor in the six countries have not been uniformly happy despite United Fruit's consistent record of providing considerably higher wages, security, welfare, and other fringe benefits than those generally prevailing in the communities concerned. In the postwar period, its operations in a number of countries have, on occasion, been seriously interrupted through work stoppages incident to labor disputes.

On balance, it is probably fair to appraise United Fruit performance in the field of labor relationships over the years as generally in advance of current practices in areas to which the tradition of labor unionism is new, its leadership relatively inexperienced, worker allegiance to union principles weak, and where political overtones tend to overshadow bargaining considerations. In several of the six countries, the company is caught between a cross-fire of criticism on its labor relations. On the one hand, there are those who hold that such organizations as the Fruit Company should be taking a vigorously active position in encouraging unionism among its workers, rather than following the conventional employer role of recognizing and bargaining with such unions after they are formed. In recent years, even the U.S. government has given official support to this position through its general endorsement of ORIT, a program for affiliating free trade unions in Latin America with the AFL-CIO complex in the United States and with other noncommunist labor organizations on a world basis. On the other hand, the company often has been criticized as unduly soft in its labor terms and policies by members of the local business communities and even by government officials in several of the six countries in which traditional attitudes are profoundly suspicious of labor organization and resentful of its encouragement by foreign corporations in their midst.

Since 1954—when the United Fruit Company adopted a positive code of labor practices and took steps to see that it was generally established throughout its operating divisions—the company's position in this field clearly has moved from one of generally benevolent paternalism to one of consciously forwarding modern employer-worker relationship procedures. It freely recognizes and deals with all union agencies through which many of its workers elect to bargain. Concurrently, it is not unnaturally apprehensive about the potentially damaging effect to its peculiarly vulnerable business of concerted international labor pressure that might be exercised on purely local disputes through an affiliated international structure of labor organizations of the ORIT type. Time alone will establish whether or not such misgivings have any substantial foundation. Meanwhile, the honest attempt of the United Fruit Company, and other similarly situated corporations, to support the sound principles of independent unionism would be made easier if those responsible for shaping ORIT's policies offered assurances that its structure of union affiliation across national boundary lines would not result in expanding local disputes to international dimension, or result in the arbitrary employment of such instruments as international labor boycotts or "hot cargo" embargos.

8. Since 1951, the United Fruit Company has been devoting an ever-increasing effort to the task of improving its public relations in the countries in which its foreign operations are centralized. The professional personnel to which this task has been entrusted operate upon the sound hypothesis that their function is to see that accurate information about the company's affairs is made available to the widest possible audience, rather than to attempt to manipulate public opinion to an attitude favorable to the company's interest.

This program has included the issuing of annual reports on subsidiary operations and a variety of educational pamphlets stressing the company's contributions to local economies through its business transactions and philanthropic activities. It has employed the publication of company newspapers to keep its workers informed, and has purchased advertising space in the local press to keep a wider public aware of what the company is doing. Increasingly, arrangements are

238

being made to invite local journalists, public officials, and influential citizens to visit the company's divisions to gain firsthand knowledge of how its affairs are conducted. To an ever-increasing degree, the responsible local personnel of the company are being reminded of the importance of discharging the "citizenship" obligations of a corporation engaged in foreign operations through extending services to the surrounding communities in general and to their local competitors in banana production in particular.

Despite the commendable vigor of these efforts, there is a long road to be traveled before the local image of the United Fruit Company conforms to the true picture of its performance, although there are evident signs of genuine progress along this line. In our discussions of the United Fruit Company's current policy and practices with heads of state and high government officials in all six of the countries visited, recognition of its signal contributions and certification of the generally high standard of its behavior far outweighed the specific criticisms that were voiced. The same result was obtained from interviews with local business representatives, including United Fruit competitors, and with most of the company's employees, although the praise was seldom unqualified.

Yet, objective reporting compels us to register the fact that Latin American esteem for the United Fruit Company and its works is far from universal. The further one moves from those who have firsthand dealing with United Fruit, the lower is its repute. This generally holds true within the countries where it operates, and its worst reputation is in the Latin American republics with which it has no active relationships. Scarcely a week goes by in which the United Fruit Company is not denounced somewhere in the Latin American press as the epitome of arrogant foreign exploitation and greed. To the average man in the average Latin American street, the name of the United Fruit Company conjures up an image not unlike that of the Abominable Snow Man in the minds of the Sherpa guides and bearers of the high Himalayan snow slopes. Few Sherpas even claim to have seen the creature. The legend of his hostile behavior is fragmentary and shadowy. And yet the conviction of his malevolence is almost tangibly intense.

The striking disparity between the reputation and the performance of the United Fruit Company deserves further exploration. Part of the explanation lies in difficulties and complexities which are shared by many other large foreign-investment enterprises operating in economic frontier areas, to which are added special complications

239

inherent in the banana business. Part stems from the historic setting of the United Fruit Company's incorporation and early development. And part, no doubt, must be charged to the company's own shortcomings and ineptitudes.

Why the Image Is Blacker Than the Record

1. From the description given in this study of the pattern of United Fruit's operations in the six countries, it is evident that it has been forced to deal with a range of human problems inordinately wider than that faced by the average corporation—whether operating at home or abroad. To establish the production end of its business, it had no other option other than to provide, at its own expense and initiative, full-scale communities with all of the physical and social utilities necessary for their support in what were essentially wilderness environments negligibly populated before it moved in.

To compound the difficulties, such operations had to be carried out in countries of less than mature political stability, and without sufficient resources to provide in such fringe areas of their terrain even a minimum complement of the services that governments normally supply in societies of more advanced economic development.

The average industrial firm builds its plant, and draws upon the surrounding community for its work force and for a host of servicing activities to support its operations. Most of its human relationship problems center on the workers in its plants during the hours of active employment. From the wages that it pays, its employees make their own arrangements for housing, food, and other purchases, and for their transport between home and job. The corporation's taxes contribute to the support of schools, health facilities, roads, and all of the public utilities that service the community life of its workers, but it has no direct responsibility for their operation.

Although such enterprises as the United Fruit Company pay the full complement of taxes with which other corporations are charged, governments provide them with relatively little in the way of community facilities in return. The terrains in which United Fruit grows its bananas fall within the do-it-yourself zones of countries in which the fabric of conventional governmental institutions is stretched unduly thin. Through necessity, not choice, the company has become enmeshed in the establishment of company towns with all of their supporting activities, and has undertaken the servicing of far broader communities with land transport, communications, port and shipping

240

services, and a variety of other activities—from facilities primarily designed to meet the exceptionally demanding logistics of its major business.

Each of these extraneous activities stretches the normal range of corporation-community relationships. Each invites its own misunderstandings and strains. No corporation anywhere in the world has ever assumed so broad a portfolio of responsibilities and managed to maintain frictionless public relations. The United Fruit Company is no exception to this rule. When consideration is given to the fact that it has carried the extra burden of operating as a foreign-owned and foreign-managed enterprise in environments that are supersensitively nationalistic, it would be a miracle if it had been able to be the exception.

2. Even so, the public relations path of the United Fruit Company might have been smoother if its operations had evolved in a happier historic setting. The company was incorporated in 1899, only three years after the Spanish-American War. The United States had just annexed Puerto Rico and the Philippines. In 1901, Cuba's sovereignty was gravely compromised by U.S. insistence on the terms of the Platt Amendment as a condition of terminating general occupation. In 1903, the United States intervened to assure the success of Panama's secession from Colombia, with the Canal Treaty as its concomitant reward. In 1904, it took over the management of customs services in the Dominican Republic when European intervention was threatened because of defaulted debts.

In this period, President Theodore Roosevelt was making pronouncements to the effect that "chronic wrongdoing, or an impotence which results in a general loosening of the ties of a civilized society, may in America . . . force the United States . . . to the exercise of an international police power." The terms "Manifest Destiny" and the "Big Stick Policy" were coined by the proponents of U.S. expansion, and "Dollar Diplomacy" by its adversaries. In 1909, the United States sent troops into Nicaragua; in 1915, into Haiti; and in 1916, into the Dominican Republic. Other interventions of several types and degrees occurred in Cuba and Central America over this period.

In short, the founding and early development of the United Fruit Company occurred at a time when Latin American confidence in U.S. intentions and policy toward its weaker neighbors of the Western Hemisphere was at lowest ebb. To them, the United Fruit Company was a visible symbol, and one of the largest and most conspicuous, of a potential northern dominance that they feared and resented. The fact that the record is singularly free of incidents in which U.S. government pressure was exerted to forward the interests of this particular company made little impression. Its image in the Latin American mind, and in many North American minds as well, was etched by the mood of distrust, on the one hand, and of guilt, on the other, induced by a stage in U.S. foreign policy that was happily ephemeral and which most of its citizens now would be glad to forget. Somewhat ironically, this guilt-by-association image that was attached to the United Fruit Company's name has persisted long after the growth of the Pan-American political structure and confidence in the good-neighbor intentions of the United States had gone far to dissipate national tensions and suspicions in the Western Hemisphere.

3. Although we believe that these historical factors are important to an understanding of attitudes, it is far from our intention to dismiss all criticism of United Fruit Company performance as a fortuitous inheritance of circumstance and historic association. While we have not attempted the forbiddingly difficult, and probably impossible, task of appraising the rights and wrongs of the voluminous chronicle of charges and countercharges arising out of the days of banana pioneering, we are willing to believe that the early "banana hands" did not always fully exemplify the virtues and rectitude associated with the ideals of chivalry. But the same could be said of the political and commercial environments in which they had to work. On balance, it is doubtful that they seriously depreciated the prevailing ethical currency.

Within a more recent time span—where we feel that we have a firmer grasp upon the facts of the record—there can be no doubt that the company has made a very earnest effort to live up to the enlightened obligations of "good citizenship" in the areas of its foreign operations. Its degree of success in registering this intention firmly upon local consciousness has varied considerably from country to country. Although the inherent difficulties of its public relations task are sufficient to make a standard of perfection unattainable, there is ground for believing that the company was somewhat tardy in recognizing the full importance of cultivating this field. Its present policy of publishing annually a factual account of the impact of its operations upon the economy of each country in which it operates is still susceptible to improvement in form and coverage. And there is still a considerable range in the sensitivity of the company's representatives to the feelings, usages, and prejudices of the local communities. It will take years of unremitting effort before the practice in all divisions equals

242

the very high level already achieved in some of them, or effectively reflects the aims of the company's central policy.

INDICATIONS OF FUTURE TRENDS

FINDINGS WERE CATALOGED in the first section of this report which were derived from the relatively secure base of measured or, at least, observed phenomena. We turn now to the far more precarious exercise of attempting to forecast trends and outlook that seem likely to shape the development of the banana trade in general and of the United Fruit Company's destiny in particular.

Future of the World Banana Market

As we have seen, the combined North American and European markets that absorb over 90 percent of world banana shipments have shown a rather rapid growth in terms of value over the postwar period, but a relatively modest growth in terms of volume measured by weight of stems imported. Most of the latter growth has taken place in the European market in which per capita consumption is still well below half that of Canada and the United States.

Population growth in these two major areas would seemingly provide a potential increase in demand of something approaching 2 percent per year. Practically, no such growth trend is likely to be realized, because in the larger North American market the per capita consumption of fresh fruits, as a whole, has been shrinking and the total weight of banana imports has been virtually static since 1940. In Europe, however, increasing per capita incomes promise to stimulate a continuing upward trend in the banana imports of that area for a considerable period of time; and within 10 to 20 years this outlet may well attain a larger dimension than the North American market. The relatively small market in other nonproducing countries may also expand. But the most optimistic reading of present trends gives promise of only a relatively modest growth in the overall weight of bananas that will be exported in world trade in the predictable future.

With most of the growth originating in Europe, where the common market-free trade area movement seems to be gaining a foothold, it is probable that much of this expanding demand may be supplied from producing areas of Africa or the Western Hemisphere where the currencies are not linked to dollars.

There is one possible development that could radically change this outlook. To date, all but a negligible fraction of bananas shipped in world trade are sold to consumers as fresh fruit. But if the experience of the North American market can be taken as representative of world trends, all of the recent growth in per capita consumption of fruits has been accounted for by the dramatic increase in the sales of processed fruits—refrigerated and frozen fruit juices and pulps, canned, dried, or otherwise preserved fruits in various forms. There are numerous and formidable technical problems in the processing of bananas. If they can be solved—if an economic and palatable product that would lend itself to wide use by confectioners and ice cream manufacturers, or as baby foods and, particularly, as an ingredient in the rapidly growing package market for breakfast cereals and cake, muffin, and bread mixes of various types can be produced—the world consumption of bananas could be enormously increased.

The United Fruit Company and others in the field have been working on this problem. Success to date has been only moderate, but the potential stakes are sufficiently high to warrant continuing and intensified effort in this direction by all who are concerned with the future of banana production and marketing.

Persistence of Large-scale Integrated Organization

Chapters III, IV, and V set forth in considerable detail the special characteristics of banana production and distribution that explain why the prevailing pattern of large-scale integrated organization has become predominant in this field and is unlikely to be displaced. The exceptionally heavy capital requirements for establishing and maintaining banana acreage, the encroachment of diseases that to date have forced successive shifts in the locale of growing areas, the recurrent blowdowns and floods that dictate multiple sources of supply as safety insurance, and the exceptionally demanding logistics of distribution for an almost uniquely perishable major trade commodity—all of these unite to make large-scale, vertically integrated organization a condition of successful operation.

One trend (recorded in Chapter VI) promises to make continuing headway that will modify to a limited degree the all-inclusive sweep of integration. It seems likely that United and other large operators will expand contract operations, under which an increasing proportion of their bananas will be produced by local farmers with the purchasing companies guaranteeing to take all acceptable fruit at agreed-upon prices and in turn providing growers with disease control and other services related to growing and shipping their products.

This procedure has at least three features of obvious merit. It preserves the degree of centralized control needed to maintain quality standards in production and handling. It encourages local entrepreneurs and importantly contributes to the sense of a responsible national stake in what has too generally been regarded as essentially a foreign enterprise. It appreciably reduces the capital investment that the integrated operators are forced to commit to the supply side of their business, and thus limits their margin of risk and improves their profit potentials.

Future Position of the United Fruit Company in Bananas

Contrary to widely held preconceptions, the United Fruit Company's importance in the world banana trade has been subject to continuous, if gradual, erosion. Its relative share of the world banana market in 1956 was only about 40 percent of its share at the turn of the century. In the North American market, where it obviously has made a major effort to maintain a foothold, its relative position has declined by about 20 percent over the same period. In 1900, it had about 20 importers competing for the trade of the United States and Canada. Today, competitors number about 160.

The evident downward trend in the United Fruit Company's relative position in the world banana market and the concomitant gain of its competitors may be salutary rather than retrograde from the viewpoint of the industry as a whole. But from the perspective of the company's own interest, and from that of the producing areas for which it provides the major outlet channel, there is room for a certain amount of concern as to where a continuation of the trend will lead. Apparently, company policy has been focused upon the major aim of holding its relative position in the important North American market. In this, it has been reasonably successful for a long period even though its share of this market since 1910 has been consistently lower than in the first 10 years of its corporate life.

With a limited supply of bananas at its disposal, this policy has resulted in the drastic loss of its relative position in the European market. Since the outbreak of World War II, the company's relative position as a European supplier has deteriorated to only about 25 percent of its immediate prewar position, and to only about 11 percent of that occupied from 1913 to 1930.

In short, there would appear to be genuine ground for debating the wisdom of the company's policy of focusing upon the North American market—in which the growth prospects are meager at best, and in which antitrust regulation assuredly will inhibit any increase in its approximately 60 percent share of recent years, if indeed it goes no further. This policy necessarily called for a variety of decisions relating to the disposition of available supplies and the areas in which programs for expanding production would be pursued. The result has been a drastic loss of position in the European market that has far greater growth potentials than the one that has been cultivated. Unless the United Fruit Company reorients its policy and takes whatever steps are necessary to win back a larger share of Europe's trade, or succeeds in developing a substantial outlet for processed bananas in the United States and Canada, its prospects for a continuing expansion of business upon any impressive scale are far from bright. More vigorous exploration of both of these matters than they have received in the past appears to be warranted, since the clear record of corporate history indicates that in the absence of growth, deterioration sets in.

It is conceivable, of course, that the United Fruit Company could achieve expansion through diversification of its activities, even though its banana operations showed little upward trend. But the record offers little encouragement to the idea that this is a promising alternative. This study has given at least some indication of the considerable variety and scope of the company's past efforts in diversifying. To date, none of its diversification ventures—in sugar, cacao, palm oil, abaca (in an agency capacity), forest, or other agricultural products—has demonstrated that they can substitute adequately for continuing growth in the company's core business of growing and distributing bananas. From none of these side activities has the company been able to match even the modest rates of profit return earned in the banana trade. It would appear that few agricultural pursuits lend themselves to the high capital outlay and high overhead pattern that is basic to United Fruit Company operations.

Future Programs for Using Abandoned Banana Lands

Earlier in this chapter, and at greater length in Chapters IV and VI, we referred to the extravagant wastefulness entailed in the abandonment of land rendered unsuitable for further banana production by the incursion of Panama disease. Neither the flood fallowing procedure adopted by the United Fruit Company in recent years nor the Standard Fruit Company's policy of planting such lands to disease-resistant varieties seems to provide the ideal solution of stabilizing banana production upon a given acreage.

Panama infection has no effect upon the productivity of soils when planted to other crops. Thus, the failure to make optimum use of fertile lands that are cleared, drained, and serviced by the full range of community and transport utilities, in areas where their lack is the chief impediment to needed agricultural development, is an inexcusably profligate waste. We have enumerated the varied measures that the United Fruit Company has taken to avoid a repetition of the social losses that accompanied giving up banana culture in the Limón area of Costa Rica, but the problem is of too great a magnitude to be handled by the action of banana-producing companies alone.

What is needed for the future is systematic planning by the governments of all banana-producing countries for the prompt resettlement of abandoned banana lands. The technical assistance programs of the United States and the United Nations should take an active interest in planning and carrying out such change-overs. These can provide an opportunity for either international or local agricultural resettlement programs which could scarcely be matched on the score of economy and general ease of transition by any existent alternatives. It is not too much to hope that the future will show far more vigorous and enlightened efforts to wed what are likely to be continuing world needs to the exceptional opportunities for satisfying them that are afforded in this field.

Gradual Emancipation from Extraneous Services

We have dealt at some length with the extraordinary ramification of services only indirectly related to the banana trade that large companies operating in virgin areas are called upon to provide. We have noted that many of the United Fruit Company's public relations problems stem from the fact that in order to grow, purchase, and export bananas, it has been forced to establish and service whole communities with housing, public buildings, roads, transport, power and communication facilities, hospitals, sanitation services, schools, recreation establishments, commissaries, and a variety of other social services. In more settled areas, many of these activities are performed by other private enterprises or by the organized political entities of the surrounding communities. It is reasonable to expect that, as the areas opened by the pioneering efforts of United Fruit Company mature, many of the burdens that it has been forced to carry may be turned over to others.

The period of transition inevitably will vary in length from country to country. It would be a mistake to push it overrapidly for doctrinaire reasons, since the delicate balance of banana export logistics could be disastrously upset if some of these services were not carried out with high efficiency. Nevertheless, it would seem desirable for both the company and the local governments to formulate definite policies for moving in this general direction with as much dispatch as practicable. Any sound progress that can be achieved should serve to reduce an almost hopelessly complex public relations problem to one of tenable dimension.

The Problem of Company-Government Contracts

One of the principal wellsprings of local criticism of the United Fruit Company is its adherence to a general practice of large corporations operating in frontier economic areas. That is the practice of entering into general contracts or agreements with the governments of the several countries in which it maintains subsidiaries outlining commitments and obligations on both sides over a given period of years.

With some justice, this procedure is condemmed on the ground that the terms of such an agreement between a private corporation and a sovereign government attribute to the former a status to which it is not entitled, and compromises the dignity of the latter. With much less cogency, the specific guarantees offered on the government side— such as abatement of import duties on capital equipment and process materials or a margin of leeway on requirements to clear all foreign exchange earnings through currency controls—are often denounced as "give-aways" or concessions unfairly extorted by a foreign colossus. The evidence presented in this study shows that the extraordinary obligations assumed by the United Fruit Company in its agreements are considerably greater than the value of any concessions granted it.

The problem is not a simple one that can be resolved in terms of principles that can be etched in pure blacks and whites. There is unquestionably an element of indignity in the posture of a government that offers a private business entity individual status, whatever its terms, instead of treatment defined by general laws relating to its category. On the other side, it is fair to note that a corporation such as the United Fruit Company is required to risk far more than the normal capital investment when it establishes a new, large-scale enterprise in a wilderness area that can furnish none of the ordinary facilities of industrialized communities. Its risks are compounded when it moves into countries in which no firm tradition of political stability has been established, and in which the record of *de facto* as opposed to *de jure* equality of treatment to foreign-owned corporations is far from secure.

Under such conditions, stockholders and directors are simply unwilling to commit large investments to such areas and bankers are unwilling to extend loans, without such added assurance as a firm contract with the recognized government of the area can offer. Many state and municipal governments in the United States offer special concessions over a term of years to new enterprises as an incentive to locate within their borders. And such institutions as the International Bank for Reconstruction and Development require government guarantees as a condition of extending loans to private development projects, often with a spelling out of terms under which the business will operate.

As a practical matter, for the immediate future it is hard to see how capital investments on a scale sufficient to establish new banana divisions in many countries may be mobilized without specific agreements. In the longer term, the establishment of stable policies and the development of international treaties and machinery for adjudicating disputes may make them obsolete. The fact that the United Fruit Company now is operating in Ecuador without a general contract may indicate a pattern of future trends.

The Significance of this Case Study

This work was undertaken as a case study of one important U.S. example of direct private investment abroad. We stated the initial thesis that, in order to justify its claim upon the hospitality offered by host countries, such an enterprise would have to demonstrate that its operations left behind a contribution to local economies greater than they could reasonably have expected to realize from the use of their own resources. The complementary thesis was that unless such investments in pioneer economies proved to be sufficiently more profitable than the normally expectable return from investments of less risk at home, there would be little incentive for private capital from mature economies to move into these channels.

On the first score, the measurements that we have been able to apply show that the contributions made by the United Fruit Company's foreign operations to the local economies have been outstandingly to the latters' advantage.

On the second count, it is clear that while the company's returns have been sufficient to keep it in operation and finance a considerable expansion, they have not matched the earnings of the average company of its size engaged primarily in domestic business.

Obviously, it is not tenable to make generalizations about U.S. foreign investment as a whole upon the basis of one case. If our study has any merit, it lies in the attempt we have made to base our findings upon measurement in a field in which subjective judgments have been largely dominant. If it serves to encourage others to apply a similar approach to other cases, we shall feel that our work has been justified.

APPENDIX NOTE

AFTER THIS STUDY HAD BEEN SUBMITTED to the National Planning Association for publication, but before its processing had been carried to the page-proof stage, the civil antitrust suit filed against the United Fruit Company in 1954 by the U.S. Department of Justice was terminated through a "consent decree" subscribed to by both plaintiff and defendant.

Thus, a final judgment was entered by the Court of jurisdiction setting forth a series of steps and outlining a set of performance standards that were agreed upon mutually by the company and by the Department of Justice as assuring that future operations of the company in the United States market would be in conformity with the competitive pattern that the antitrust laws seek to preserve. It was specifically stipulated that the terms of the final judgment, arrived at without a hearing of testimony, without trial, and without decision upon any issue of fact or law raised in the government's complaint, implied no admission of law violations in the company's past practices.

The positive steps that United Fruit agreed to take, and which were ratified by stockholder vote on April 16, 1958, may be summarized as follows:

1. It agreed to divest itself, through sale not later than June 30, 1966, of all of its stock ownership in the International Railways of Central America, and not to reacquire any direct or indirect interest in this Guatemalan railroad enterprise. (For background discussion, see Chapter VI.)

2. It agreed that by midyear of 1966, it would submit for Court approval a plan, to be carried through to fulfillment within four years after approval was obtained (presumably by not later than 1970), for turning over to a new company operating independently of any United Fruit control, a sufficient part of United's producing lands and purchasing arrangements combined and of its integrated facilities for shipping to and distribution in the United States to furnish that market with approximately nine million stems of bananas generally equivalent in size, variety, and freedom from disease to those that United is then shipping.

Three optional arrangements were specified through which this commitment might be fulfilled:

A. United Fruit might itself organize the new company under

251

arrangements that would assure its subsequent independent operation, and distribute its stock upon a prorata basis to United's own shareholders.

B. It might sell to any buyer in which United Fruit has no direct or indirect interest (other than the Standard Fruit and Steamship Company) the necessary production and transportation assets to provide the specified shipment volume. If this option is chosen, United is relieved of obligation to transfer to the new company managerial or other personnel or any distribution facilities.

C. It might work out an arrangement that combines features of the other two alternatives, by organizing the new company, as under Alternative A, but by selling a partial interest to an independent investor, as defined in Alternative B, who commits not less than $1 million to the enterprise. In this case, also, United will be relieved of the obligation to transfer managerial or other personnel.

3. United Fruit agreed to liquidate, within nine months, its Banana Selling Corporation, a subsidiary engaged in jobbing operations in the area of Mobile, Alabama. This was the last remaining subsidiary of its type that, according to company statements, had been set up to experiment with and demonstrate improved methods of handling, ripening, and merchandising fruit to its regular jobber and wholesaler clients.

In addition to these three positive commitments, the consent decree specified that United Fruit must refrain from engaging in a long list of practices of the variety generally considered to be inconsistent with healthy competition. They included, as is customary in such documents, the listing of various procedures that had been attributed to United Fruit in the complaint, although the company had denied using them, along with others included merely to safeguard the maintenance of sound competition in the future. Thus, United Fruit was enjoined from engaging in jobbing operations; from maintaining exclusive sales contracts with jobbers, or exclusive purchasing contracts with independent banana suppliers for longer than five years without an escape clause; from acquiring proprietorship, ownership, or control of any of its competitors or of any substantial part of their business assets; from entering into collusive agreements with competitors, or using coercive tactics against them; from attempting to control the resale price policies of jobbers or other wholesalers; from obtaining preclusive treatment from common carriers; from requiring its customers to employ specified transport media; from refusing to sell in specified markets to any purchaser at its regular terms of sale such bananas as it might have after supplying the needs of regular customers; or from tying up refrigerated space on vessels, other than through bareboat, time or voyage charters, in a manner that prevents competitors from obtaining space needed for their shipments.

Finally, the judgment provided that the Department of Justice be afforded such freedom of access to the accounts and records of the United Fruit Company as might be necessary to assure compliance with the consent decree's provisions.

The sharp rise in the price of United Fruit stock on the New York Stock Exchange that followed the announcement of the terms of the consent decree indicates a market judgment that the advantages to the company's interest of having the suit settled far outweigh any adverse effect upon its future prospects of the provisions to which it subscribed.

Of the three positive mandates, the divestment by United Fruit of its stockholdings in the International Railways of Central America and the liquidation of its sole remaining jobbing establishment represent overdue actions that probably would have been taken in any event.

The provision for the establishment of a new company through the spinning off of a portion of United's assets accounting for approximately nine million stem imports for the U.S. market will eventually create another competitor of about the same size as Standard Fruit and Steamship Company. Time alone will demonstrate whether or not such additional competition will be of positive benefit either to this distribution market or to the regions that supply it.

Since, under the terms of the final judgment, the actual establishment of the new company does not become mandatory until around 1970, many developments may take place in the interim that can modify the impact that such a move would have if it were made immediately. If the scope of United Fruit's banana procurement operations meanwhile expands by an equivalent amount, the surgery will not reduce its absolute size below present dimensions. The growth potential of even the North American market could provide this leeway, not to speak of the larger margin that the European market holds forth. It also is possible that the future will provide more profitable opportunities than have been seized in the past for United to grow through a diversification of activities in other lines than banana production and distribution.

If another interest can be found to purchase at a fair value the assets that United Fruit may elect to sell, the company's stockholders will be adequately compensated for the amount of the divestiture. If such a purchaser is not forthcoming, the required formation of the new company by United will merely transfer to United Fruit's stockholders an ownership right in assets of the new company equivalent in value to the assets transferred to it by the United Fruit Company.

The matter of intangible values is, of course, more difficult to weigh. Whether or not the new company will be more or less successful than United has been can only be conjectured, and this in important measure will determine the degree of competition that it will offer United and United's other competitors. It is worthy of note, however, that the size of the entity that is to be formed is sufficient to allow the type of vertically integrated operation based on at least several sources of banana supply that seem to the authors of this report to be a major requisite for successful operation under existing conditions.

Appendix Table

World Trade in Bananas 1955

Area	Exports		Imports	
	Million pounds	% of world total	Million pounds	% of world total
North America:				
Canada...........................	—	—	311.2	4.6
United States......................	—	—	3,292.5	49.2
Total...........................	—	—	3,603.7	53.8
Europe:				
Austria...........................	—	—	23.3	0.4
Belgium-Luxembourg.................	—	—	112.1	1.7
Denmark.........................	—	—	60.2	0.9
Ireland..........................	—	—	16.7	0.2
Finland..........................	—	—	16.8	0.2
France...........................	—	—	598.2	8.9
West Germany.....................	—	—	469.9	7.0
Italy............................	—	—	98.6	1.5
Netherlands......................	—	—	73.7	1.1
Norway..........................	—	—	17.1	0.3
Spain............................	—	—	149.6	2.2
Sweden..........................	—	—	96.0	1.5
Switzerland......................	—	—	44.1	0.7
United Kingdom...................	—	—	691.9	10.3
Total...........................	—	—	2,468.2	36.9
Central America:				
British Honduras..................	1.1	—	—	—
Costa Rica.......................	726.1	10.7	—	—
Guatemala........................	250.5	3.7	—	—
Honduras.........................	546.5	8.1	—	—
Mexico...........................	63.4	0.9	—	—
Nicaragua........................	21.1	0.3	—	—
Panama..........................	606.5	9.0	—	—
Cuba............................	2.7	—	—	—
Dominica.........................	32.6	0.5	—	—
Dominican Republic................	94.1	1.4	—	—
Guadeloupe.......................	146.4	2.2	—	—
Haiti............................	1.9	—	—	—
Jamaica..........................	381.3	5.6	—	—
Martinique.......................	114.2	1.7	—	—
Trinidad and Tobago...............	4.2	0.1	—	—
Total...........................	2,992.6	44.2	—	—

(More)

Appendix Table (continued)

Area	Exports		Imports	
	Million pounds	% of world total	Million pounds	% of world total
South America:				
Brazil	465.2	6.9	—	—
Colombia	462.1	6.8	—	—
Ecuador	1,344.8	19.9	—	—
Argentina	—	—	350.0	5.2
Chile	—	—	38.2	0.6
Uruguay	—	—	40.6	0.6
Total	2,272.1	33.6	428.8	6.4
Asia:				
Taiwan	77.0	1.2	—	—
Japan	—	—	53.7	0.8
Total	77.0	1.2	53.7	0.8
Africa:				
Belgian Congo	66.4	1.0	—	—
Canary Islands	427.2	6.3	—	—
Egypt	1.6	—	—	—
Eritrea and Italian Somaliland	107.5	1.6	—	—
French Cameroons	167.9	2.5	—	—
French Guinea and Ivory Coast	275.6	4.1	—	—
Gold Coast	1.4	—	—	—
Mozambique	23.6	0.4	—	—
British Cameroons	151.2	2.2	—	—
Nigeria	150.1	2.2	—	—
Sierra Leone	0.6	—	—	—
Algeria	—	—	19.7	0.3
French Morocco	—	—	23.4	0.4
Tunisia	—	—	6.4	0.1
Union of South Africa	—	—	n.a.	n.a.
Southern Rhodesia	—	—	n.a.	n.a.
Total	1,373.1	20.3	95.0[a]	1.4
Oceania:				
New Zealand	—	—	47.5	0.7
Total	47.5	0.7	47.5	0.7
World total	6,762.2	100.0	6,696.9	100.0

[a] Estimated.
n.a.—Not available.
Source: U. S. Department of Agriculture, Foreign Agricultural Circular, FDAP 5-56, Sept. 12, 1956.
Note: Import figures for the United States and Canada were adjusted upward slightly.

THE POLICY COMMITTEE'S STATEMENT

IN UNDERTAKING THIS PROJECT the National Planning Association is not attempting to assess or describe how U.S. business enterprises generally operate abroad. Rather we are concerned with an objective study of some selected cases in which U.S. business management has, in pursuance of normal and profitable operations abroad, taken positive steps toward raising living standards and helping to integrate into countries less developed than the United States the foundations of a more mature economy. We are attempting only to sketch out those aspects of typical managerial efforts that contribute to the general economic and social progress of a host country. In confining ourselves to this facet of the problem of United States private enterprise abroad, we are not deprecating or belittling the other side of the coin, nor are we trying to write the "success" stories of nonprofit operations.

Underlying this project are the following assumptions concerning the relationships between U.S. private enterprise and the interests of the countries in which this private enterprise is operated:

First Assumption

We assume that certain, though not all, U.S. private enterprises operating in foreign countries have made contributions to the welfare of those countries and that these contributions have resulted from the foresight of management. We are convinced, therefore, that well-operated and profitable businesses abroad can establish patterns of behavior that contribute materially to the welfare of the countries involved without unduly disturbing native cultures, living patterns, and ideologies.

Second Assumption

Properly managed private enterprise abroad contributes to its market and economic area an organizational pattern, within which new enterprises are developed by people native to the host country. This chain reaction helps to create a manageable, more productive economy. In other words, well-run U.S. enterprise abroad not only can be self-sustaining, but also can give birth to or stimulate the development of corollary enterprises as a result of the private enterprise pattern taking hold.

Third Assumption

A basically private enterprise economy in less developed countries, of which well-managed U.S. private enterprises can well be a part, provides strong insulation against Communism, totalitarianism, and political instability. Therefore, it is to the national interest of the United States to have "policies" that promote enlightened and well-managed U.S. enterprises abroad. Conversely, it is in the best interests of all parties concerned that the United States Government use its influence to promote cooperation between U.S. private enterprises abroad and democratic countries in which they operate.

Fourth Assumption

The soundest way of assuring continued access in the less developed countries to those vital raw materials which the United States needs is to take cooperative measures to help those countries improve their standards of living and strengthen their economies. One of the most practical ways of doing this is to provide encouragement to U.S. private enterprises to help these countries develop their resources insofar as they want the assistance of U.S. management organization, private capital, knowledge, experience, and technical skill.

Fifth Assumption

In the long run, the "success" of an enterprise abroad must be judged in the light of its relations to the host country. The ultimate success and permanence of the enterprise must necessarily be related to the importance of its contributions insofar as the host country is concerned, since enterprises typical of those we are studying do not exploit host countries, but create wealth which is shared by their citizens. If U.S. private enterprises abroad are managed in such a way that the host countries are convinced they are also promoting their economic and social development, then it is most likely that they will receive the cooperation essential to long-run survival.

Since the above assumptions are general considerations, it is unlikely that any specific *Case Study* will bear directly on all these points. All *Case Studies,* however, will be measured against the fifth basic assumption. Our inquiry, therefore, is an area that until now has been almost wholly neglected.

The files, information, and services of our governmental departments, numerous agencies and special commissions, the Export-Import Bank and the International Bank for Reconstruction and Development are replete with current and historical information helpful to the businessman contemplating operations in foreign lands. In addition there are many private agencies —particularly commercial and investment banks maintaining foreign departments—engaged in counseling on legal, financial, trade, transportation, and local political conditions throughout the world. Our *Case Studies* will not aid the student or businessman seeking out specific answers to questions in the legal, financial, political, and related subjects. We are under no illusions as to the many difficulties that beset management in initiating and maintaining operations abroad.

We do not assume that U.S. enterprises will go abroad unless they believe they can return a satisfactory profit on the capital placed at risk, although collateral considerations may be involved. In pursuing profits, however, the "successful" enterprise finds it pays dividends to strive consciously to contribute to the social and economic life of a host country. For this reason, there should be no misunderstanding of what we are studying. We are not delving into the business transactions of any company under study except as they may relate to these contributions in our area of inquiry.

We frequently hear these days of the unsettled conditions abroad, that little or no basis exists for private investments in foreign countries, and particularly that the world is hostile to U.S. capital and our production methods (though not to our achievement!). This may be true among certain segments of the world's population, but an increasing number of foreign governmental and private leaders are consciously trying to create and maintain an economic climate favorable to such ends. Most of the world is short of capital and very short of dollars—yet at present it is only from the United States that they may obtain both to a degree necessary to their continued growth.

Capital that goes abroad without management—as much of it did in the early twenties—often constitutes a poor risk. That which goes abroad under American management—through U.S. business firms establishing branches or subsidiaries—usually shows better results both from a profit standpoint and in terms of economic and social contributions to the host countries. Governmental guarantees by this country are not nearly as effective in safeguarding such investments as the enlightened attitudes of the U.S. businessmen who manage the investments. This country has much to offer the world in business organization, technical know-how, and creative capital. The building of economic units in foreign countries that are not only profitably managed but also provide a positive economic and social contribution to their host countries are the surest guarantees that such capital will not be subject to abnormal risks.

The rapid expansion of industrial capacity here and abroad has enormously increased the need for raw materials throughout the world. On this basis alone, it is in our self-interest to encourage private capital to seek profitable opportunities in underdeveloped areas. And in so doing, we can demonstrate that we are creating new outlets for electric power, transportation and port facilities, increased industrialization, greater demand for U.S. capital goods, and contributing to the increase in international trade in general. However, unless we can come to a more realistic "import" policy, the export of U.S. capital will shrink and with it will go one of the principal ways to meet the present critical "dollar gap." This dollar shortage abroad is already seriously threatening our nondefense export trade.

Because we live in a world of state trading, exchange controls, export subsidies, import quotas, and intensified nationalistic aspirations there is special need for correlating private and governmental action in the exportation of U.S. capital. Everyone, including the taxpayer, benefits when governmental action constructively complements the flow of private capital abroad; when such action anticipates and helps create the appropriate climate, and when it fosters the long-range development of economic and trade relations of this and responding host countries.

The fact that we are only studying successful companies certainly implies that they have been profitable to their stockholders, and therefore we will not concern ourselves directly with this facet of their success. Our concern is rather how these selected though typical companies have earned the title "successful" insofar as they have benefited the host countries. For convenience, we may outline these principal possible benefits in the order of greatest ease in ascertaining their existence:

I. *Contribution to the basic economy*

    A. Additional resources (land, minerals, etc.) brought into use for the country.

    B. Transportation, energy, communications which are built, fostered, subsidized, or otherwise created by the company or by virtue of its operations and available to the use of the country in whole or in part.

C. Products of the company consumed or used in the host country.
D. Related industries developed with company assistance or which are attributable to the company's operations.
E. Service industries and trades dependent on and arising because of the operations of the company and the additional purchasing power of the labor force.

II. *Contributions to living standards*
A. Improvement in wages, hours of work, and employment conditions.
B. Better housing.
C. Improved health and sanitation.
D. Greater opportunities for education and recreation.
E. Higher levels of nutrition.

III. *Institutional benefits*
A. Formation of and use of local capital.
B. Improvement in skills.
C. Changes in patterns of doing business.
D. Tax, social, and other legislation encouraged or fostered.
E. Changes in public administration.
F. Greater civic responsibility.

IV. *Cultural*
A. Are the company operations as a whole tending to increase the middle class?
B. Is initiative passing to more responsible groups?
C. Are class conflicts decreasing?
D. Is there greater respect for human rights?

Unfortunately many of these broad areas of benefits cannot be measured or even detected except over a considerable period of time. They will be present or absent in varying degree according to the type, size, and purpose of the capital investment and the stage of the country's development at the time the initial investment was made. Certainly the cultural benefits will emerge gradually and probably only will be measurable by the influence of the total impact of all managed capital—foreign and local— rather than any one part of it.

In addition to these external factual areas, we are vitally interested in studying the relationships and attitudes that have made these practices successful:

How has the company met the obstacles which it has encountered?

To what extent has the company introduced U.S. managerial skills and methods cut to fit the operating picture abroad?

How has the company sought and obtained the co-operation of employees, government officials, and community; and have the views of these people changed markedly since the company first started operations?

Has the company sought to identify itself with the community as a friendly institution?

Has it sought to train native labor for the higher skills, for supervisory and executive positions, and have such efforts resulted in higher productivity, greater responsibility, and understanding on the part of labor?

Have the company's practices in investing capital and securing return of profits been made progressively easier?

Has the company brought know-how, technical assistance, and business management that could not have been provided at all—or as effectively—by government programs?

Above all, we shall be describing U.S. business management attitudes toward its job of conducting successful operations abroad, its flexibility and patience in meeting the great obstacles that are presented in so many fresh and challenging ways. Let no one be deceived by these *Studies* into believing that the way of business management abroad is all romance, huge profits, and success, purchasable in the market place. The rewards are adequate, the work is hard but interesting, and, as at home, the results are created, not bought.

NPA'S PUBLICATIONS POLICY

NPA is an independent, nonpolitical, nonprofit organization established in 1934. It is an organization where leaders of agriculture, business, labor, and the professions join in programs to maintain and strengthen private initiative and enterprise.

Those who participate in the activities of NPA believe that the tendency to break up into pressure groups is one of the gravest disintegrating forces in our national life. America's number-one problem is that of getting diverse groups to work together for this objective: To combine our efforts to the end that the American people may always have the highest possible cultural and material standards of living without sacrificing our freedom. Only through joint democratic efforts can programs be devised which support and sustain each other in the national interest.

NPA's Standing Committees—the Agriculture, Business, and Labor Committees on National Policy and the Committee on International Policy—and its Special Committees are assisted by a permanent research staff. Whatever their particular interest, members have in common a fact-finding and socially responsible attitude.

NPA believes that through effective private planning we can avoid a "planned economy." The results of NPA's work will not be a grand solution to all our ills. But the findings, and the process of work itself, will provide concrete programs for action on specific problems, planned in the best traditions of a functioning democracy.

NPA's publications—whether signed by its Board, its Committees, its staff, or by individuals—are issued in an effort to pool different knowledges and skills, to narrow areas of controversy, and to broaden areas of agreement.

All reports published by NPA have been examined and authorized for publication under policies laid down by the Board of Trustees. Such action does not imply agreement by NPA Board or Committee members with all that is contained therein, unless such endorsement is specifically stated.

NPA issues regularly the *PLANNING PAMPHLETS* and *SPECIAL REPORTS* series which present the findings of NPA's Board, Standing Committees, staff, or cooperating specialists. Information on titles, prices and quantity discounts of these—as well as several other special series—will be provided upon request.

NATIONAL PLANNING ASSOCIATION

A Voluntary Association Incorporated under the Laws of the District of Columbia
1606 NEW HAMPSHIRE AVE., N. W., WASHINGTON 9, D. C.
JOHN MILLER: *Assistant Chairman and Executive Secretary*
EUGENE H. BLAND: *Editor of Publications* 7